KU-166-704

The World of Simon Raven

PRION HUMOUR CLASSICS

* for copyright reasons these titles are not available in the USA or Canada in the Prion edition.

The World of Simon Raven

Selected and edited by
HOWARD WATSON

with an introduction by
ANTHONY BLOND

This collection published in 2002 by
Prion Books Limited,
Imperial Works,
Perren Street,
London NW5 3ED
www.prionbooks.com

Copyright © Simon Raven
Introduction copyright © Anthony Blond 2002
Edited and selected by Howard Watson © Prion Books 2002

All rights reserved

No part of this book may be reproduced, stored in a retrieval
system, or transmitted in any form or by any means, electronic,
mechanical, photocopying, recording or otherwise, without the
prior written permission of the publisher.

ISBN 1-85375-493-5

Jacket design by Bob Eames
Cover image: *A Society Gentleman*, original photograph by
Maurice Ambler. Reproduced courtesy of Mary Evans Picture
Library.

Printed and bound in Great Britain
by Creative Print & Design, South Wales

Contents

INTRODUCTION

In 1958, when I had just started in publishing, I asked a young, eager Hugh Thomas, who although a protégé' of Harold Nicolson, was a rising star of the Left and was then seeking nomination as Labour Parliamentary candidate for Ealing, to edit a collection of essays to be called *The Establishment*. Henry Fairlie, who may have invented the term, wrote about the BBC, John Vaizey, who like Thomas was to turn right and become a peer, wrote on the Public Schools and Simon Raven, 'sometime captain in the King's Shropshire Light Infantry' was chosen to write an essay on the military. *The Establishment* was a success – we even sold the translation rights to Franco's Spain – and established me as a certain kind of publisher and confirmed the view of those not yet called the chattering classes that Hugh Thomas was worth chattering about. At some point along the line Hugh had suggested that I commission Simon, whom I knew of slightly as a genial figure of doubtful reputation, to write a novel and this I did, paying him £10 a week conditional on him living at least fifty miles from London. This temporary arrangement lasted, with variations, to the satisfaction of both parties for forty years or so, for, as the battered typescripts rolled in, punctually, week after week, we, the publishers, began to realise that we were sailing in special waters for which special arrangements had to be made.

The reviewers shared our opinion and *The Feathers of*

Death sold out in a few days, earning Simon a reputation and a following which never left him.

We published his subsequent twenty-six novels and our office took care of his bills from haberdashers and dentists, until fame and fortune as a writer of TV plays rendered our concern unnecessary. None of this exempted us from the flow of satire which welled up in him as naturally as milk in a cow. Simon delineated his friends and acquaintances in his novels and few were kindly limned: William Rees Mogg, who, admittedly, had shopped him at Charterhouse, is found dead in his bath; Dickie Muir, a patient supporter, is killed by a slate falling off the Paul Getty Museum, to the relief of his daughters, (he had two in real life), and I, the Jewish publisher, am crucified in a disused church in the Veneto. Miss Thornton, our office manager, a spinster of seventy-eight summers, is penis-obsessed and fatally mugged. Only my late partner, Desmond Briggs, his literary executor, is spared.

Simon Raven was not much kinder to characters in the real world outside his novels which he viewed with Olympian, or Roman, disdain from his modest lodgings in Deal. (In a rather grand house next door lived the eximious art connoisseur, David Caritt, famous for discovering a Tiepolo ceiling in the Egyptian Embassy in South Audley Street.) They never spoke. Simon, whom David referred to as "the man who lives in the kennel", being without any visual awareness, despite obligatory pre-prandial cultural outings when abroad. I later discovered that Simon's minute quarters had actually been a kennel.

Simon, though his prosperity in the middle years derived from television, never owned a set, and the refusal of the licensing authority, attempting to levy its due, to believe this, was the source of continuous acrimonious correspondence. He did always keep by his bed copies of the Loeb editions of the classics which he read regularly, with pleasure, and without affectation in the original Greek and Latin. He admired, if he was not always able to practise, the Roman virtues of dignitas, auctoritas and caritas and was always temperate and courteous.

Journalists from London sent down to interview him were astonished to be entertained to luncheon for their pains at the Royal Hotel in Deal. Apropos of which, having eaten more meals with Simon in more countries than with any other man of my acquaintance I can testify that he had no palate and was only concerned that the food be copious and punctual and the wine abundant, and, if possible, costly. The psychotherapist Andrew McCall who accompanied him frequently in later years, not in a professional capacity, remembers that Simon tried to order two half-bottles of the same wine on the grounds that if they were more expensive than one whole bottle, they must be better. Simon disapproved of the world around him and tried to insulate himself from its effects. He cocooned himself in a circle of preparatory school masters, of which his brother, the gentle, timid, virginal, bulky, half-blind Miles was the fulcrum, and took his pleasure in gossip, beer, point-to-point race meetings and cricket matches. But he was not a hermit. He was not interested in current affairs and never read newspapers but he was happy and effective on BBC chat shows and was never short of a soundbite. He disapproved of the ease of modern travel and communications, preferring his Morris Minor to airborne packages, relishing letters of credit and having recourse to the telephone only when he needed money.

He was not a snob in the ordinary sense but believed everyone should stick to their place in a medieval, hierarchical way: the rich man in his castle, the poor man at his gate. He had no illusions about his own gentility, but, touchingly, was worried about mine and when writing *The English Gentleman* told me that he would rate me as one, though a Jew, because I had my own publishing house, which could count as an estate! Although he revered wealthy, landed figures of ancient stock – rather like the novelist Disraeli who preferred them Catholic – Simon's moral approval was only accorded to the salt-of-the-earth modest fellow, such as CSM Mole in *The Feathers of Death*, who stabs to death, as a deus ex machina, the young officer who so fatally admired Drummer Hartley's bollocks; or the Pay Corps Colonel who keeps the peace in Simon's description of a row among officers in his essay in *The Establishment*. Both are early works but they strike a note that never faltered and never altered for thousands of words from that steadily eloquent pen. He admitted that as the grandson of a manufacturer of socks in Leicester – Granny had a Rolls and a chauffeur whose leggings he much admired as a boy – he could not himself rank as a gentleman though he cultivated what he considered to be upper-class attitudes such as distaste for package tourists, contempt for the lower classes for their whingeing voices, reluctance to question the bill and so forth... all actually more concerns of the middle classes. (When I fathered a child out of wedlock and casually told Simon that he was down for Eton, Simon was indignant maintaining that, as a bastard, he would never be accepted, a severe misreading of current, or, indeed, any other mores.)

The collection which follows is a glittering harvest of Simon Raven's works which can only inspire admiration for his talent, nay genius, as a wordsmith and it may not be wrong to protest the lack of compassion or any emotion other than the most classic of sentiments, but I do remember the slightly frightened individual who, as he lay dying in the City hospital near the Charterhouse, which had taken him in, cried out "Who's paying for all this, I'd like to know?" – before pulling out the plugs.

Anthony Blond 2002

Apology

from
The English Gentleman

I myself am not a gentleman. If I were, I would almost certainly not be writing this book, for one of the marks of a gentleman is that he seldom mentions the question of gentility, whether in application to others or to himself. There are a number of reasons why I am not a gentleman, some of which will become abundantly plain in the following pages; but chief among them is that I have no sense of obligation. I am happy to enjoy privilege: I am also prone to evade or even totally to ignore its implicit commitments. This defect would not necessarily disqualify me from being 'upper class', but it does mean that I can never be a gentleman, which is a very different thing.

As it happens, I am not 'upper class' either. The reasons for this range from middle-class parentage, through chronic and perpetual lack of ready money, to a sneaking fondness for baked beans on toast at tea-time. But somewhere among them lurks the most powerful reason of all – guilt. For although I am prepared to arrogate privilege and disown obligation (in itself a very upper-class way of behaving), I always feel guilty about so doing. This is not to say I make any attempt to mend my ways – I am much too fond of comfort for that – but it does mean that I am uneasy about the advantages which I receive and so cannot enjoy them with the full relish and assurance proper to an uncompromising member of the upper class. Thus I have the worst of both worlds. Exiled for ever from the courts of gentility by a kind of ingrowing dishonour, I am yet ineligible to play the shameless aristocrat, even when I have the means, because I am sadly conscious of that dishonour and so must always be making grovelling gestures to allay my guilt. For example, I always overtip; not out of generosity, which would be all right, nor even out of a desire to show off, which would be tolerable, but because deep down inside me I am afraid that the waiter has in fact detected my vileness and may, unless heavily bribed to refrain, at any moment turn and rend me for it.

There are, of course, consolations. Belonging to neither party, I need be loyal to neither. On the one hand, being known to be no gentleman, I am not blamed by my acquaintance when I behave like a cad, maltreating a woman or failing to return a loan; it is what is expected of me, and is received with equanimity by all. On the other hand, since I am known to lack the steely self-sufficiency, the boundless ability to overlook the feelings or welfare of others, that is perhaps the purest characteristic of the upper class, no one is disposed to mock me for some pitiful display of bourgeois weakness, like apologizing to the restaurateur if a member of my party has been sick on him. My upper-class acquaintance simply recognize my lack of assurance, and then deprecate but tolerate my condition.

Still, you see my problem. I should like to be a

gentleman, or, alternatively, I should adore to be a member of the upper class: both aspirations are entirely vain. After long thought, however, it has become clear to me that it is possible, if not to alter, at least to rationalize my predicament by demonstrating that it is nowadays irrelevant and almost out of the question *to be a gentleman at all*, and that such gentlemen as survive, though honourable and decent men, can only be seen as futile anachronisms when once one properly appreciates the present conditions of society. The mere member of the upper class, as distinct from the gentleman, needs no further castigation these days; we all know how disgraceful *he* is. But the gentleman still retains, in some quarters at least, a title to respect, and he is still, therefore, a worthwhile target of attack. It is thought that he behaves well, is dutiful and responsible, accepts only so much in the way of privilege as his dignity and office strictly necessitate, and would not dream of exploiting or boasting about such superior talents as he may possess – this last a great comfort to the envious and the democratically minded. It is also averred that, as his name implies, he is 'gentle', i.e. mild, in his dealings. The last conception, as it happens, is based on a misunderstanding of the adjective 'gentle' (Latin: *Gentilis*), which in this context simply means 'worthy or typical of a kind (or *genus*)' and has nothing to do with meekness: but this misunderstanding, by its very existence, only pays further tribute to the good character of the gentleman. The gentleman, then, unlike the already discredited aristocrat, is fair game. He still has a name to lose; and it is the purpose of this book to take that name justly and finally from him.

I have owned that my motives are partly those of wounded *amour propre* – someone else would have said so if I hadn't. But even so, my pique is not directed so much at surviving gentlemen *in ipsis* as at the state of affairs which has rendered them incongruous in survival. For while I am jealous of gentlemen because I am not of their number, I nevertheless admire them deeply and find myself out of sympathy with an age which in essence rejects them. The plain fact remains that *we are of our age* and that this age, properly understood, has no use and no regard for gentility. And so, while this book may have had its origins in personal frustration, its arguments have some claim to balance: if I resent the gentleman, I am no friend to his common detractor; and in dealing with either of them I have made some effort to eschew prejudice and to argue from the observed social facts of our time.

Anyone who writes about society should first place himself in relation to society. So far I have only done this in a very general way; here are some of the more relevant details.

I was born in 1927 in a nursing home in Welbeck Street; and as this venue implies, my parents were well-to-do. My father was the son of a self-made industrialist, whose factory and effects, being turned into ready money after his death, had realized close on a million pounds which was then divided equally between the ten-odd children of his two marriages. My mother, coming of a Cambridge family of long-established but only middling tradesmen, had brought no money to her wedding; but my father, though he did no work, had quite enough to support a family in solid comfort. Thus on one side I was two generations out of the gutter, while on the other I had a petty bourgeois inheritance of at least a hundred years. I grew up in Surrey stockbrokers' country, was sent to a smartish Surrey prep. school (sixty guineas a term – a high fee before the war), was evacuated in 1940 to a competent and rather cheaper school in Somerset, and in 1941 won top scholarship to Charterhouse. Hence I was expelled for homosexuality in the autumn of 1945, but not before I had won a Classical Scholarship to King's College, Cambridge, and played in the same school cricket XI as Peter May. There followed a happy time in the rough and ready Army of the immediately post-war period. Since the war was too recently concluded for people to worry much about morality, my disgrace at Charterhouse did not prevent my being sent to India as a cadet and then duly sent back again with a commission in the Oxfordshire and Buckinghamshire Light Infantry, a regiment of sound if hardly brilliant social standing. I was consequently forgiven by the authorities at Charterhouse and allowed to join the old boys' association. Meanwhile King's College, in its benign traditional tolerance, had never made much of my expulsion, and indeed by this time had probably forgotten all about it; so I was allowed to come up to Cambridge, after being demobilized in 1948, with the privileges and emoluments of a Foundation Scholar and with the boundless anticipation of pleasure and enlightenment proper to my extreme youth.

Of King's I shall have more to say later in this book. Enough to remark here that my expectations were little disappointed, but that I repaid the kind attentions I received by getting dangerously into debt and badly confounding my tutor's hopes in my final Tripos. Even so, I was elected to a Studentship so that I could stay on at the College and write a thesis in competition for a Fellowship. To this piece of consideration, for which I was genuinely grateful, I responded by getting even deeper into debt and totally neglecting my research. For I had begun to have outside aspirations; I was being allowed to write reviews for a well-known weekly, I had written a novel of which I thought highly (it never appeared, I am thankful to record), and the anonymous routine of low-paid and conscientious research sorted ill with my new character of cosmopolitan literateur. As Cyril Connolly has it, I required to be paid - and still more important, praised – on the nail. I had my deserts: a little cash, a little praise – and the total collapse of my hopes of a Fellowship, which I had foolishly seen as something one might dawdle into with the insouciant idleness of a latter-day Petronius. Being disabused of this illusion, I saw it was time to go. King's College and I had had enough of each other for the time being. But go where?

I then took one of the few decisions I have never regretted. It was at that time very easy for any graduate who had previously held a temporary commission to return to the Army, with a regular commission and back-dated seniority, after completing his university course. After four years at Cambridge this seemed just the thing. Travel, action, a breath of fresh air…My application was accepted, and within a few months of deserting my research I found myself a senior lieutenant in the King's Shropshire Light Infantry. Of this excellent corps, as of King's College, I shall have more to say later. For the present I shall only say that by my regiment, as by my college, I was treated with every kindness and given every opportunity – treatment to which I reacted, after some four and a half years, by becoming so deeply indebted to so many bookmakers that I was assured of total ruin. At this juncture my seniors, so far from showing ill will, used all their influence to speed my resignation through what are normally very cumbrous processes, it being their wish to get me safely out of the Army before the scandal became so openly obtrusive as to require official action – which in this case would have meant my trial by court martial for conduct unbecoming the character of an officer and a gentleman. Their efforts were successful: the Army Council's acceptance of my resignation reached the regimental headquarters a few days before the first of the bookmakers' emissaries, and I was therefore free, as a private person, to repudiate my debts without any punishment more severe than being warned off the Turf.

And so, at the age of thirty, I had successively disgraced myself with three fine institutions, each of which had made me free of its full and rich resources, had trained me with skill and patience, and had shown me nothing but forbearance and charity when I failed in trust. Small wonder I was becoming a prey to guilt. Small wonder I was beginning to realize that, whatever else I might become, I was now discredited far beyond the point where I could claim to be a gentleman. True, my defects were negative, consisting in vanity and weakness rather than in active malice. Even so…But there were now other and more pressing considerations. For one thing, I had to eat. Money must be procured, some sort of career contrived. I must clearly take up again the literary connexions which had made me so vain of myself while still at Cambridge. For in a literary career there was one unfailing advantage: no degree whatever of moral or social disgrace could disqualify one from practice – and indeed a bad character, if suitably tricked out for presentation, might win one helpful publicity. It wouldn't even matter if one went to prison. The abdication was final: by becoming a writer one bade farewell at once to ethical restraint and to any kind of conventional status in society.

In all fairness to myself, I should add that I did have a modest talent for the pursuit of letters. I enjoyed writing, and it was my pride to render clear and enjoyable what I wrote. A reader, I thought, must pay in time and in money for his reading; both courtesy and equity therefore required, not indeed that one should defer to his possible opinions, but that one should attempt to entertain him while demonstrating one s own. This is a matter of the simplest common sense, but as relatively few aspirant writers ever seem to grasp the point, those that do set out with a distinct advantage. But let all this be as it may, my fortune has been moderately kind in the three years since I 'resigned' from the Army and commenced properly as author. I am allowed to write reviews and even long essays for certain established periodicals; and I have, up to this time, published three novels, one of which at least has been kindly received.

Now, I have given this potted autobiography in order to let the reader know where I stand. In the same way as it was only fair to confess to some personal pique at being neither a gentleman nor a member of the upper class myself, similarly it is but proper that I should present other and more detailed circumstances of my life, so that anyone who wishes may count the chips on my shoulder and then discount what follows in this book to allow for such prejudices as he may think my career and background have induced in me. For my part, I can only say that I have attempted to see to my prejudices myself; and I should also like to point out that of the three institutions – school, college and regiment – that have in various degrees and with good reason rejected me, for none do I feel *personally* anything save the warmest

8

affection, whatever criticisms I may offer on other levels. Finally, it should be clear from the foregoing account that I am qualified to write of those whom society calls 'gentlemen' in this respect at least – that I have, after all, passed most of my life in their company.

It now remains, since this apologia is also an introduction, that I should say something more of the thesis of this book – should give broad notice of its argument and division.

In Part I, which I shall call *Tradition*, I shall attempt to assemble and discuss the principal elements, cultural, historical and social, which I believe have gone to form the traditional English notion of what constitutes a 'gentleman'. These separate elements, some of which have been imported from distant races and ages, some of which are truly indigenous, will be seen, for all their diversity, to combine into a coherent and consistent whole. I shall demonstrate this fusion and conclude Part I with a generalized portrait of the English gentleman – his manners, morals, origins, occupations, code of honour and beliefs – as he might have been seen at the beginning of this century and can still, in rare cases, be seen today. I shall also be at some pains to distinguish between those who are gentlemen in the full and demanding sense of the word and those who, through accidents of birth, office, appearance or property, are loosely referred to as such, although they have few of the real qualifications. For while there is a certain social level below which no one can properly call himself a gentleman, this level lies qui e low in the scale (just how low I shall try to make plain); and I cannot over-emphasise that to be a gentleman it is not sufficient, and is not indeed even necessary, to belong to what is known as the 'upper class', itself to be investigated more closely later on.

In Part II, *Degeneration*, I shall show how the ideal presented in Part I has either declined or become obsolete during the last fifty years. As a start, we shall go back to the upper class, define it more exactly, and show that the tendency of its members is to rely on externals, such as prestige, power, rank, money or privilege, whereas the gentleman, whether or not he also belongs to the upper class, has always been more concerned with justice, obligation and duty. I shall then point out that there has been in this country for some time an increasing popular concern with overt status and material goods, that the main social emphases are now fixed in such things, and that in consequence men are judged largely in relation to them. From which it follows that a man's quality is far more likely to be assessed, not with reference to his character, courage and probity, but in accordance with such upper–class criteria as 'pounds sterling and strawberry leaves'. To make matters worse, such standards are applied in the most vulgar and philistine fashion: after all, one might tolerate a world in which a man was revered as a relative of the King or for his collection of antique statuary, but it is not easy to acquiesce when prestige is conferred by the ownership of a Bentley or an expensive greyhound.

We shall then consider, since it is closely linked with the above phenomenon, the contemporary distrust of personal excellence. On the whole, people do not resent other people's possessions, if only because they might at any time 'come up on the pools' themselves: but what does stir up jealousy and ill feeling is the idea that someone might be, *in himself and for his own qualities*, superior to the general run. Now, the type of excellence demanded of a gentleman is very limited; but excellence it nevertheless remains, particularly in matters of character and conduct. The average man will no longer suffer that someone else should appear superior on this or any other personal ground, and so one way of settling things is for *everyone* to announce that he is a gentleman. Since the necessary integrity and sense of honour can hardly be assimilated overnight, recourse is had to externals. One man has been a temporary officer during the war and now joins the territorials for the prestige of the commission; another can just manage a B.B.C. accent; a third has a habit of dress or drinking which he considers elegant; a fourth runs a tired hack in the local Point-to-Point. Thus face is saved; by apeing the gentleman in one external respect – however trivial – every Jack is made a gentleman and, once more, we are all equal. After all, everybody nowadays is addressed as 'esq.' on his letters and goes through a door marked 'gents'.

And so we shall have seen how the general adoption of material standards and the general resentment at personal quality have combined to cheapen the notion of gentility. But the case is even worse. For the trouble is that even if a man admires the true ideal of gentility and wishes to conform to its canons, he will find that it is now either impossible or irrelevant to do so. It has always, for example, been the mark of a gentleman to lend public support to the established religion of his country – however strong his private doubts. But if ever there was an irrelevance in English life, it has been, since 1918, the Church of England. Or again, a gentleman recognizes his obligations to those less fortunately placed – all of which obligations have now been firmly shouldered by the State. Good manners will more likely prove an embarrassment than an asset: offer your seat in the tube to a woman or an older man, and some young lout will probably crash down on it while you are still being thanked. (This has happened in my presence twice in the last three months.) To be grave on a grave occasion is to be seen as 'pompous': discipline is viewed either as 'provocation' or 'thwarting of personality': the display of courage as 'what we'd *all* have done if we'd been there'. Let me labour the point no further: the ideal of gentility has widely declined, and those who are still true to the banner will find themselves the victims either of mockery, envy or indifference, and in no case able to render the services they wish.

So far the discussion will have been largely theoretical. In Part III, *Illustration*, I propose to offer concrete evidence for my thesis. It will be the longest section of the book but needs only a short description here. I intend, quite simply, to give accounts of certain people and circumstances in my own life. I shall describe how I was trained, at school, to adopt the correct gentlemanly ethic, how I betrayed this ethic, but how I have since seen the ethic itself, rendered futile by the times, betray those who were true to it. I shall give an account of some of the 'upper–class' cavortings which I have witnessed in London and elsewhere – concrete instances of the decay of manners and morals which has perverted public taste and brought disrepute on an imperial class. I shall also tell of some gentlemen I knew in the Army – how they were still able, in the artificial conditions which prevailed, to assert themselves usefully under arms, and how they were ruthlessly beaten down when, for one reason or another, they emerged into the outer world. Finally, I shall say something of my time at King's College, Cambridge; my purpose in this being to show that tolerance, learning and scepticism, the paramount virtues of the place, may inculcate an ethic which, flexible yet not dishonourable, will equip a man to deal with present realities in a practical but seemly fashion that cannot be taught by the defunct codes of gentility. I am sorry that the gentleman has passed; after telling the manner of his passing, I shall be at some pains (though I expect no thanks for them) to suggest how we may fill his place.

The Green Years

from
Shadows on the Grass

'Pittifer Joe' Potts was also a modest man. Forty years of teaching Classics and Cricket at St. Dunstan's Preparatory School at Burnham-on-Sea had made him, one might hazard, more contented and more humble by the year. And yet there was much of which he might have boasted. He was, for a start, a brilliant teacher of Greek, and managed to push enough of it into me, starting from scratch and during the single year I was at St. Dunstan's, to win me a Scholarship to Charterhouse during the summer of 1941. What was more, Pittifer Joe was a marvellous instructor in that most difficult of all strokes, the Leg Sweep. Yet he took no undue pride in these attainments, just attended quietly to the needs of his pupils, swift to correct but slow to anger—until one day in that summer of '41 he revealed a streak of violence and brutality which, latent and unsuspected over the full forty years he had served the school, now burst over our astonished heads like Vesuvius over the lotus-eaters of Pompeii.

It happened in this wise. At the end of the Easter Term

the maths master had very properly followed the call of the bugle, and the school had been compelled to employ a middle-aged temporary called 'Wally' Wallace. Although Wally knew little mathematics and less science, he was quite a plausible bluffer and had the wit to discover straight away which boys had some reputation at his subjects and then, as it were, to pace himself by them. If he were uncertain how to solve a problem, he would not flounder about trying to do it himself, he would set the whole class on to it and then announce that the school swot had come up with the correct answer. The school swot ('Lotty' Loder he was called) would then be invited to come up to the blackboard and demonstrate his solution to the accompaniment of grateful and approving nods from Wally...who, however, was calamitously found out on the day when Lotty had been introduced by his neighbour to the delights of self-abuse.

Wally by now had such trust in him that he summoned him to the blackboard without even bothering to look at his work; whereupon the wretched child came limping forward with a huge erection clearly visible under his grey shorts and no solution to propose to his audience. After a few feeble efforts at improvisation he asked to be allowed 'to go to the bog, sir, please', stayed there exploring the full possibilities of his new-found hobby, and left Wally to do his own job for once.

And a sad mess Wally made of it. However, no one complained, because we all liked Wally and those of us who were cricketers much admired his graceful batting and the excellence of his instruction in the nets. Whatever his maths might be, his cricket, in a phrase of the time, was the real McCoy. And this it was which eventually led to his explosive confrontation with Pittifer Joe Potts.

Wally had very properly been appointed assistant cricket master on his arrival, and for some weeks conducted himself as modestly and as prudently as a lieutenant should. The only slight trouble was that Wally was a 'Leg Glance' man who delighted, at the wicket as in the class room, in letting others do the work and deflecting their power to his glory. Now, Pittifer Joe, as I have already mentioned, was a 'Leg Sweep' man: he believed that one should positively hit the ball and that there was something unmanly, un-British and even un-Christian in merely deflecting it. From this it will be plain that the difference between Wally and Pittifer was not just technical or even stylistic—it was fundamental and it was moral. Nevertheless, such were the efficiency and the deference with which Wally filled his subordinate role that for some weeks, as I say, all went well. Both men sensibly contrived to avoid making Leg Sweep versus Leg Glance into any kind of issue…until the day of the Scholars' Picnic.

This took place early every June in honour of those boys who had won Scholarships to Public Schools in the May examinations. Before the War the school had travelled to Cheddar Gorge or Dunster Castle for the celebration: in 1941 it was held a few hundred yards down the beach by which we lived. The great feature of the day was to be The Dutch Game, as we called it. For this the school was divided into fifteen groups of five boys; each group ranged in age from eight to thirteen, and spent the entire day from eleven in the morning constructing a fort of sand to resist the tide, which would begin to encroach on our labours some time around four p.m. The fort which was judged to have held out the longest would win the competition, and the group which had constructed it would receive a florin a head—half a crown for the group leader.

Of all the childhood games which I remember, I think The Dutch Game was the most thrilling. The tension mounting as the tide rose, the desperate reinforcements and adjustments as the first trickle lapped up some tiny channel, the haste and huddle of the final retreat within the walls of the fort (obligatory, by the rules, when the first proper wave reached the ramparts)...it is these I would choose if the gods offered me a few hours back as a boy. But matchless as The Dutch Game was, there was one other game which ran it pretty close and obviously, in the view of Lotty Loder, beat it altogether. Since his induction into masturbation on the day of Wally's unmasking, the ingenious fellow had refined a series of subtle and varied methods which he confided and later actually exhibited to such of his acquaintance as expressed interest. Hitherto, for whatever reason, there had been no question of 'doing it to each other' or even of 'doing it together'; one was simply permitted to watch. But the Scholars' Picnic, in this matter as in others, was to prove a feast of revelations.

Now Lotty Loder (who despite his auto-erotic frenzies had achieved an exhibition to Blundell's) was a group leader in The Dutch Game. Even quite early it was observed by Wally Wallace and others that Lotty's fort was progressing very slowly. Wally, an oddly innocent man, could not imagine why: the rest of us could have told him that it was because Lotty kept whisking one or other of his group into the sand dunes for a look at 'Lotty tickling his pee', as the exercise was currently dubbed. After the third of these expeditions, this made with an intelligent and sultry ten year old, Lotty returned in a state of some bewilderment and came lolloping along the beach to talk to me.

18

'It's even more fun,' Lotty said, 'if you tickle one another. Young Hayward suggested it. I can't think why I never thought of that before.'

'*I* thought of it before,' I said.

'Why didn't you tell me?'

'It makes *them* cross. It happened at my last school and there was a dreadful row. We were told it might ruin our whole lives.'

'Oh. Does it ruin your whole life if you just do it to yourself?'

'No. But they're not too keen on that either.'

Lotty went thoughtfully away. But clearly my warning had not gone very deep, as soon after lunch I saw him disappear again with 'young Hayward'.

Pittifer Joe came on the scene.

'Where's Loder?' he said. 'His fort's jolly feeble.'

'He's gone to the bog in the dunes, sir.'

This, as I had supposed, for the time being satisfied Pittifer Joe, who now hung around giving me unwanted advice about the design of my own fort. But at last,

'Loder's taking a long time,' he said. 'Wallace,' he called to Wally, who was ambling along under the dunes, 'just have a look for Loder, please. He's somewhere in there and he's neglecting his fort.'

Wally turned without enthusiasm to climb the steep dunes. Pittifer, noticing Wally's reluctance and not entirely satisfied with delegation of duty, started walking up the beach after him. Something must be done very fast. Always a slow thinker, I was paralysed, my mind a blank. Fortunately there were quicker wits than mine in the group.

'Sir,' said Broxton I (a tall, morose, precocious boy, with legs like tooth-picks), 'Sir,' he called to the departing Pittifer, 'can you please explain something?'

Pittifer turned.

'If the Leg Sweep is better than the Leg Glance, why did Prince Ranjitsinjhii always do Leg Glances?'

'Who told you that?'

'Mr Wallace, sir. In science yesterday.'

'*Did* Mr Wallace say that, Raven?'

'Yes, sir,' I lied, by now having some notion of Broxton I's tactic.

'Wallace—please come here.'

Wallace, half way up the dune and not at all sorry to be recalled, plodded down through the fine sand and back on to the beach. Pittifer Joe went to meet him.

'Did you tell the Sixth Form in the Science Period yesterday,' said Pittifer levelly as they met, 'that Ranjitsinjhii always played the Leg Glance and not the Leg Sweep?'

'I might have done,' said Wally amiably. (Having no science, he usually allowed the period to turn into a conversational miscellany and in his own casual way imparted a lot of valuable general knowledge.) 'Yes, I might have done,' he said. 'It's true, you know.'

'It is not true,' said Joe sternly.

Although I could not see his face, I could tell from his tone that he had thinned and primmed his mouth into what we called his 'confiscating' expression. ('Nasty little boy, eating sweets in form. Watch me now. I'm going to put them all on the fire. One by one. One...two... three...')

'Oh, come along,' said Wally. 'You know that photo in the Jubilee Book of Cricket. "Ranjitsinjhii glancing the ball off the Leg Stump".'

'There is also a photograph, in the Lonsdale Library book on Cricket, of Ranjitsinjhii sweeping to leg. He did not *always* glance.'

'That photo,' said Wally earnestly, 'has no definite caption. It only says "Ranji playing to Leg".'

'He was playing off the front foot. He must have been sweeping.'

'It is quite possible to *glance* off the front foot.'

'His bat is at an angle for sweeping.'

Lotty came out of the dune with Hayward. Hayward looked jubilant. Lotty looked even more bewildered than he had the last time, and rather haggard with it. What was that story, I thought with some alarm, about the brain turning to water?

'He could perfectly well be glancing,' said Wally, mild but persistent, 'even with his bat at that angle.'

'He was not glancing,' rasped Joe; 'he was sweeping.'

'All right, have your own way,' said good-humoured Wally. 'All I really meant was that Ranji glanced much more often than he swept.'

'Not true. Lies. Beastly lies.'

For some reason, Wally's concession had infuriated Joe more than anything yet. His face, I reckoned, must now be at its 'Filthy little pig' stage, which it normally reached only in cases of cheating or theft.

'Lies,' said Joe, low but intensely malignant. 'Where have you been, boy?' he yelled at Lotty as he slunk past towards his fort.

'Going to the bog, sir.'

'Lies,' shouted Joe, transferring his rage, apparently without even noticing, from Wally to Lotty. 'Horrible lies. Look at your face, the rings round your eyes, you've been polluting yourself, you'll go blind, you'll go to hell—'

'—Steady on,' said Wally. 'You can't go accusing people of that sort of thing.'

Luckily Hayward had got out of Joe's arc of vision

before Joe spotted Lotty. Otherwise, I thought, his accusations would have been far worse.

'I hate LIARS,' howled Joe. (Yes; howled.)

He seized Lotty by the hair and jerked his head backward and forward, faster and faster.

'Stop that,' said Wally.

He hit the inside of Joe's elbow very hard with the wedge of his hand. Joe released Lotty's hair, nursed his arm, and bowed his head. Wally nudged Joe off along the beach. No reference was made to the incident, nor did Pittifer Joe lose his temper, ever again.

During later discussion of the day, while all mention of the quarrel was carefully avoided, questions were nevertheless asked about why Lotty Loder had loitered so long in the sand dunes. A normal 'Lotty session' took three minutes flat: this time he and Hayward had been gone fifteen.

'What on earth was going on?' we insisted.

Lotty sweated and blushed, refused to gratify the curiosity of the general, but later confided in myself. What had taken so long, it transpired, was that Lotty had had his first adult orgasm ('White stuff coming out') and had nearly fainted from pleasure.

'I had to hang about and pull myself together,' Lotty said.

Hayward had been delighted, relishing the unusual nature of the performance and attributing Lotty's ecstasy to his own skill. But Lotty was bothered. What was this remarkable phenomenon? Always before he had had 'the feeling', along with a lot of 'throbbing and juddering', and then it had 'sort of exploded' and gone away, leaving a slight discomfort 'in my pee', as he explained, which, however, vanished in ten minutes or so, whereupon he was immediately able to start up again. But this time he had felt—well—as if he had been 'drained', and hadn't 'got keen again' for nearly an hour, by which time he was sitting in his fort with his team surrounded by the sea. He had been about to suggest that they all did it together, only the Headmaster's wife had been paddling in that area and it had seemed unwise. But the real point was, Lotty said, that he must know exactly what had happened to him in the dunes. Hayward had been vaguely reassuring and had quoted a rhyme which his elder brother, now at King's School, Bruton, had taught him:

> First it tickles and it prickles,
> Then it trickles:
> Then it squirts and it spirts
> For hours and hours
> When you see Harcourt Minor in the showers.

But there was an element of hyperbole here which Lotty mistrusted, and in any case the thing was too frivolous to carry the authority for which he craved. Now, I seemed to know a lot about all this, with all the talk of the row there had been at my last place: could I please enlighten Lotty? Was this afternoon's occurrence in the natural order, or had he been overdoing it?

So then I told him. It would seem, I said, that he *had* been doing it rather a lot by other people's standards, but otherwise everything was as it should be. It hadn't yet happened to me, I went on, because I hadn't yet got 'hairs down there' ('Ah,' said Lotty); but sooner or later I would and it would, and it was the same for everybody. 'For girls?' said Lotty. *Mutatis mutandis*, I replied. I then went on to explain the mechanics of sexual intercourse and the conception of children, which was, I said, what the whole apparatus was meant for.

'It seems to me you can have a lot of fun without any nuisance of that sort,' said Lotty, who was not an Exhibitioner Elect of Blundell's for nothing.

In fact, it now appeared, Lotty found the whole arrangement so ridiculous ('I mean, imagine trying to stick it in your mother.' 'You're not *supposed* to stick it in your mother.' 'Well, in Matron or Mrs Mack the cook. You'd look absolutely *daft*.') that he suspected me of having him on. What was the *provenance* of the information, he wanted to know? In what circumstances had I come by it? How could I authenticate it? Since he would not be satisfied save by the most accurate, detailed and logical account of how I came by my knowledge, I was compelled to give him the full story...

...Which can conveniently begin at the Oval in August, 1938. A boy called Crawford, a friend of mine at my first prep. school, had a father who had tickets for the timeless test against the Australians. I was invited to accompany Crawford *père et fils* to several days of the match, and there we now were, watching Hutton as he plodded towards his world record. Whatever you may hear to the contrary, take it from me that it was a pretty dreary performance; I was far more interested in the man on my left, who kept peeling great strips off his finger-nails with other finger-nails. How long, I wondered, before he had none left? This question was not to be answered, as the man left shortly afterwards, as soon as Hutton broke Hammond's record. But by that time there was a much more absorbing drama in the offing, something which we had been working towards ever since we arrived in the Stand at eleven o'clock that morning.

Imagine us there. Crawford and myself, in gray shorts and turned down knee socks topped by our school colours (red and green), airtex shirts and horizontally striped school ties, gray jackets and big gray floppy sunhats which sported the school riband…imagine us there, Crawford and me, one on either side of Mr Crawford, who was in a dark blue chalk-striped suit, and had iron-grey hair cut very short and an iron-gray Hitler moustache. There we had been sitting, as I say, since eleven o'clock, and now at last Mr Crawford was about to put the boot into his son's belly in the manner which he must have been planning ever since we sat down.

Mr Crawford had set the thing up by asking for an account of the 1st XI Cricket season at our school. Both Crawford and I, though only ten, were in the XI, and we started on an artless history of the matches played, interrupting and supporting each other, strophe and antistrophe, sticking mostly to fact but occasionally issuing half-baked tactical or general judgments.

The first match had been against Fan Court, where all the boys were Christian Scientists and constantly dying, we assured Mr Crawford, of ruptured appendices because they were never allowed a doctor. Fan Court had made 57, which was a pretty feeble score. One of their batsmen had wet himself with fear of our fast bowler and had then fainted. We afterwards heard (said Crawford) that he died of sunstroke because he wasn't given any medicine, only prayed for. No, I said; it couldn't have been sunstroke because it was a very chilly day in early May; it was infantile paralysis. What happened in the match? prompted Crawford Senior.

'We won with 4 wickets down,' said Crawford. 'I made 62.'

'How can you have made 62 if the other side only made 57?'

'We played on after we'd won.'

25

'How many had you made when you passed their score?'

'Nineteen, Daddy.'

'Then that's all,' said Mr Crawford with evidence satisfaction, 'that counts. Nineteen not out. *That* is what goes into the averages. How many did you make, Raven?'

'Didn't bat, sir. I'm a bowler.' (As, in those days, I was.)

'Did you get any wickets?'

'Three, sir.'

'Jolly useful. They say one wicket equals 20 runs. Say 15 in prep. school cricket. So you got the equivalent of 45 runs—much better than 19 not out.'

And so the morning had gone on.

By the time we reached the Bigshott match, two patterns had become abundantly plain: the pattern, dismally familiar to all cricketers, of poor Crawford's form as a batsman, which had started brilliant but turned steadily sour; and the pattern of Mr Crawford's inquisition, which consisted of probing into every one of his son's performances, eliciting the maximum disgrace from the bad and somehow contriving to discount or even discredit the good.

'At Bigshott,' said Crawford, setting his teeth, 'they don't have proper lavs. They go in pails. They make the boys empty them themselves.'

'Only as a punishment,' I put in.

'What about the match?' insisted the remorseless Crawford *père*.

Well, we had made 136. Crawford had made 2 and I, batting at No 10, had fluked 17. Then they went in to bat. I had taken 2 wickets; Crawford, who was given a trial bowl, had taken none—*but*, I pointed out loyally, had had two sitters missed off his second over.

'I hate bowlers,' announced Mr Crawford, 'who whine about missed catches.'

'I didn't whine,' said Crawford. 'I didn't even mention it. Raven did.'

Mr Crawford appeared not even to have heard. I then went on to describe how their best bat had been in with their last, how their best bat had got the bowling and had a whole over left in which to make the 7 runs needed to beat us, how he had hit a brisk four off the second ball, and had then driven the fourth ball so hard that you could hear it hissing and everyone thought it must be another four—only Crawford at extra-cover had thrown himself down to his left, to take a miraculous catch six inches from the ground and win the game for our school.

'Sheer fluke,' said Mr Crawford.

'Mr Edwardes said that it was very lucky—'

'—Sheer fluke—'

'—But,' continued Crawford patiently, 'that I deserved the luck for being quick enough to get my hands there.'

'Mr Edwardes should know better than to encourage small boys to get conceited.'

By this time I was beginning to dislike Mr Crawford very much indeed. The odd thing was that he hadn't behaved at all like this during the earlier days of the match; he had been a bit sombre but perfectly agreeable, remembering to hand out ice cream money and quite prepared to smile (if not without patronage) at our brash little jokes. Why had he suddenly turned so nasty?

That is a question I couldn't answer then and still cannot. Perhaps he had received one bill too many in the post that morning; perhaps he had failed to satisfy his wife the night before. However that may be, the fact remains that he became more and more unpleasant to his

27

son as the day went on and by the time that the applause for Hutton's record had subsided he was ready to stick in the knife and twist it.

We had now arrived at the Lambrook match, the penultimate of the season. Lambrook had made 97. At the start of our innings wickets fell swiftly but Crawford, who was beginning (too late) to run into form again, had batted steadily and after 45 minutes was apparently in a position to win the match for us, his own score being 23 and that of the team 59 for 5. But at this stage he had stepped back to pull a short ball, slipped and skidded into his wicket...after which disaster we were all out for 72.

'Jolly bad luck,' I said.

'Sheer carelessness,' said Crawford Major. 'Anyway, people who play cow shots deserve everything they get.'

'I was trying to hook,' said Crawford miserably.

'Hooking is for people who can play the game. You didn't even get your Colours. Did Raven get his?'

Raven had got his. So would Crawford have, had he not made a blob in the last match (a shooter), given away 24 runs off his first over, and missed two skiers (out of the sun).

'I wonder you weren't sick on the pitch,' said his father, 'to top it all off. It would have made an apt comment on your entire season's play.'

Now, I hope I have made it clear that Crawford was a jolly nice boy. Although all in all he'd had a wretched season which had ended in cruel humiliation, he had made no complaint and had clapped as cheerfully as anyone, in the circumstances, could possibly expect of him when the rest of us went up the Assembly Room to receive our Colours. But now he had had more than he could bear. Even his one great achievement, the match-winning catch against Bigshott, had been treated by his father with contempt. He needed to get his own back; he needed someone to blame for his misery; he needed a plausible excuse, other than mere 'bad luck', for his failure. And so, like many before and after him in similar predicament, he drew a great big stinking red herring right across the trail, diverting the hounds that tormented him to the pursuit of others.

'It wasn't my fault,' he said: 'I was worried about Colonel Killock.'

There was a long silence.

'Colonel Killock? What about Colonel Killock?'

'Oh, nothing. Nothing, Daddy, nothing.' But it was already too late.

Lieutenant-Colonel Killock, a married man with two sons, had retired from the Indian Army three or four years previously and had come to our school to teach football, rugger, P.T., mathematics and English. He was extremely good at teaching all of them; he was one of the finest natural schoolmasters I ever met, a man whom one would wish above all things to please and would obey as if one's life depended on it; a firm man yet flexible and tolerant, of apparently inexhaustible good humour and good will.

He liked playing with little boys' penises, and he did it so deftly that we positively queued up for him. He also liked letting us play with his own, an object of gratifying size, agreeable texture and startling capacity. One of his particular favourites had a tent which he put up in a remote part of the pine woods which surrounded the cricket ground; and as soon as cricket for the day was over, Crawford and I would hurry through the warm pines to 'The Tent' (as it was known), inside which several boys, ranging in age from nine to thirteen, would already be lolling about with their shorts round their ankles, exploring one another's anatomy and waiting for the arrival of 'Colonel K'. It was a scene of great erotic fascination, vividly memorable to this day, of Petronian power and indecency.

It may be imagined, therefore, that the information which Crawford's father now had from him really set the fuse sizzling. To be fair to Crawford, I think the uneasiness of mind of which he had spoken was genuine: there was obviously something not quite right, to say the least of it, about five boys and a grown man practising circular *fellatio*: however much one enjoyed it at the time, one felt a bit dubious when it was over. Whether or not this uneasiness had affected Crawford's cricket is another matter again, and in any case irrelevant. For what was happening, as I have already tried to convey, is that Crawford was instinctively using 'Colonel K' to create a diversion as a result of which he would be exonerated, at someone else's expense, from any blame for his failure. In fact, of course, he found that he was not only exonerated but was actually deferred to—as long as he kept the revelations coming. Crawford, then, did not stint: any guilt he might feel at his treachery to his companions of 'The Tent' was swiftly allayed by assurance that it was his moral duty to tell all; and so, gleaming with self-righteousness and self-importance, tell all he did.

'They' made a very good job of hushing it all up. The evident approach of war was cleverly exploited in order to arrange that Killock should rejoin his old regiment, which was only too pleased to have a good man back before others grabbed him. It could therefore be egregiously announced, when Colonel K did not appear among the Surrey pines next September, that he had been requested to return to military duty in India. It is a matter of record that he had a 'good war', after which he and his wife started up a 'pre-preparatory' school for boys aged between six and ten. He must have died (which he did suddenly some fifteen years later) an exceedingly happy man.

As for the rest of us, we were dealt with by a combination of enlightenment and threat. In the first place, we were told the full 'facts of life' from Alpha to Omega, in order to straighten us out about the precise (and perverse) nature of our recent experience. We were then told that if ever it all got out none of us would be allowed to go on to his public school. Because we were all so young, 'they' said, 'they' were prepared to forgive us: others would not be so accommodating, so from now on just keep your dear little hands to yourselves and hold your busy little tongues, *or else…*

Mr Crawford and Master Crawford were full of nuisance, Master C because his pleasure in the role of principal delator had made a strutting little monster of him, and Mr C because he was the only parent in the know and was constantly threatening to tell others if the affair was not handled exactly as he thought it should be. Since this would involve calling in the police and the public burning of Colonel K, 'they', who abhorred the idea of publicity and incidentally liked Colonel K as much as the rest of us did, had a problem on their hands…which 'they' managed to solve by agreeing to educate young Crawford free till the end of his time. Thus Crawford *père* was silenced and the boy perforce tolerated. Since he was, *au fond*, a thoroughly decent boy, he returned before long to his natural and agreeable self, from which indeed he would never have departed, had it not been for his father's malice at the Oval. Although Crawford and I often discussed the possibility of 'doing it together again', we decided that 'their' warning was too savage to be neglected. From now on, pleasure under the pines was strictly solitary.

Thus and thus it came about that I was competent to inform Lotty Loder of the full facts of life and to reassure him that his experience in the dunes on that afternoon of the Scholars' Picnic had been, physically at least, entirely *en règle*. 'They' would certainly pass a wet orgasm: what 'they' would not care for, I said, was the idea that young Hayward's ministrations had brought it on. For the rest—well, now he knew.

I had, on the whole, a satisfied client. Lotty's initial incredulity about the facts I offered him had been overcome by the evident sincerity of my tale of how I came by them.

'It must have been fun at your first school,' Lotty said wistfully, 'before it all came out.'

'It was. Tremendous fun.'

'I can't see it happening here. With Wally or Pittifer Joe.'

'Pittifer Joe would have had a fit if he'd caught you and Hayward.'

'Gosh, it was lovely. When that stuff started coming out….'

'I haven't seen that—not since Colonel K. Come on, Lotty; show me.'

And good-natured Lotty obliged.

Charterhouse Pink I

from
Shadows on the Grass

It had all started at a House Match.
It happened that year (1945) that my House (Saunderites) could field five members of the School XI, two of whom, Peter May and myself, had already got our 1st XI Colours. Then there was a particular friend of mine called Ivan Lynch, who was Captain of the House XI, James Prior himself, and one now dead, alas, called Hedley Le Bas, who was Head of our House and, incidentally, of the whole school as well. As may be supposed, Saunderites, with such supplies of talent, had started clear favourites to win the House Cricket Cup, and Hedley, Ivan and James were exceedingly keen we should do so. Myself, I did not care very much, so long as I had some fun and cut a creditable figure; and what Peter May thought in the matter no one ever knew, as he was not, at the age he was then (something over fifteen), much given to utterance. Judging by his later form, I should say that he was determined to do his level best to help us to win without being inclined to recrimination or resentment if we did not.

All that aside, however, the thing had turned sour on us. Talent notwithstanding, we had performed pathetically in the first two rounds (a heavy loss and a shady draw); and in order to retain any chance of winning the Cup we absolutely had to win the match in which we were presently engaged. We were no longer favourites, though in some quarters, so it was said, a recovery was still expected of us. If so, such expectation was fast fading; for now, on a languid evening in mid-June, our situation was desperate.

Our opponents had made 130 all out, a score we should have passed blindfold. Peter May was already the best schoolboy batsman of the century; James and Ivan both purported to bat at 1st XI level; so did I; and there were some promising younger players in the tail. But Peter had been bowled by a vicious shooter; James had been unluckily run out by Ivan; Ivan had been caught on a short boundary having tried to hook a six; and I myself had been stumped off my first ball, having leapt out like Trumper (or so I conceived) to drive the thing over the bowler's head. Our score was now 47 for 4, and Hedley Le Bas, a bowler and a reserve wicket keeper, was going in to bat at No.6.

'An irresponsible stroke of yours,' said Ivan to me pompously, 'considering the state of the match.'

'I didn't think much of yours,' I said.

'I had at least made 17, and it wasn't my first ball.'

'Well at any rate,' I said, 'I didn't run anyone out.'

'You weren't there long enough to run anyone out. Though your stroke was so ridiculous that you could almost be said to have run yourself out rather than to have been stumped.'

'Stop squabbling, you two,' said James.

It was about then that the trouble started.

'Sorry, old man,' said Ivan, and nudged my knee with his.

'Sorry, Ivan,' I said, returning the nudge. 'And now I must go and have a pee.'

'I'm afraid you can't, Raven,' said one of the younger boys who was waiting to bat: 'the rears in the pav are out of order. There's a notice.'

'Then I shall have to go behind the pav.'

'You can't, Raven,' said another boy with infuriating smugness: 'the Scouts are practising putting up their tents behind the pav.'

'Then I shall have to go back to House. What a slog.'

'You can't do that,' said Ivan. 'People will think you're sloping off in a sulk because you've made an egg and we're losing.'

Losing we were worse than ever. Hedley Le Bas was out the next second to a drooping full toss which he fatuously tried to scythe away to leg.

'Look,' I said; 'I'm sorry, but I must have a pee. The only place left seems to be at the side of the pavilion.'

'All the players will see you,' said a pert little blond of thirteen who was keeping the score book.

'I'm too desperate to care.'

So I had my piddle on the side of the pavilion. The only person who noticed was Hedley Le Bas, who was walking in from the wicket and was thus pointed straight at me.

'You oughtn't to do that,' he said, as soon as he'd taken off his pads. 'It makes a bad impression on the younger boys.'

'It's not my fault that the pavilion rears are fucked up. They all understood.'

'Did they?'

'Well, James didn't mind. If there'd been anything wrong he'd have said so.'

Even in those days we all had enormous faith in the wisdom and equity of James Prior. Hedley grunted in what seemed to be assent.

'Forgiven, Hedley?'

'But not quite forgotten. I do not like my monitors to make a public spectacle of themselves, with or without the approval of James Prior.'

'You're the only one that actually saw.'

And this, of course, was the trouble. *As a result of being out*, Hedley had seen. Hedley was in a bad temper because he had only made 3; Hedley was in an even worse temper because we were going to lose the match and with it our last hope of the House Cup; and all this rankled to such an extent that Hedley, although an easy-going and intelligent man, was making a production out of an episode which he would normally not even have noticed.

'What,' he said, 'do you suppose Peter May thought?'

'I suppose he thought that here was a chap who badly wanted a piss…having a piss.'

'Boys as talented as that are highly strung.'

'Rubbish. He's not Mozart or somebody.'

'He could be Bradman or somebody.'

'Bradman wouldn't care. Australians don't care where you have a pee. They're far too coarse. Anyway, May didn't actually see me.'

'He must have heard. God only knows what he thought.'

On this cantankerous note our last wicket definitively fell for a total of 61. Defeated, disgraced, disgusted we trailed back to Saunderites. Hedley said no more about the peeing incident but started to elaborate a theory that a surplus of talent had led to facile over-confidence.

'Anyway, that's that,' he said. 'Now we must concentrate on the Arthur Webber.'

The Arthur Webster Cup was awarded annually to the best all round House Platoon in the Junior Training Corps. (In those days Public Schoolboys belonged to the J.T.C., residual legatee of the old O.T.C., while everyone else was in the Army Cadet Force.) Hedley, as Under Officer and Platoon Commander, had a great deal of personal prestige at stake here, and now sought to hearten the dismal little band of cricketers by persuading them that great things were in store for them on the field of honour. None of this impressed me, as I was immune from military zeal and indeed belonged to the Air Training Corps (a sloppy outfit which wore shoes instead of Ammunition Boots) especially in order to avoid the martial excesses which Hedley was now extolling; but I was delighted to think that the dear fellow had found a new interest so quickly, and fondly imagined that my urinary gaffe (if gaffe indeed it were) would now be dismissed from his consciousness for ever.

And so I think it would have been, had not Fate decreed a most unlikely and unlucky sequence of events which was put in train on the next day but one.

The Charterhouse XI was on its way from Godalming to play Tonbridge School at Tonbridge. A change of train had been made at Guildford. The train in which we were now travelling had no corridor and no convenience attached to the compartment in which we were seated… 'we' being Peter May, Ivan Lynch, Hedley Le Bas, James Prior and myself, the whole Saunderite set, plus my friend and fellow-scholar of the Classical Sixth, a merry-witted boy called Robin Reiss.

After we had been travelling for about three quarters of an hour with many halts,

'You're not going to believe this,' I said, 'but I must have a pee.'

37

'Oh God,' said Ivan.

Hedley looked up sharply but said nothing.

Peter May looked straight in front of him as if he hadn't heard.

'Why didn't you go at Guildford,' said Ivan.

'No time.'

'Plenty of time if you hadn't insisted on buying that *Lilliput* at the book stall.'

Lilliput, Men Only and *London Opinion* were the three wicked monthlies of my youth, crammed with coloured pictures of nearly naked ladies, decorous indeed by modern standards but in those days passing fierce and inflammatory.

'*You* liked looking at that *Lilliput*,' I said.

As indeed they all had, except Peter May, who, when offered it, had not lifted a hand to take it or moved a single muscle of his body in any direction.

'Much better,' said Ivan, 'that you should have had a pee.'

Hedley scowled. Peter sat. Ivan pouted. James pondered. Robin Reiss twinkled. I shifted sweatily from ham to ham.

'Does anyone know,' said James, 'how long it is before we reach Tonbridge? Robin, you live round here, don't you?'

'Yes,' said Robin, twinkling more than ever. 'Tonbridge is about forty minutes.'

'Many stops?'

'Lots,' said Robin gaily, 'but none of them long enough for anyone to have a pee.'

'That settles it,' I said.

I stood on my corner seat, crouching to avoid the luggage rack, took out my piece, and made pretty good shift to aim my jet through the gap between the ventilating panels—a narrow target even though they were open as wide as they would go.

'Bravo,' said Robin.

The train slowed and lurched into Tonbridge Station while yet my golden stream showered from the window.

'Mind that Postman,' Robin said.

'Why didn't you tell me we were almost at Tonbridge?'

'Time to get out,' James said.

We gathered our gear and slouched up the hill to the school.

That was the first time I ever saw the Head at Tonbridge, a ground on which I have been many times since and come to know as well as any in the Kingdom. Trees and a long expanse of playing fields to the West; a green bank and then a lawn to the North; more trees, with margins of grass to the East, and beyond these the undistinguished yet satisfying nineteenth-century buildings, which sit so well in their place; and to the South the roofs of Tonbridge dipping to the Weald, the Weald rising to a ridge, and the white clouds scudding along its spine on the bright and breezy days when the Head is at its best.

But such days were far in the future. *That* day in 1945 was not bright or breezy: it was gray, still and very damp. Tonbridge, having won the toss, elected to bat and were all out for 37; and the rest of the morning and most of the afternoon was spent by me in watching Peter May and our Captain, Tony Rimell, while they piled up superfluous runs which would not even, once the Tonbridge total was passed, count in their own averages. Still, I had my Colours safe, so it didn't matter much that I had no chance to shine. No chance to shine, after all, means no chance to be eclipsed. No doubt I should have passed that gray afternoon pleasantly enough, sitting on the balcony of the Tonbridge pavilion, had not Hedley Le Bas arrived up there in fierce remonstrance.

'Disgusting exhibition on the train,' he said.

'I couldn't help it, Hedley. If it was going to be forty minutes to Tonbridge—'

'I—It wasn't forty seconds.'

'But Robin Reiss said—'

'Robin Reiss is a well known joker. Couldn't you have used your intelligence? If the train was really going to take forty minutes more to Tonbridge, we should not have reached Tonbridge Station until well after 11 .30—the time at which the Match was due to start. And you know very well that Tony Rimell would never have arranged a scruffy performance like that.'

This was a valid point.

'I'm sorry,' I said.

'What do you suppose Peter May thought?'

I was getting thoroughly sick of this particular question.

'He didn't seem to notice.'

'And what do you suppose he thought when you offered him that Lilliput?'

'The same. He just didn't seem to notice.'

'He was probably dazed by shock,' Hedley said. 'It was almost as though you were pimping for the girls in that paper. God knows what damage you may have done to Peter.'

'He's made a pretty sharp recovery,' I said, as Peter drove the ball up the Northern Bank to complete his fifty.

'Mental damage.'

'Because he was offered a *Lilliput*? They're lying about ten inches deep all over the House.'

'The other thing.'

'Because he saw somebody peeing out of a window?'

'Not so much that…though it wasn't a pretty sight… but because he saw someone whom he is supposed to respect behave with complete lack of self-control and discrimination. You nearly hit that Postman. Someone might have sent for the Police. As Head of the School, I shall have to instruct Tony Rimell, as Captain of Cricket, that you are not a fit person to represent Charterhouse in the 1st Eleven.'

'For Christ's sake, Hedley.'

'I mean it. You've put yourself beyond the pale.'

Hedley departed. James Prior came and sat down next to me.

'You look awful,' he said.

I told him of Hedley's intention.

'Will Tony Rimell listen to him?' I said.

'He'll have to. Hedley's Head of the School. Anyway, everyone listens to Hedley. He has a way with him.'

'I cannot understand,' I said, 'what is this endless drivel about Peter May. My crime seems to be that I have shocked or damaged Peter. What nonsense,' I said, as Peter sent the ball hissing through the trees to slam like a siege missile into the Chapel door.

'Haven't you understood?' said James.

'Understood?'

'Hedley keeps wicket—but we have Oliver Popplewell as our wicket keeper, and a bloody good one. Hedley bowls out-swingers which swing the whole way from his arm in a slow curve like a slack banana. Hedley bats like an imbecile gorilla. In short, Hedley is only in this side until somebody in the 2nd Eleven makes some runs or takes some wickets, and very well Hedley knows it. Now, this is his last quarter and he hankers, he yearns, for his 1st Eleven Cricket Colours. Since he will do nothing spectacular enough to earn them, his only hope is to survive in the side till the end of the season, when Tony will have to follow the custom and make up the number of Colours to a full eleven.'

'I see. And his only chance of surviving that long is a shortage of players. So he's decided to get me out of the way for a start.'

'Right.'

'Oh, *James*.'

'It serves you right. You've given him the chance. You were in an impregnable position as far as cricket went— but you've gone and lost your name with all this stupid pissing.'

'You didn't mind it.'

'I was brought up on a farm. And of course Hedley doesn't give a damn either—he's far too upper class. But your behaviour, if denounced with suitable moral fervour and deplored with sanctimonious reference to the innocence of Peter May, could certainly disqualify you from playing for the XI for the rest of the season— making a better chance of a permanent place for Hedley.'

'All those days out with you and Ivan…I couldn't bear to miss them.'

'Well then. If you promise me to pull yourself together from now on and hold your water like a man, I think I can arrange matters.'

'Oh James. How?'

'The thing to remember, old man, is that Hedley is keen on his *Colours* rather than on actually playing in the side. He is not a cricketer at heart.'

'How do you know that?'

'Because he is not sentimental. All real cricketers are sentimental men.'

A day or two later Hedley appeared with his wrist in a heavy bandage. It was announced that he would not be able to play cricket again that season, but that in recognition of his services already rendered he would be awarded his Colours as Honorary Twelfth Man and allowed, as such, to accompany us on all our away fixtures.

'Which means,' said James, 'that when Tony Rimell comes to make up his lists at the end of July he'll have to make the First Eleven up to Twelve. Eleven chaps in the side—and Hedley comes extra. Twelve Colours are not really in order. I had a terrible task persuading Tony.'

'But surely…it is rather bad luck on Hedley, not being able to play any more.'

'I have already told you. He's not that keen on playing. So he was quite happy to go along with my little scheme and wrap up his wrist in a bandage.'

'Oh.'

'Also, he was relieved that he'd have no further reason for doing *you* down. He hadn't really fancied that. Although he may not be sentimental, he isn't a shit.'

'No. Only a fake.'

'Not even that, perhaps. He desired his Colours so much that he was prepared to give up leading the House Platoon to victory in the Arthur Webster Competition; because obviously if he's not fit for cricket he's not fit for Corps. You know how much the Arthur Webber meant to him in terms of prestige. Yet he was prepared to give it all up to make sure of his cricket Colours—so perhaps,' said James, 'he is a sentimental man after all.'

I am afraid lest I have given rather an unfair impression of Peter May, who has so far figured in these pages as a po-faced booby who batted like an automaton. What I should now like to make very clear is that Peter, as a man, had intelligence and a good deal of charm; and that as a batsman, so far from being a robot programmed always to select and play the most efficient stroke possible in the given circumstances, he had an individual brilliance which often led him to select and play the most satisfying and beautiful, even the most spectacular, stroke possible in the given circumstances—and sometimes in direct defiance of them.

Of the latter gift, more in a moment. First a little tale to demonstrate the fundamental good sense and sensibility of the man.

Although he came to Charterhouse in the Autumn of 1942, Peter May was still under fourteen in the summer of 1943. He was therefore still young enough to sit for a Junior Scholarship, and indeed too young, by the Headmaster's decision, to play for the School Cricket XI, though the cricket master, the Captain of Cricket and George Geary, the professional, were all convinced that he was good enough.

Peter accepted the Headmaster's decision with equanimity and played with great content for the Under 16 XI...where he learnt a great deal more about cricket than he would have learnt, at his age, in the First: for the master who ran the First was a nice but nugatory sort of man, whereas R. L. (Bob) Arrowsmith, who ran the Under 16, had a rare gift, reinforced by picturesque and memorable utterance, for impressing the necessary disciplines on talent, or even (as in Peter's case) on genius.

However, the substance of this anecdote lies, not in the benefits which accrued to Peter through being kept down for a while, but in the interpretations which were variously made of the matter. It was known that it was the Headmaster's veto which kept Peter out of the Eleven, but it was not known on what moral or social ground the veto was based. Some said the Head Man had judged Peter to be in danger of injury if he played among boys so much older, some thought that the danger was not of injury but of Peter's own conceit or others' insalubrious attentions; some opined that the Head Man did not want a Lower School Hero round the place nor yet an object of envy, and some that he was afraid the Press would get hold of the story and run annoying articles about a thirteen-year-old prodigy. On the whole, however, the view which prevailed was the most pedestrian: the Head Man, it was generally asserted, did not want Peter's work to be interfered with and his chances of a Junior Scholarship impaired by the demands of the many whole-day and away matches which, even during the war, were still played by the First Eleven.

In the event, Peter did not win a Junior Scholarship. I remember hearing at the time that he came very near it but that his performance was somewhat tenuous and lacked flair. The general and immediate view was that Peter had got 'the worst of both worlds'; that having been denied his pink First Eleven cap in order that he might win intellectual laurels, he had in the end been crowned with neither. The obtrusive were not slow to express this sentiment to Peter himself. I was the first.

The list of Junior Scholars Elect had just been posted in the Cloisters. Peter, having examined it, was walking away with a subdued air. I was going the opposite way in order to quiz the list.

'Any luck,' I said, as Peter passed me.

He shook his head.

'Pity,' I said fatuously. 'You've been made to give up your chance of a pink hat and got nothing in return. You've got the Head Man to thank for that.'

Peter was a shy boy, who during the two and a half

quarters (terms) he had been in the school had said very little indeed. Now, reluctant to speak but determined that justice should be done, he struggled to present his own notion of the affair.

'I think,' he said very slowly and carefully, 'that the Head Man decided as he did, not to stop my cricket wrecking my hash [work] but to stop my hash spoiling my cricket. I could hardly have made much showing in the Eleven while I was worrying about a scholarship, but I could manage all right in the Under 16.'

In short, Peter was attributing to the Headmaster the kindest and most sensitive of all motives: the Head Man has seen, Peter was trying to say, that the big thing in my life is cricket, and he has made sure that this has not been spoiled for me by my being too early exposed in high places while I am under other and necessary pressures.

Whether this was or was not the Head Man's true motive, I never found out; but it has always seemed to me that Peter's defence of the Head Man, in the face of my loud-mouthed comment, was grateful, generous, and, for a boy of his years, exceedingly subtle.

Whatever the reason behind the Headmaster's edict, Peter continued to play for the Under 16 instead of the First Eleven even after the Scholarship exams were done; and in consequence l am now able, as a member of the same Under 16 side, to give an eye-witness report of an incident which vividly proclaimed the genius of Peter's batting and also illustrated the combination of anticipation, perversity and panache which informed it.

Not long after the conversation in the Cloisters, I was Peter's partner at the wicket during a crisis in the Under 16 Match against Eton. I was having a bad season, out of luck and out of form, was batting low in the list, and was most unlikely to do much to dig us out of disaster. But I could, I told myself, be of service if I could only *stay there* for a while, giving Peter time to gather runs. In the end, I was too feeble and too futile even to defend my wicket for more than a few minutes, but during those few minutes I saw an unforgettable sight.

I was at the bowler's end, while Peter was facing the very fast deliveries (for our class of cricket) of a tall and fibrous red head called Bob Spear (later in life a distinguished judge of racing). Peter was having no trouble with Bob, who pitched the ball well up on a wicket that was fast and true; and what followed may even have been an indication of boredom on Peter's part, an attempt to get entertainment out of doing the easy thing the difficult way. In any event, having efficiently driven the first two balls of Bob's over to the long off boundary in the approved manner and off the front foot, Peter took a quick look at the third, which was an obvious half volley just outside the off stump, and then, instead of making another routine front foot drive, elected to hit it for four off the back foot, with the same ease and accuracy as he might have despatched a very long long-hop, mid way between mid-off and the umpire...greatly to the astonishment of both, who watched the ball pass between them with huge, goggling eyes, as though it had been an emanation of the devil.

Now the great point about Bob's bowling, as I have already suggested, was that it was, for boys of our age, very fast indeed. The speed and co-ordination required to hit it, when well pitched up, off the back foot yet in front of the wicket, very hard and straight back where it came from, were only less remarkable than the perverse ingenuity which conceived and selected such a stroke. The showmanship with which it was carried off was superb, consisting in a total lack of overt enjoyment or sense of the unusual, merely in a slight shake of the head as though to indicate mild displeasure at not having lifted the ball for six instead. Anticipation, perversity, panache.

And, of course, genuine modesty. The quiet and sometimes embarrassed manner in which Peter behaved in the midst of his triumphs reminded one of the poet Horace when he disclaimed personal merit for having written his poetry and gave credit for all to his Muse:

Totum muneris hoc tui est
  quod monstror digito praetereuntium
Romanae fidicen lyrae:
  quod spiro et placeo, si placeo, tuum est.

This is all thy gift
That I am pointed out by the fingers of those that pass
As the minstrel of the Roman lyre.

That I am filled with the breath of song,
And that I please, if please I do,
Is of thy bestowal.

Reading these lines, one understands why everyone liked Horace. It was probably for much the same reason that we all liked Peter May.

Mummy's Boy

from
Shadows on the Grass

But back to the Autumn of 1946. My embarkation leave was rather distressful. Here was I, a grown man and now an Officer Cadet, deserving and desirous of a fortnight of independent and sophisticated pleasure; and here was my leave pay, all £14 of it—and not even as much as that because in theory I was to give some of it to my mother for my 'maintenance'. As for *her*, she was no help at all in sustaining me in my chosen role of aspirant officer about town: she still regarded me as a schoolboy, who should and must come straight home now the term was ended and stay there with no nonsense until it began again.

Neither of my parents was impressed by my posting to India. My mother regarded it as all rather 'silly' and as liable to give me 'silly, independent ideas'. My father thought it was 'bad and silly and bad' that the nation should be paying good money to send 'someone like you' all that way to be trained for a Commission. It wasn't, he said, as if I were going into the Indian Army—not that there would have been much point in that either. When I remarked that Subalterns were still badly needed in the Far East, and that most of us would probably be posted to British Battalions in India itself or in south-east Asia, my father expressed peevish scepticism about the function of such Battalions and the function of anyone as 'floppy' as myself within them, while my mother became exceedingly resentful at the further opportunities I should have, at points East of Mandalay, to incubate 'silly independent ideas'—to say nothing of the fact that when I got leave I could neither be expected nor compelled to come home for it.

That was the sort of parents I had. My sister was too young to understand or comment. Only my brother Myles took interest or pleasure in my situation, partly because he realised it was just the sort of trip I should enjoy, and partly because he could now tell the boys at Charterhouse that I had smashed to pieces the supposedly unbreachable sanctions imposed by my expulsion: for beyond any question I had now become an Officer Cadet and would shortly become an Officer, appointments of honour which tradition declared to be for ever beyond the reach of a man who had been 'sacked', especially if it had been 'for the usual thing'.

Having touched this topic, I should add that people's attitudes in this regard were very revealing. The Army itself simply did not want to know whether one had been sacked or what for, but it did issue every candidate for a Commission with a formal certificate of moral character which must be signed by a priest, schoolmaster or J.P. of his acquaintance before he presented himself at W.O.S.B. Since, in the circumstances, I could hardly apply to the Headmaster for a signature, and did not want to embarrass Bob Arrowsmith or the Uncle (both of whom would have taken such a formality rather seriously), I simply forged Sniffy Russell's autograph on my certificate, knowing that while he too would have been reluctant to sign it in the cold light of day, so to speak, he was yet far too good-natured and loyal to denounce one should reference ever be made to him by the authorities. He would probably, I thought, laugh the same high, dry laugh as he had when Hodgsonite Yearlings were cheated by William, and disappear fast in another direction. In the event, of course, my speculations were never put to the test; the certificate was simply filed and forgotten as the irrelevance which it was—though it still gives me pleasure to reflect that my Emergency Commission, and much later on my Regular Commission, were both made possible, in the original instance, by my own crudely forged moral testimony in my favour.

The Headmaster, when he eventually heard of my Indian prospect, was, I think, rather puzzled. He knew that a moral certificate had to be signed in such circumstances, as he had signed hundreds himself. He had not, he knew, signed mine, so presumably somebody else had. Who and why? These questions, though never uttered, were somewhere at the back of his voice when I rang him up to say good-bye, in itself an entirely natural proceeding, as we had remained friends and corres- ponded as such despite the dismal sentence he had been bound to pass upon me. His sentiments were probably very much those which he entertained towards King's College after the College Council had pronounced my offence trivial and my admission certain: he was glad, as my friend, that things were going as I would wish, but also rather indignant that my wickedness, though punished by him with the gravest penalty in his power, was made so light of elsewhere.

The simple fact was that the immense popularity, over

many years before the war, of the ludicrous Billy Bunter and his friends at Greyfriars' had made the whole punitive apparatus of the Public Schools, flogging and expulsion, the lot, a universal joke. Even Public School men themselves, though grateful and dedicated *alumni* in other areas, could not be got to regard corporal punishment or condign dismissal as anything other than an hilarious 'jape'—which would in any case be forgotten by the next issue of *The Magnet* (as it were), in which Coker the school rotter, publicly whipped and cast forth at the end of the last number, would be back again after some shadowy process of reinstatement lurking among the studies as slimy and villainous as ever. And of course if expulsion was such a light matter, so was what you were expelled for. Never, after my expulsion from Charterhouse, did anybody so much as raise an eyebrow when the thing was mentioned. Most people merely giggled.

But enough of this digression.

When my leave still had four days to run, I received two letters in the same post: the first, accompanied by a cheque for £10, was from my grandfather (maternal) who himself had been a soldier and took vicarious pleasure from my exotic posting; the second was from Hedley Le Bas, suggesting that I should join him for a day or two at Lord's, or even for all three days, during some Festival Match which was to be played early that September. Since these were the last three days of my leave, I wired Hedley that I would meet him by the Tavern the following afternoon and announced to my family my intention of leaving for London early the following morning.

My father, who had seen about enough of me, took this in good part. My brother, although a little sad, quite understood, he said, that I needed a change of scene. We then spent the whole of my last afternoon at home playing a game of small cricket, which we had first devised as children, on an enclosed terrace in the garden, and after Myles had made 402 while impersonating J. D. Robertson he was resigned to the indefinite suspension of play (which was, in fact, never resumed, for when I came home again as an Officer I found small cricket beneath my dignity). Thus all was well—except with my mother. At first she had heard of my intention with apparent good grace: 'It'll be so nice for you to meet your old friend at Lord's,' she had conceded. But as the afternoon went on she had been busily distilling discontent inside herself, and when Myles and I came in from small cricket she fizzed and steamed like a witches' cauldron.

'This boy, Le Bas,' she said: 'I know the name.'
'You do. Head of the School my last summer.

'Yes. One of the boys who got up to filthy tricks, like you.'

'Can't we forget all that.'

'If only we could. But now you're going off to get up to those filthy tricks again at Lord's.'

'We're simply going to watch the cricket.'

'Cricket. Nothing but filthy boys like this Le Bas, playing filthy tricks in the changing rooms…etc, etc… and anyway,' said my mother half an hour later, after poor Hedley was finally disposed of, 'what are you going to use for *money*?'

'I've got ten pounds.'

'Where did you get it?'

'Grandpa sent it.'

'GRANDPA…*sent you ten pounds*? Without asking me? We'll see about *that*.'

She flew to the telephone and excoriated her unfortunate parent for fifteen minutes flat.

'I've made him agree to cancel the cheque,' she said when she came back: 'he quite sees, now, that he shouldn't give you money to encourage *silly ideas of independence*.'

'Too late. I cashed it at the bank this morning. Special clearance.'

'You…deceitful…little…pig,' mouthed my mother, with all the venom (rather a lot) which she had in her.

But the show was over. Game, set and match to me. My mother, although one of the most infuriating and possessive women I have ever known, knew when she was beaten (which in those days wasn't often) and was skilful at assuming a kind of hurt and sorrowful quietude which, with cleverly interposed acts of kindness, was intended to make one feel guilty—and did. By ten o'clock that evening, so tender had been her concern about what I would like to eat and to do 'on your last night at home', so wistful had been her asides about how 'Myles and I will miss you', that I was on the verge of renunciation. However, Myles saw this coming and took me on one side:

'Don't give in,' he said. 'You know how you'll enjoy yourself at Lord's. You mustn't let yourself be blackmailed any more than you let yourself be bullied.'

Good words and true; but justify myself as I might, I had not a moment's mental peace during the whole journey to London.

'Happy days are here again,' said Hedley Le Bas outside the Tavern. 'A pity about that infernal row down at Charterhouse, but I think we're over the worst of it.'

Hedley, skilful operator that he was, had managed to

make his part in the Great Scandal appear marginal, whereas in truth it had been central. He was helped by his already having left the school when the scandal broke, which meant that he could not be summoned and grilled like the rest of us but at the same time could always protest, from a safe distance, that he was being misrepresented. The end of it was that Hedley had been forbidden to appear on Carthusian territory for one calendar year but was not otherwise penalised. Since the year would very soon be done (mid-October) he was indeed 'over the worst of it'. I, on the other hand, was not. It might be many years before I was admitted to the Old Carthusian Club, about which I did not particularly care, or allowed to play cricket for The Friars (the old boys' touring side) about which I cared very much. But I saw no point in going into that now: Hedley would only think I was being envious and dreary, and he would be right.

'Take my word for it,' he was saying: 'old Bags [Birley] knows the ways of the world as well as anyone living. Although he may be playing it rather stiff and stuffy just now, he'll come round just as soon as he sees that we're not letting it get us down. In my case, I was accepted for a Commission in the Life Guards, then they found my heart was a bit dicky, so I was given an immediate place, in mid-term, at Jesus—returning heroes or no returning heroes, they found room for me fast enough. All done by money, of course, and Bags knows that as well as I do, but *it looks pretty good in the score book*: so I'm more or less forgiven already, and by October it'll all be as if it had never been. More beer?'

'Yes please, Hedley.'

'As for you, they'll take you back into the fold just as soon as you get a Commission—and never mind how you got it. The India thing will impress them too. To be an Officer in India is in fact about as unsmart as you can get, but it sounds all right to the middle classes, and Bags is nothing if not middle-class. Have a whisky with that beer. You drink half the beer in one go, then all the whisky in one go, then pour the whisky drops into the rest of the beer and then drink *that* in one go.'

'Where did you learn that trick? In the Life Guards or at Jesus?'

'In a pub by the Mill Road. Some of us from Jesus go there to pick up women.'

'I hope you don't pick up anything else.'

'Been lucky so far. Anyhow, all that's got to stop because I'm thinking of getting married.'

'Why on earth?'

'Must have a son, old boy. Le Bas must have a son.'

'But already? Surely, if there's one thing more unsmart than another, it's an early marriage?'

I had him there; but Hedley was saved, as the likes of Hedley are always saved, by sheer chance, which this time took the shape of Gerald Carter, a plodding but good-humoured member of the XI the year previous to our own.

'What cheer, old chums? Let's have another of what you were both having. Dismal match, this. I thought it was meant to be a Festival.'

'They're all trying to look good in the score book,' I said, 'to fatten up their chances for next year. Although they may call this a Festival, the new era we live in has no time for all that sort of amateur rot. It's graft and grind from now on.'

'I rather think you're right,' said Hedley, taking a beer and a whisky from Gerald. 'Have you noticed that none of the amateurs are wearing club caps or sweaters, Free

Foresters or Harlequins or anything like that? They always did before the war, but now they've been told to wear county colours or nothing. Democracy, you see. It upsets the pros to look at them in their pretty striped blazers.'

'It never upset George or Rainsford,' I said, and drank the second half of the beer Gerald had given me (complete with whisky drops).

'George was too good a player to worry about that kind of thing, and Rainsford was too bad. The sort that are complaining are the mediocre lot—they're always the ones that carry the chips. Blight, P., of Notts—that kind of crap.'

'Exactly,' said Gerald, accepting a fresh beer and whisky from my hands. 'Look what happened the other day down in Kent. Ladies' Day at Canterbury, sun shining, band playing Blue Danube on the boundary, everyone as happy as larks in the sky, and then what happens? Some grimy little pro complains that the music is putting him off. "Fuck that," says the Umpire, "it never put Frank Woolley off. You just play on." (Thank you, Hedley: same again). Then blow me, ten minutes later the same beastly squirt says that the sun shining on the instruments is upsetting him. "You mingy bugger," says the Umpire, "why don't you send for yer cap? That's what it's for, to keep the sun out of yer eyes." "I haven't yet got my cap," says Ferret-face, "and what's more I never shall if I have to play in these conditions." "Conditions?" says the Umpire. "Look you here, laddie: if Les Ames and Arthur Fagg could put up with a band now and then, so can a manky sod like you." So of course the little brute didn't get his way, but you see what a pass things have come to? Some puking junior pro, who hasn't even got his county cap, daring to complain about the

Band at Canterbury. They'll start a Union next. Don't they know they're simply there to entertain us?'

'I fear,' I said, 'that we have been born into the wrong age. Just a hundred years too late. (Thank you, Gerald, I don't mind if I do.) We should have been happier with top hats and round arm.'

'And proper grovelling from the Lower Classes,' said Hedley.

Later on, after some of the base mechanicals also drinking at the Tavern had become hostile to our little group, Hedley drove me to the Norfolk Hotel near South Kensington Tube Station, at that time a creaking and crumbling private hostelry which my family always used when in London. As we rounded Hyde Park Corner, I said,

'I'm terribly thorry, Hedley old bean, but I musht have a pith.'

'A pith?'

'A weedle-weedle.'

'A weedle-weedle?'

'For Chrisht's shake, man: a PEE.'

'God,' said Hedley: '*that* again.'

'It'th quite all right, old faggot. The Law shays I can go on either of your off-shide wheelsh.'

'In Knightsbridge?'

'It's either in Knightshbridge, or it'sh in your car.'

Hedley stopped (in those days you could, wherever and whenever you wanted).

'Make it the rear wheel,' he said: 'it's rather muddy.'

'The Byelaw,' said James Prior, 'under which you thought you were permitted to urinate on the off-side wheel of a stationary vehicle, has long since been rescinded.'

'Why?'

'Notions of public decency. Increase of public provision for relief. Sheer bloody hypocrisy and prudishness. But the fact remains that it *has* been rescinded, and that you could have been arrested and charged with perpetrating an obscene nuisance—and then good-bye to your Commission. For Jesus Christ's sake, stay out of trouble until you've passed out of Bangalore.'

James and I were on the deck of the Troopship *Georgic*, watching the flying fish as they played among the waves of the Indian Ocean. James had done his Primary and Infantry training with the Greenjackets: by a marvellous stroke of luck (for me at least) the potential officers of his intake had been posted to Bangalore with the same draft and in the same Cadet Platoon as myself.

'I've been finding out about Bangalore,' James said now. 'It's not like an English O.C.T.U., where they'll toss you out for showing a fly-button. By the time they've transported you to Bangalore, they've invested so much money in you that they've got to pass you through with a Commission. All you have to do, Simon, is to sit there politely and let the thing go on; and after the prescribed number of weeks you will march off the parade ground as Second Lieutenant Raven. For Christ's sake, and all our sakes, do it. Do it, and everyone will forgive you everything, because a Commission means success and success means exculpation. Do it, and Bags Birley, Bob Arrowsmith and the Uncle will stand in line to welcome you down to Charterhouse again with open arms and beaming faces.

'But if you make a mess of this,' James rumbled on, 'if you are so wilful or perverse or plain stupid as to make a fuck-up where it is, by common consent, almost impossible to make a fuck-up, then you'll have ditched yourself for good and all, and bloody well serve you right.'

'Hedley said much the same at Lord's.'

'Of course he did. He knows the way the world goes round.'

'But we must...well...have *some* fun at Bangalore.'

'Of course we must. We'll have all the fun that's going, we will have food and drink and expeditions and parties of pleasure, but what we will not have is sex. Repeat after me, Simon: NO SEX.'

'NO SEX.'

'No sex with the other Cadets, because even at Bangalore they'll draw the line at that. No sex with white women, even if readily available, because British women in India are, by and large, idle, conceited, pampered and promoted far above their proper class. They are therefore even more prone than most of their sex to interference and malice, and are to be avoided at any cost. And no sex with native women, if only because they stink.'

'What about half-castes? I'm told they're very appetising.'

'So they may be. But they probably have the pox and they certainly have native mothers who chew betel nut.'

Raven Sahib

from
Shadows on the Grass

When we arrived in India we were sent to a Transit Camp called Khalyan (near Bombay) to await transport that would take us South to Bangalore. The only features of the place which I can still remember are a weird conical mountain which spiralled up over it and a seedy fair ground with a Death Wall Rider.

'Transit Camps mean idleness and trouble,' said James; 'we must organise occupations for ourselves.'

'I'm told we can get twelve hour passes to go to Bombay,' I said.

'And what would you do when you got *there*, I'd like to know? We shall stay here, Simon, and I shall go to the Officer who is in nominal charge of us, and we shall have football matches and cricket matches and swimming matches and cross country running matches and—'

'—Isn't that enough to be going on with?'

Some of these things we certainly had, and in this way James continued to keep most of us out of trouble during the very long three weeks during which we lingered in Khalyan. The cricket match in particular was a huge success because of the spectacular come-uppance with which it served Spotty Duvell.

Spotty Duvell (M.M.) was an ex-Sergeant-Major (very much with a 'g') and Glider Pilot. Now, as a general rule, Warrant Officers who were found fit to hold combatant Commissions at that time were commissioned straight away in the rank of Lieutenant and did not have to undergo training as Officer Cadets. But the authorities had clearly decided that Spotty needed a bit of polishing first, and to India he duly sailed in the good ship *Georgic* with the other 300 odd of us. There was a good deal of controversy as to his exact status. Spotty maintained that until we arrived at Bangalore he would still hold the King's Warrant and enjoy the rank of Company Sergeant-Major (after all, he was still being paid as such) and that he was therefore entitled to the absolute obedience of the rest of us who were still only Private Soldiers. Nonsense, we said: we had now been instructed to assume the insignia of Officer Cadets; *all* of us had been so instructed, including Spotty Duvell, so he could jolly well take down his crown and laurel-wreath (in 1946 C.S.M.s still wore both) and put up white shoulder tabs along with the fellow-Cadets who were now his peers.

Spotty did indeed put up white tabs, and also fixed the complementary white celluloid disk behind his regimental cap badge, but he did not take the crown and laurel wreath off his sleeve. All right, so he was an Officer Cadet: he was also a Sergeant-Major. As it happened, this concept very much suited the Officer who had been given the charge of us while we remained in Khalyan: he was short of Warrant Officers, Cadets in transit were notorious for putting on airs with non-commissioned ranks, so let them have their own Cadet Warrant Officer to keep the little buggers in order. Thus authority upheld Spotty's claim, which was thereafter reluctantly conceded.

It followed, of course, that it should have been Spotty who formed up to suggest the programme of games and matches, whereas it had in fact been James. For Spotty was not an initiator, he was a natural other rank loiterer, who would have been only too glad to hang about, vacant and atrophied, for our entire stay in Khalyan. He therefore resented James's action on several levels, and set about trying to discredit the activities which James had put in train by giving loud-mouthed imitations of the Public School accent ('Bah Jove, what a supah toe-ah, Aubrah old sport, whaaaat') and, more harmfully, by ordering people to leave the field in mid-match or mid-race and report for some nugatory fatigue which he had got up out of sheer malice.

Of all the fixtures which had been set up, the one Spotty Duvell most loathed was the cricket match. ('Bah Jove, the mater and the pater are coming to watch us play crickah at Lord's, whaaat. Don't forget your topper, Claude, etc, etc.') No sooner was the first over bowled than Spotty came strutting down to the ground (a murram square with matting wicket) accompanied by his henchman, Syd Tasker, an ex-Sergeant of Military Police.

'Now let's see, Sergeant,' said Spotty. 'We need five men to clean out the latrines.'

'Sir.'

'I think we might detail these men who are sitting here doing nothing. Men, did I say? More like a row of little girls at their first dance, legs together in case they piss their knickers...You,' yapped Spotty, 'you you you and you, report to the latrines at the double.'

'Excuse me, Sergeant-Major,' said James, who was

Captain of the side that was batting; 'these Cadets are members of my team and are waiting to go in to bat.'

'You speak when you're spoken to, Cadet Prior,' said Sergeant Tasker. 'You you you you and you.'

'If you take them,' said James civilly, 'you will spoil our match.'

'Oh, jolly poor show, whaat, fraightful shame, Monty old chap, and what will his lordship the Marquis say,' snarled Spotty. 'Got ears, have you, lads? You you you you and you.'

I myself was the third 'you', and I did not like the way things were going. For a moment the match continued, but uneasily. By now the fieldsmen were fully aware what was up, and when 'Over' was next called they crossed with furtive, scurrying movements, as if about to be detected in criminal conspiracy.

'There are plenty of people available to clean the latrines,' said James equably, 'who are not playing in this match...which, incidentally, has been organised with the permission of the Officer i/c Draught.'

'Who you went crawling to when I wasn't looking,' said Spotty with naked malignance.

'Only because you arranged nothing for us...sir.'

'Watch yourself, Prior. You're not too important to be put in close arrest...and have those pretty white tabs taken off your shoulder. Now then, you lot: for the last time: you you you you and you.'

'I suppose it's no good my appealing to your kindness?'

'Christ almighty, it brings tears to my eyes, it really does. Poor little toffs, and did the horrid, wicked mans spoil their nice cricket game. You, *you*, YOU, *YOU* and—'

'—I have a note here from the Officer i/c Draught,'

said James, producing it, 'which specifically exempts from to-day's fatigues all those selected to play in this cricket match, including the two twelfth men, and also two umpires, two scorers, and two men to operate the tally-wag. Here is the list, sir: these five Cadets are all on it.' And then to us, 'Please do not disturb yourselves, gentlemen.'

I think it was this last sentence that really did it—possibly just the last word of all, so quiet and so clear, so evident and total a repudiation of Spotty Duvell…who now completely lost his self-control.

'Why didn't you tell me at once,' he yowled, and snatched at the list. 'You fucking, stinking, slimy little cunt, you—you and your shit-eating nancy friends.'

There was a very long silence. Play ceased as all the players turned to gaze in our direction. Syd Tasker shifted from heel to toe and licked his upper lip. Spotty's face wobbled and then fell apart.

'I…I…' he mouthed.

'As a man of your experience must be aware,' said James, 'you are forbidden to address any soldier in this fashion. If sworn at with good will and good humour, the rank and file will tolerate and welcome a little rough language. If insulted, indeed slandered, in obscene and malevolent terms, they will not. I have only to report this disgraceful exhibition to the Commandant, supported as I shall be by these witnesses, for you to be deprived of your Cadetship and almost certainly degraded to private rank. However, gentlemen,' said James to the rest of us, 'I think we know how to make allowances. You, Sandy, and you, Barry: you're batting well down in the tail. Just accompany the Sergeant-Major to the latrines, would you, please, and be sure he makes a good job of them.'

'Well,' I said later, 'why didn't you tell him at once? About that note? You were leading him on.'

'Oh no. I just wanted to give him a chance to show us his better side.'

'Would they really have degraded him if we'd reported the incident?'

'I doubt it. *He* believed it, because at bottom he is the sort of under-dog who believes anything which he is firmly told by his betters. My own view is that he might well have got off with a severe reprimand. Still, it certainly wouldn't have done his career any good. I think he was wise to accept the proffered bargain.'

The next day, Sergeant-Major Spotty Duvell dismissed his jackel and arranged with the Officer i/c Draught for James to be made up as a Local, Acting, Unpaid (O/Cadet) Colour-Sergeant. From now on James was to be Spotty's constant aide. Clearly Spotty, though not an initiator, was an opportunist and a philosopher; he would make (James reported as the days went on) a far better Officer than we had thought.

Certainly, he never forgot himself again.

'You taught me a thing, you did,' he said to James one night when mildly in drink: 'you taught me there's nothing like Class, and if a man hasn't got it he better borrow a bit. That's what you are, Jimmy boy—my bit o' borrowed Class.'

Although the O.T.S. at Bangalore had been founded to train mature and experienced civilian volunteers, and was therefore adult in its attitudes and sparing of regulation, the authorities were aware by now that the Cadets coming into their care were far younger and more vulnerable than they had been in the early 'forties. The Commandant had therefore decreed that, while the traditional tolerance of the institution should not be renounced, the Cadets must nevertheless have as many amusements as possible 'laid on' for them during their leisure, in order to distract them from the perils of the town. One such entertainment was an educational visit, scheduled to extend over a whole long week-end, to the Gold Fields at Kola. James and I and Sandy and Barry (two Greenjacket chums of James who were wary of me but not unfriendly) were all going, not for the technical enlightenments on offer, but to take part in a Gala Two Day Cricket Match.

'I want no snobbiness from any of you,' James said as we set off in an O.T.S. bus. 'Some of the chaps there will be absolute oiks, of course, the sort of people you'd expect to be mixed up in gold digging, but we must remember that we are the ambassadors of the O.T.S. and the Army, and we must do our best to strike up cordial relations.'

'Yes, James,' we all said.

It was early in the evening when we arrived at Kola, where a crowd of white employees was waiting by the central offices to greet us all and escort us to the various houses in which we should be entertained. As luck would have it, I was separated from James, Sandy and Barry, who were swept away by a stubby and over-bearing manager of senior aspect. Meanwhile, I was taken on by a modest and brittle young man, who led me off to his bachelor bungalow and filled me up with gin, curry and whisky, in that order, as a preface to telling me about his life.

This had been somewhat less than satisfactory: his father and mother had drunk the money left by his grandfather specifically to provide him with a decent education, and had then resented and bullied him when he succeeded in winning for himself scholarships just sufficient to put him through a grammar school and Sheffield University. His father accused him of being a parasite on the household and his mother called him a traitor to his country (his call-up had been deferred as he was studying Metallurgy), and the only girl friend he ever had used to arrive in his lodgings at Sheffield shortly after breakfast every morning and stay with him there or follow him wherever he went until eleven o'clock at night, talking incessantly of the 'home' they would have as soon as he had the sense to leave the University and get a 'proper, paying job'. In order to be rid of her he had to feign three epileptic fits, during the last of which he had banged his head so hard on the fender that he went to his final examination in a state of shock. What with that, and what with having had his work constantly disrupted for the last three months by the alternate quacking and whingeing of the girl friend, it was, he told me, hardly surprising that he managed to obtain only a Pass Degree.

However, Metallurgists were in short supply, and when the Army had absolutely turned him down for service (advanced and ubiquitous nervous eczema, first aroused by the attentions of his girl friend and later long nourished by her memory) he was accepted for overseas employment here at Kola. So in the end things hadn't turned out too badly, you might say. He was quite liberally paid (in order that he might keep up his end as a white man), he had two native servants (to the great envy of his mother and the fury of his father), and a cosy little place of his own (and cosy it was) to drink his whisky in peace and quiet. What, I enquired, did he actually do in exchange for these privileges? Well–er–well, he was in the Security Department. A trained Metallurgist...in the Security Department? Yes: you see, they needed an expert to recognise the presence of gold dust in the clothes or on the persons of native workers who tried to smuggle it out of the compound. He looked at me heavily, took a long swig of whisky, laughed out loud, and,

'After all that solemn grind at Sheffield,' he said, 'I now spend my entire professional life looking up black arseholes and under black foreskins—some people's idea of heaven, I suppose.

He was, in fact, a pretty good sort of man who had no illusions about his own dinginess and absurdity. I often wonder what happened to him when Independence came to the Kola Gold concern, and I rather fear for the worst.

As soon as I arrived with him next morning at the cricket ground, I was taken on one side by Sandy.

'Something awful has come over James,' Sandy giggled, passing his fingers rapidly in and out of his short blond hair and exhibiting a positive sheen of pleasurable excitement on his fourth form face: 'he's taken against the Mem.'

'Taken against the what?'

'The wife of that man who's putting us up. He calls her "The Mem", or "Mem" in the vocative. Apparently she's the "doyenne"—that's the word he uses-of all the Kola wives. She snooted us up last night because we're Greenjackets. *She* pretends to think that the Fusiliers are much smarter—her father was one. James is very put out.'

'Surely he won't rise to that bait? After all his talk about our being ambassadors. She's just the sort of person we've got to be nice to.'

'I know. But when you get a look at her you'll see why we're finding it difficult. There,' said Sandy, and pointed.

A sort of giant upright pug-dog, on two legs like barrels, was dismounting from a tonga. It carried a parasol and was supported by two native bearers. An enormous straw-hat, smothered in botanical decoration, crowned and sheltered it; the massive, white-stockinged legs, jammed into white brogues, somehow, incredibly, propelled it; a kind of shrill drawl announced its arrival, in a series of prolonged hoots.

'Can't...you seaah...I'm heaaah,' it said: 'jildah, jildah, cheah...bairaah.' (Can't you see I'm here. Jilde, jilde (quick, quick), chair bearer.)

'I do see,' I said. 'Has there been a row yet?'

'No. Though there nearly was when she called the Rifle Brigade a "Parvenu Regiment".'

'So it is.'

'I know. But James says a woman like that can't be allowed to say so and get away with it. He's planning what he calls a "Heffalump Trap".'

I remembered the technique from nursery readings of *Winnie the Pooh*. In order to trap a Heffalump, one arranged a piece of ground to look particularly pretty and well kept, and so particularly tempting to an ill-conditioned Heffalump to trample on. And when it did, it went crashing through into the trap beneath, where it was left bellowing furiously until at last it quietened down and promised to mend its manners.

'From the look of her,' I said, 'he'll have to get up quite early in the morning to construct it.'

'It seems that her husband is Captain of their cricket team. James is working on that.'

'But he's about a hundred years old.'

'That's what James said. "No fool like an old fool",' he said: ' "we should be able to fix something." '

'But what's got into James? He knows he mustn't

tamper with elderly managers—however disagreeable their wives may be.'

'I thought I'd tell you,' said Sandy, jittering with expectation, 'because you've known him longer than any of us, and you might be able to do something to stop him. Though I don't think you will be,' he added happily.

As I walked across the ground towards the Pavilion my host (Ted) rejoined me.

'You'll find our lot's a sporting team,' Ted said, 'but tough. They remind me of some of the Sheffield League sides I used to watch. The only trouble is our Captain. He is fascinated by the personality and practice of W. G. Grace. He thinks that he's W. G. reborn.'

'A fairly harmless delusion?'

'But don't you remember? W. G. was a marvellous cricketer, but he was also omniscient, arrogant, and over-fond of refreshment at lunch time…all of which turned him into a bully and even a cheat.'

'Ah.'

'Kola Bert—that's what we call our skipper—Kola Bert reincarnates the very worst of W. G. But no one can do anything because he's so senior. And as for his Mem…'

Ted shuddered.

As I passed this lady on the way into the Pavilion (with some difficulty as she was parked slap in the doorway) four bearers appeared with cold drinks, pots of tea, plates of cakes (etc), and set them up on a series of tables which substantially increased the obstacle to entrance. Her husband now came up (wearing an Old Carthusian blazer) and diffidently recommended a slight shift of her apparatus, but was told 'not to be a bloodah fool, Bertah, Ah've onlah just got comfah.' He departed with a muffled snort, clearly about to take this defeat out on someone else, while I hurried on to the

Visitors' Dressing Room.

'He's wearing an O.C. blazer,' I said to James, who was putting on the specially thick white socks that were knitted for him by his mother.

'Who is?'

'Bertah—the chap you're staying with. He's wearing an O.C. blazer with thick stripes—like a wop ice cream.'

'Is he?' said James dangerously.

'James…what has *he* done to you?'

'It's his wife. Great rorting carnivore. But he's as bad. O.C. blazer indeed. There's no such thing. Bob Arrowsmith once told me.'

'But I tell you he's wearing it.'

'Then he's had it made up. As bad as wearing a made up evening tie. *Worse.*'

'Ted, my host, says he thinks he's W. G. Grace. And cheats to prove it.'

'Come over here, please, Barry,' said James to sinuous, sinewy Barry Tooman, our first spin bowler.

Barry came.

'Now listen carefully,' James began.

The first day's play in the Kola Match was pretty dull, but left the possibility of an interesting finish. Giles Peregrine, our Captain, had won the toss, put us in to bat, and declared at tea-time at 372 for 6, an average opening score for the ground, which was very small and very fast (whence the dulness of the play, which was apt to be a monotonous succession of easy boundaries). The Kola XI had reached 180 for 3 in reply when stumps were drawn for the day. On the form they were showing, they would probably bat on to equal our score by about lunch-time the next day, thus leaving the afternoon to settle the issue.

At close of play on the second day, there would be a quick buffet, after which we Cadets must leave at once for Bangalore. On the evening of the first day, just concluded, there was to be a Gala Dinner for both teams, we had been told, in the Board Room of the Company. Men only. Thus it seemed unlikely that James would again encounter the Mem in any substantial fashion, and I was hoping that absence, making his heart grow fonder or at least less loathing, might lead to his abandoning his scheme for the humiliation of her husband the next day.

This consisted in getting Barry Tooman, with Giles Peregrine's connivance, to bowl very high donkey-drops, which would descend almost vertically on the old man and show up his incapacity in shame-making slow motion. It was, on the face of it, a harmless enough idea, but it seemed to me that it could lead to just the sort of ill feeling which James himself had told us must in no case be conjured, and it also seemed that this whole business was somehow unworthy. Why did James have to bother himself about this dismal couple in the first place? True, the Mem was about the most appalling example of her species ever put on view, but Kola Bert was just ageing and pompous, nothing worse, and in any event at all they would both vanish from our lives for good and all at dusk tomorrow. It did not seem to me that her mild (and accurate) jibe at the Rifle Brigade and his donning of a vulgar and unauthorised blazer need give rise to vengeful stratagems. So at least Sandy and I were telling James as we walked up the steps of the building (Graeco-Buddhist) which contained the Board Room, and so, I was happy to observe, he now seemed to be thinking for himself.

'Right you be,' he said: 'I was just being childish.'

Then we entered the Ante-Room. The first thing we saw was the Mem. Enthroned amid a crowd of Kola cricketing sycophants and wielding a Tom Collins like a sceptre, she gazed down with sumptuous disdain on all which and whom she beheld, ourselves among them.

'What is that fucking woman doing here?' muttered James. 'A men's dinner, they said.'

'She,' I hazarded, 'is bound to be the exception…the one who may not be excluded, the one to whom the Laws do not apply, just as the Queen of England, alone among women, may enter the Pavilion at Lord's.'

'That could be it,' said James. 'The Head Bitch.'

Clearly he was outraged and even rather frightened by the Mem's appearance at this masculine function. So was I. Who knew what vile processes of bullying, nagging or blackmail she had deployed to get herself there? We were also outraged by the behaviour of the husband. He surely was in a position to stop her. If he had not done so, it meant either that he was downright feeble (in this area at least) or that he enjoyed according such lone privilege to his wife and so by extension to himself. Either way he must be punished: the plan for tomorrow would now, after all, go forward as it had been conceived; and it was greatly hoped among us that before the sun next set the Mem would have been brought as low as her lord, by the humbling of Kola Bert.

In the event, Kola Bert came in to bat at No.7, when the score was 280 and the time half past twelve. Thus the Kola team had 92 more to make in order to equal our first innings' score, and until a few minutes previously none of us had doubted they would get them by luncheon (1.30 p.m.). But the arrival of Kola Bert at the wicket was definitely encouraging; for it would appear to indicate that we were now into the tail. To judge from Bert's flaccid fielding, he had long been too far gone for cricket, and if his position as No. 7 was in true accordance with his relative merit as a batsman, there could only be even worse rubbish to follow him. If, on the other hand, Bert had put himself in at No.7 out of vanity or selfishness, then here at any rate was a quick and easy wicket. We grinned self-indulgently as Bert asked for guard and took up his 'W. G.' stance with left foot cocked. Barry Tooman took a three pace run and launched the first of his hyperbolic donkey drops.

Even a good player finds it hard to deal with Dollies. They take for ever to arrive, they are very trying to watch in the air, they madden otherwise cool men into desperate, ill-tempered swishes, and even if perfectly struck they do not fly sweetly off the bat but either stop dead after twenty yards or, if lofted, sag dismally into the hands of long off. We all waited for Kola Bert to wind himself up like an arbalest for some clownish stroke which would end with his falling on his wicket (or something of the kind)—and were a good bit mortified when he leaned easily back and hooked the ball full toss, as it descended, clean out of the ground. He then did the same thing twice more, at which stage Giles whispered to Barry, who reverted to his normal style of leg break bowling. Not that this troubled Kola Bert. To the fourth ball of the over, which was on a good length and turning just outside the off-stump, he played quietly and precisely back, getting a sight of the new Barry, and both the fifth and sixth balls, which also turned outside the off stump, he cut very late and most exquisitely for four.

Barry's over had cost 26 runs. Bert remained

unhumbled, quite conspicuously so. How could we, I thought, how could we have made such a stupid mistake? We had surely been playing the game long enough to know that an elderly man who does not put himself out in the field may yet be a most accomplished batsman. Ted had not said that Bert was no good, just that he had a fantasy, which could sometimes prove tiresome, about being W. G. Grace. Fantasies of this order could inspire as well as derange: I remembered Myles's 402 on the terrace in the role of J. D. Robertson ('Another spanking boundary for "J. D." ').

'Jollah gad shah, Bertah,' honked the Mem from the midst of her manifold refreshments in front of the Pavilion door: 'you shah the little baggahs.'

It was impossible to distinguish whether the last word intended beggars or buggers. Whichever it was, it conveyed an almost physical disgust.

Not to go into the details of our discomfiture, I shall say *tout court* that Kola Bert made an immaculate 49, which included every stroke in the book; and that when he was given out l.b.w., one run short of his fifty and on a highly questionable decision (he almost certainly snicked the ball before it hit his pads), he went with a good grace and without hesitation, as a gentleman should. No ugly flush of the face, no shaking of the head, no reproachful look at the umpire, no slamming and slapping of bat on pad as he departed: he simply went, followed, I'm happy to recall, by a huge volley of clapping, and received by the Cadets on the boundary (who had now concluded their educational tour of the mines) with a cheer to warm his heart till the day it turned to dust.

As he entered the Pavilion, he stooped to give his wife a quick and sweaty kiss on the cheek. 'Bravah, bravah,' she bleated, 'oh bravah, dear old chap.' Watching from the boundary for the next batsman to emerge, I saw that a single tear (of pride? love? gratitude? pity?) was running down her ogreish jowl, and I forgave her all.

'What I never understood,' said James, when we were discussing the incident a long while later, 'was why that man Ted told you that Bert was an ill-tempered cheat.'

'He explained, after the game, that it would have been a very different matter if Bert had done badly. He might even have refused to go out. It had happened—according to Ted.'

'Seems odd to me,' James said. 'If he was that sort of chap, he'd have shown *some* sign of annoyance or recalcitrance at being given out even when he had done well. He might have pulled himself together pretty quick and gone with a smile in the end, but for a few seconds at least the bad sportsmanship would have shown. It always does. But not in this case—not for a single flick of the eyelid.

'It's my view,' James went on, 'that Kola Bert was absolutely pukkha right through. That was what I got wrong at the time. I thought that if Barry got him all knotted up with those high lobs, he'd lose his rag and make a fool of himself Then, later on, I thought, at luncheon perhaps, the Mem would push herself in on the act, reckoning aggression to be the best form of defence as such a woman would, and that with a little luck she too would lose her wool and give me the chance to pick her off.

'But the origin and basis of the entire scheme was the notion, promoted by Ted and confirmed by that horrible O.C. blazer, that Bert was hairy at the heel-which simply wasn't true.'

'I dare say Ted got it all wrong,' I said; 'he had chips along both shoulders, to say nothing of nervous eczema.'

'But what about that made up blazer?' said Sandy. 'That was real enough.'

'I've written to check the record,' said James. 'There's no doubt Bert was at Charterhouse. He was a Saunderite—contemporary of Ronald Storrs.'

'But as you pointed out,' Barry persisted, 'there is no such thing as an Old Carthusian blazer, or at any rate it is not officially recognised. Bert was out of order there.'

'But was it really so very dreadful?' said James. 'I was furious at the time because I was narked by that bloody Mem woman. Another day I'd just have laughed. It was probably she that had it made for him—stupid kind of cock-up these women make when they will interfere. Particularly a stuck up blowsy old bitch like that.'

'She wasn't so bad,' I said. For the first time I told them about the tear.

'Crocodiles put on the same performance,' said James: 'it only meant she was going to eat another piece of him when they got home.'

'I don't know. Tough she may have been, but then you've got to be if you're going to live out here.'

'Fat lot you know about living out here,' said Barry.

'I wish,' I said, 'that I was going to have the chance to learn a lot more. Seems such a damned shame—to go home after only six months.'

For the appointed day had duly come and gone, and now we were all four Second Lieutenants, four brand-new Second Lieutenants just about to go home. Independence was to be bestowed on India earlier than anyone had thought; Attlee's Labour Government was 'bringing the boys home', not only from India but from other parts of the Far East, as fast as possible; and so far

78

from being urgently despatched to points East of Mandalay (as I had boasted to my parents we should be) we were sitting in the most run down and visibly rotting Officers' Mess (Napier Mess) of all the four such in the Transit Camp at Deolali, waiting for a passage back to England with the lowest possible priority.

'What makes you think we shall ever get home?' Sandy now said.

Deolali was so famous for frustration and delay that it had given its name to a form of madness—Deolali (sometimes pronounced Doolali) Tap. Men were abandoned there for ever, the legend said: your papers disappeared through a crack in the floor, after which you lost your official identity and with it your pay, your rations and any possibility of a passage, so that there was nothing to do but turn your face to the wall and die. But generally there was an intermediate period: before you took to your bed for ever, you made a last effort, uttered a final protest, which took the form of hideous fits of gibbering and foaming—Deolali Tap.

We had been there three weeks. At first the Field Cashier had looked kindly upon us and advanced us plenty of money against arrears of pay: now, when we skulked into his office, we were peremptorily waved away by a Lance-Corporal. Clearly we had no further claim; we were losing our substance, our identity…Any minute now we should be attacked, as inexorably and mortally as if by rabies, by Deolali Tap. Something must be done to revive us, to make us aware again, or we were surely lost. It was in this predicament, as the result of an idle boast by Spotty Duvell that he could out-drink any man in Deolali, that James issued his Challenge and A GRAND DRINKING MATCH was proclaimed along the Lines.

At last life had meaning and interest enough to make us bustle again.

James and Spotty were both to deposit Fifty Guineas, making a Purse of One Hundred Guineas for the winner. (Although everyone else was counting his Annas, James and Spotty, each being the man he was, had ample resources.) The Match would take place at Nine p.m. on the night of June 10, 1947, in Napier Mess. Two Judges were appointed by common agreement; and the Laws which they had to enforce were these:

I. At Nine of the Clock on the Afternoon of the Day Appointed, the Two Principals should present themselves on the Ground (Napier Mess); and at Ten Minutes after Nine they should come to the Scratch (the Mess Bar), where they would exchange Compliments in a gentlemanly fashion.

II. At Fifteen Minutes after Nine the Judges would supervise the pouring of the first potation, a Double Whisky for each Contestant. Each Contestant must then drink his Whisky, neat from the glass, by 9.20, at which time the Judges must be satisfied that both potations had been absolutely consumed, and would then cause to be poured two more of the same amount of the same Liquor. These in turn must be consumed by 9.25, when two more potations would be poured, etc, etc, etc.

III. The First of the Principals to puke on the Ground (i.e. anywhere in Napier Mess), to faint, have a fit, fall and be unable to rise, die, or declare himself unable to consume, in whole or in part, a properly presented potation, would be disqualified and The Match and The Purse would thereupon be awarded to his Opponent. But if both Principals puked on the

Ground (i.e. anywhere in Napier Mess), fainted, had a fit, etc, etc, etc, *after consuming an equal amount of Liquor* (in which matter the Judges' Computation would be absolute and final), the Match would be pronounced a Tie. It was to assist the Judges in this respect (e.g. in the assessment of partly consumed potations) that the Contestants were required to drink their Whisky neat from the glass. However, there would be no objection raised against the Contestants' drinking chasers of water, or any other liquid they might favour, from separate glasses.

IV. Spectators would be admitted, but they must keep a distance of not less than Five Yards from the Principals and the Judges; and the Stewards would ensure that a passage of Four Foot wide was clearly marked and respected by all, to enable the Contestants to reach the Jakes without let or hindrance. *Nota bene*: Voiding of Bladders or Bowells by the Principals would be perfectly in order, always provided:

a) Such functions were performed in the proper Offices of the Jakes;

b) Contestants were back on Scratch (i.e. at the Bar), having fairly finished their current potation and being ready to receive the next, by the time allotted;

and c) Contestants admitted one Judge to accompany them into the Water Closet to determine whether or not they threw up (*vide* Law III).

V. Bets might be struck with the Principals up to the time appointed for the Match to commence. Once the Principals had arrived on the Ground they might no longer take or lay the odds on or against themselves or each other. Spectators, however, might wager among themselves ad lib both during 'orders' and 'in running'.

As the days passed and excitement mounted among gentlemen of the fancy, Spotty emerged a clear favourite at 6 to 4 on, though respectable sums were invested on James (by those who could still find them) at 7 to 4 against. As much as 100 to 1 was offered in some quarters against a tie, and 500 to 1 (generally thought to be rather mean odds) against the death of one Contestant. I myself staked two Rupees (about three shillings), at 2,000 to 1, on both Principals' dropping dead and ten Rupees (all I could raise for the purpose) on a victory for Spotty at even money—a price briefly on offer when a rumour that Spotty had the clap (started by me) caused fluctuations in the market.

'Damned disloyal I call that,' said James when he heard.

'One has to take the practical view. I know you're a reliable drinker but you haven't quite had Spotty's experience.'

'I don't get drunk, if that's what you mean.'

'It's exactly what I mean. There's nothing in the Laws saying the winner has to be sober, only that he mustn't be sick or pass out. Spotty has had practice—almost every night he has practice—at getting drunk, i.e. drinking the stuff by the bucket, *without being sick or passing out*. You have had no such practice. You're not even having it now.'

'I don't have to make a hog of myself just because of the Match.'

'But you will have to make a hog of yourself in order to win it. You might at least find out what it feels like…have the odd net, so to speak.'

'But *you* don't want James to win,' said Sandy spitefully; '*you've* backed Spotty Duvell. So why are you giving him all this advice?'

'Because I don't want to see Spotty Duvell walk all over him. The honour of Charterhouse is at stake here. James must put up a good show. What on earth will Hedley Le Bas say,' I said to James, 'if he hears you've collapsed after the first few rounds of a public Drinking Match? Whatever would Bags Birley feel about it?'

'I fear lest Bags would deprecate the whole proceeding,' said James, 'whatever the result.'

'Not if you win. To win is to succeed, and as you yourself once told me, success brings its own exculpation.'

'So in the last resort…you really want me to win— although you've had a bet against me?'

'That's about it.'

'It makes no sort of sense.'

'It makes admirable sense,' I said: 'it means financial emolument in case of personal disappointment. By the same token, I've also had a bet that you and Spotty will both fall down dead. Should this sorrowful calamity occur, 2,000 Rupees would at least be some kind of compensation.'

The day before the match it became clear that if everyone who wanted to attend were to be allowed in, Napier Mess would totter to the ground. The entire Transit Camp was buzzing with almost hysterical excitement, and literally hundreds of pounds' worth of bets had been struck by men of all ranks from the Commandant himself (or so it was rumoured) down to the very punkah wallahs. Since Napier was one of the Officers' Messes all non-commissioned spectators were automatically excluded, but even then the crowd would be enormous. In the end, it was decided that the Principals and the Judges should have the right to make a certain number of nominations, and that for the rest a further 100 cards of admission would be distributed by ballot. Ticket holders, when their names were made known, were offered anything up to £20 by crooked Quartermasters who were making important books on the event or by senior Officers either in transit or on the Staff. I myself was one of James' nominees.

'You don't deserve it,' he said as he handed me my pass, 'and if you sell it I'll kill you.'

'I wouldn't miss this for a dukedom,' I said, and almost meant it.

'In that case,' said James, 'I invite you to be one of my seconds.'

Next to hearing the news of my Scholarship at King's and of my 1st XI cap, it was the proudest moment of my life.

At exactly nine p.m. on the appointed evening, James entered Napier Mess attended by Sandy and myself. All of us were wearing Tropical Service Dress, in those bleak days the nearest one could come to Full Dress or Ceremonial. James' lapels carried the insignia of The Norfolk Regiment (the Greenjackets were not accepting anyone back from Bangalore as Officer of theirs, and thank you for your kind application); while Sandy sported the Petard of The Royal Fusiliers and I displayed the Bugle Horn of The Oxfordshire and Bucking-hamshire Light Infantry (Wellington's beloved 43rd). Though I say it myself we made a brave group—and so, I am glad to report, did Spotty Duvell and his seconds, who were already on the Ground. Lieutenant Duvell (for he had been granted two pips straight away in recognition of his former seniority) flaunted the Rose of Yorkshire, while the two Ensigns who flanked him both bore the Sphinx. (Take heed, take heed, for we shall see such heraldry no more amid the drab artisans who man the Army of our age.)

The two groups bowed to each other, then stood easy and talked low and nervously among themselves. The crowd buzzed and seethed; the Stewards marshalled it well back, and marked the route to the Jakes with white ropes; the Head Barman, in high turban, stood strictly to attention behind two rows of twenty glasses; punkah wallahs plied their fans with a frenzy as if the penalty for sloth were death. No doubt about it: Napier Mess, like Todger's, could do it when it tried.

At 9.10 there was a long roll of kettle drums, followed by total silence. The two Judges (one of whom wore the crepuscular Kilt of The Black Watch, while the other carried the Harp of Ulster on his breast) beckoned to James and Spotty. The seconds of either party backed off, to a special row of seats by the double door which led to the verandah. James and Spotty advanced to the Bar, bowed again to each other and shook hands; then each retired to his own place, some three yards respectively to left and right of the Head Barman, whither he was attended by one Judge. There was another roll of kettle drums; the Head Barman measured two exact doubles into the left hand glass of either rank; the Judges stepped up to him, agreed the measures, and carried them to the Principals; and at a sign from the Senior Steward a rocket went up from the verandah to notify the masses outside the Mess that The Grand Drinking Match was now in train.

Spotty took his double in one go. (I thought of Hedley and Gerald at the Tavern.) He did not chase it with water, as his theory was that the bulk of the water increased the likelihood of his throwing up. James, on the other hand, drank his whisky in sips, taking a gulp of water from a separate glass between each sip; for *his* theory was that the water rendered the Usquebaugh less toxic and therefore more readily assimilable. Thus Spotty had nearly five minutes to wait, after taking his bumper, until James had sipped his way through his first glass, which the Judge at his elbow announced had been fairly drained with twenty seconds to spare. A green flare was then fired from the verandah to inform the crowd that both Contestants were safely through the first round; the kettle drums sounded once more; and the Head Barman measured double whiskies into the second glass of each rank of twenty.

And so the thing went solemnly on for the first six glasses. Spotty continued to drink in single sconces; James continued to sip whisky and gulp water. Both had unquestionably put up empty glasses within the time and the conditions ordained: neither showed the slightest sign of having been affected by what he had drunk: neck and neck, nothing to choose.

But after draining his seventh glass Spotty belched very fiercely; and towards the end of his eighth James had to re-swallow a sip which had obviously come back. During the ninth round both parties were in trouble with their bladders; both retired with a Judge apiece, Spotty after his customary bumper, James when he was about a third the way through his glass; and both returned, certified by the Judges to have pumped only, James just in time to sip and chase his way (with some bulging of cheeks) through the remaining two thirds of his portion.

And so the ninth green flare rose toward the eastern stars, proclaiming that after nine rounds neither Champion was yet unhorsed.

Meanwhile the 'layers' inside the Mess were doing brisk business 'in running'. The quiet dignity of James' demeanour had caused the odds against him to ease a shade, and at one time they were as low as 5 to 4; but his slight disorder in the eighth round brought them swiftly back to 6 to 4. As for Spotty, his crudity of method at first put the backers against him, and at one stage you might have had even money about him, for the first time since the discredited rumour of his clap. His mighty belch, however, somewhat reassured the punters, on the ground that it was better out than in. 6 to 4 on was now standard about Spotty, while James was slipping away, because of a slight sweatiness in his appearance on his return from the 100, to 7 to 4 against and even 2 to 1.

'Your man's fraying at the edges,' said one of Spotty's seconds to Sandy.

'Our man will stick it till he busts,' Sandy staunchly replied.

The tenth drink was a very dicey one for both competitors. Spotty retched in agony after his self-imposed sconce, and once again, for a couple of minutes or so, you might have had even money. But not for long, because Spotty shook his head and grinned, having evidently recovered for the time being, while James' sweating sickness was getting worse every second. Great glistering pools gathered beneath his eyes, then cascaded down either side of his nose, along the clefts between his nostrils and the corners of his mouth, then over his chin and on to his tunic, which was already darkened, round armpits and shoulders, by the creeping stain of the perspiration which had worked through his shirt. Then at last, despite all social and sartorial habit, he decided to loosen his tie—a concession which improved his looks a little and enabled him, though not without much heavy breathing, to finish his tenth glass.

At this stage both men seemed, for whatever reason, to get another wind. Grimly but not desperately they despatched their eleventh and twelfth glasses (having by now consumed about a bottle apiece), each sticking to the method he had used from the beginning. James was keeping up a good rhythm of sip and gulp, I noticed, while Spotty got through his two periods of waiting in a relaxed yet alert posture which promised ample capacity still in reserve. But at this very moment of apparent steadiness and calm there was a sudden and ugly transformation.

For just as the book-making Officers were offering 33 to 1 against either Contestant's consuming more than 20 glasses, James's face turned to something like Captain Hook's 'rich, green cake', and Spotty, having given two or three deep and uneasy swallows, came groggily to his feet. By now their thirteenth glasses were before them. Spotty seized his, downed it in one, then sat again, swivelling his eyes and contorting his mouth, looking all in all as though he were watching his wife in flagrant adultery while himself under heavy constraint. No question about it, though: his thirteenth glass was down. How would James respond? Most nobly. Realising that he would never get his glass down by slow stages, he rose to his feet, flung back his head, then tossed the dose off and clamped his mouth shut like a vice.

Thus James, standing, and Spotty, sitting, faced each other at the crisis of the drama. At first it seemed to me that the Match now turned on who could keep his stomach down the longer. But then did it? The Laws said that if both Contestants 'puked on the Ground (i.e. anywhere in Napier Mess), fainted, had a fit, etc, etc, *after consuming an equal amount of liquor*, the Match would be pronounced a tie.' Obviously, in order to win, James not only had to hold down his load longer than Spotty, he also had to get it out of the Mess before he chucked it up; equally obviously, he could not move until released by Spotty's prior incontinence, except to the loo whither a Judge would attend him; finally, one had to remember that in three and a half minutes' time both of them would be served with a fresh drink, the arrival of which would raise problems on several most interesting levels.

In the end, both buckled at the same time. Spotty simply opened his mouth, like a drunk don in a Rowlandson print, and sat there while vomit cascaded vertically between his thighs. As for James, his cheeks and lips bulged and bulged and bulged...until his lips must surely part or his face explode into fragments...had not Sandy, inspired, called out,

'OVER HERE,'

and pointed to the double door which led on to the verandah. Quick to take a hint even *in extremis*, James hurtled through the door, opened his lips, and squirted thirteen double whiskies and twelve tumblers of water in a proud and graceful arc, high over the balustrade of the verandah and on to the massed soldiery below.

There was now grave controversy between the two sets of seconds. True, both Principals had been sick at the same time and after consuming equal amounts of whisky; but (said we) James had deposited his burden *outside* the Mess, whereas Spotty had incontestably fouled the Ground itself. Granted (said they); but since James's person was on the Mess verandah, i.e. still in the Mess or on Mess territory, when he 'laid his kit', he must be counted to have 'puked on the Ground' even though the 'kit' itself had landed outside.

The Judges, when the matter was referred to them, inclined against James. This business of the vomit's landing outside the Mess, they opined, was a pure technicality: morally and judicially James's performance was on a par with Spotty's. And indeed a tie would assuredly have been proclaimed, bets paid out accordingly, and their respective contributions to the Purse handed back to the Contestants, had it not been for the magnanimity of Lieutenant Spotty Duvell, who lifted his head from the Bar on which it was uneasily reposing and said, like the Englishman and the sportsman that he was:

'Give him the Match. I catted on the carpet. He did it dainty, off the verandah. That's manners, that is: that's self-control. Like I always said, our boy Jimmy's got Class.'

Whether the crowd immediately below the verandah would have agreed with this opinion, I do not know; but so the matter was ajudged. A red flare was fired to indicate that the contest was decided, and then a single white flare (it would have been a pair for Spotty, matching his pips) to signify that the victor was James.

In this fashion was concluded The Grand Drinking Match between Jim Prior and Spotty Duvell, contested at Deolali in the June of 1947, when good King George the Sixth was Emperor of India, a whole generation ago. They asked me to tell the story on television some weeks back, for a programme they were getting up about the Right Honourable J. M. L. Prior, Privy Councillor. I duly told my tale to the camera, but was not altogether surprised when it was omitted from the finished film. It has an Hogarthian air which offends the prim nostrils of our time. But I for one think it a good tale which does honour (of a kind) to two good men; and if any should perchance accuse me of having embellished or improved it in the telling, well, I still preserve, at the bottom of my old Indian tin trunk, the slips for the two losing wagers which I struck—to witness if I lie.

Deolali Tap or
The Devil's Cadet

from
Bird of Ill Omen

In the autumn of 1946, His Majesty's Troopship
Georgic sailed from Liverpool bound for Bombay and
carrying thousands of disgruntled soldiers of all ranks,
300 of them, rather more attractive than the rest, being
officer cadets of infantry, among these Jerry Constant
Stanley and myself. We were all to attend the officers'
training school at Bangalore in the state of Mysore
(South India) because there were not enough officer
cadet training units in Britain. Thank God there weren't,
we said to one another: British OCTUs were dank, dull
and ferocious, with a failure rate of twenty-eight per
cent; in Bangalore (or so the rumour went) you could not
fail, so much money had been spent on transporting you
there, unless you died, went mad, or got the pox—three
times at that. This rumour, it should be said, was pretty
near true, but not quite, a qualification which may be
remembered later in this story. By the end of 1946, of
course, it was much too late to turn us out as officers of
the Indian Army, which henceforth (and God help it, we
all said) would be officered by Indians; all of us would be

commissioned into British regiments of the line and distributed round the many British battalions still in India or the Far East. More of this intention presently; just now, back to the 300 cadets and in particular to Jerry Stanley, a tall, clean, amiable, well-mannered cadet, rather weak-minded and pampered (too pretty for his own good), conceited when sober, loud and fatuous when in his not infrequent cups.

Jerry's failings, like those of the rest of us, were not diminished by the easy circumstances and indulgent treatment which we enjoyed on HMT *Georgic* and later in a Transit Camp called Khalyan, near Bombay. We were paid as serjeants, addressed as 'Sir', and waited upon, as soon as we reached India, by one quarter of a native bearer or servant per cadet. Even as early as Khalyan, a good month before we reached the OTS at Bangalore, the characters of all of us had deteriorated, and nobody's so conspicuously and, in a way, so attractively, as that of Jerry Stanley.

'Jerry Stanley is the Devil's Cadet,' my old school chum, James Prior, used to say.

'Have you heard what he's done now?' said a budding Morgan Grenfell. 'He took a day's leave in Bombay, found himself without money, marched into Barclays DCO and asked to see the manager. And they let him. It was his riding whip which did the trick – he carried it with such *panache*.'

'No officer in the infantry under field rank, unless he holds a mounted appointment such as that of adjutant, is allowed to carry a riding whip,' said puffy, pedantic Giles Benson.

'Jerry Stanley was carrying his like a colonel of cavalry,' said Morgan Grenfell. 'He looked so splendid, I'm told, that we might even have let him into one of *our* banks. But I don't think we should have let him have any money – which the manager of this branch of Barclays DCO was silly enough to do. Jerry said there was a draft on the way for his credit with Barclays DCO in Bangalore, so could he have some cash *here*, the sum to be debited to his account *there*. The manager nearly melted under Jerry's gaze, lent him twice as much as he first asked for – twenty pounds' worth of rupees – and was rewarded with a stylish flourish of the whip and a magnificent salute. But this morning the bank manager in Bombay telephoned the Commandant here and Jerry was summoned. It seemed that his account in Bangalore was a complete invention, and as for the draft – mere fantasy. Like Billy Bunter's postal order.'

'Disgraceful,' pouted Giles.

'How did Jerry get out of it?' I said. 'I've just seen him, large as a lion, piping up a huge round of gins in the cadets' mess.'

'He said,' said Morgan Grenfell, 'that it was all an unfortunate mistake. The branch of Barclays which his family used in England had either misunderstood or mismanaged his father's instructions. And of course the expense and bother of checking this with England were so enormous, and Jerry's face was so innocent, and his uniform so crisp, and his manner so pleasant and tactful (no riding whip today, of course, only a modest Cadet's split cane), that the Commandant was only too happy to accept Jerry's explanation and order that the money should be paid to the manager in Bombay and debited to Jerry's account with the army paymaster. Not a single hard word – and Jerry invited to curry tiffin on Sunday with the Commandant and what's left of his wife. He'll be moving into the Commandant's quarter before you can say *burra peg*.'

'Where did he get the cash to pay for all those gins in the mess?' said Giles peevishly. (Even in the Indian transit camps they weren't so absurd as to give the cadets drink on credit.)

'He asked me for a small loan,' giggled the scion of the House of Morgan Grenfell. 'I hadn't the heart to say "no".'

'The Devil's Cadet,' mused Jim Prior with a grin that ran the entire width of his huge moon face. 'God be praised for the variety of His creatures.'

A little later came the row about Jerry's performance on the fairground. Like all garrison towns in India at that time, Khalyan had a fair which it was hoped (absolutely in vain) would divert the soldiery from the native bawds. The two main attractions in this fair were the 'dive-bomber', when not out of order, and the 'wall of death', when the death rider was sober enough to mount his motorcycle. On one occasion when he was not, Jerry, who understood the anti–gravity principle of this simple proceeding, volunteered to take his part. After a brief period of practice, he was pronounced competent and rode to several audiences with some distinction. All of which might have been well enough, had he not, at the conclusion of his last performance, taken the motorcycle as well as his pay and driven off into the native bazaar (as opposed to the military one).

'And what did he do then?' enquired James Prior placidly.

'No one knows. Though most have been uncharitable.'

'The native bazaar is out of bounds,' announced Giles Benson vengefully, 'as Stanley very well knew. The penalty is to be deprived of his cadetship and sent home – or to some British unit in India – as a private.'

'Oh dear, no,' said Morgan Grenfell. 'The authorities

wouldn't like that after taking such trouble to get him here. They'd say that Jerry hadn't been properly looked after. So the Commandant has been easily persuaded that Jerry's brain had been confused by the prolonged gyration, and that all he meant to do was to ride the bike to its shed and park it there for the night, but somehow he lost control.'

'He had no business performing on the fairground anyway,' said Giles.

'Oh?' said James. 'And would you ride the wall of death?'

'It's just a trick; everyone knows that.'

'Not a trick I'd care to try,' said James.

'That was what the Commandant said,' said Morgan Grenfell. ' "Bravo, my boy," said the Commandant. "But please, Mr Stanley, let us have no more controversial goings-on between now and when you leave for Bangalore. Dinner on Friday? My wife would like to say goodbye to you."'

'What it is to have favour,' sighed 'Lusto' Lovibond, our platoon melancholic.

'Luck, I think, in this case,' said James. 'Lucky soldiers should always be indulged; they're much too useful to lose.'

'That's what Napoleon thought,' said Morgan Grenfell. 'He made them marshals of France.'

'The first step is to become a second lieutenant,' said Giles. 'As to that, we'll see.'

In the event, Jerry got clear of Khalyan without any more 'controversial goings-on' – unless you count being carried on to the train by loyal fellow cadets after a farewell overdose of Parry's Military Rum.

'It will be interesting to see what happens to Jerry in Bangalore,' said James, 'when he's had time to settle in and take a good look at the wicket. I always felt that his scope has been far too confined in Khalyan – that he didn't, so to speak, have "World enough and time".'

The first person Jerry saw in Bangalore, almost the moment he got off the train, was the prefect for whom he had fagged at Cranford five years previously.

Bruce Brewster had not prospered in the army. This was not for want of trying, nor even for want of ability (at that time exceedingly little was required); it was simply because he possessed not one amiable quality. Nor, for that matter, did he have any notably unpleasant qualities either. He was not odious; he was, so to speak, nullity— nullity on two stout legs, nullity with a quacking voice but one quite adequate to marshal soldiers on a parade ground or bring them up to attention on the arrival of the officer who was to address them about team spirit or tropical disease.

Obsessively clean, Serjeant Brewster always looked slightly dirty; he did not smell, but smelt so officiously of nothing (almost as though he had a neutral zone round his entire body) that one would much have preferred a little warm, human BO. He was of an intelligence so precisely average, so mathematically medial, that, while he seldom erred, he neither initiated nor achieved. He could instruct but not teach; walk in front but not lead; issue orders but not command. A decent and conscientious man, he made his superiors feel so guilty by his virtuous presence that they longed for his absence and as soon as he was out of the room forgot him absolutely – or rather, remembered him with mild uneasiness for just long enough to arrange for him to be posted elsewhere; but never where he wished to be posted – to an OCTU or an OTS as an officer cadet. He fought his way through, by sheer persistence, to selection board after selection board, but none would pass him; each one just passed him over or at best on to another.

Brewster was pleased to see Jerry and shook him by the hand on the platform.

'I've been looking forward to this,' Brewster said. 'I saw from the roll that you were coming and as luck will have it you'll be under me for weapon training.'

He looked at Officer Cadet Stanley, who looked back at Serjeant Brewster.

'But not for long, I think,' Brewster went on, truthful, earnest, without forwardness or conceit. 'I'm to have another board at the end of the month. I'm hoping they'll send me to the OTS at Quetta – this one would be out, of course, as I've been training cadets here – or even to receive an immediate commission in recognition of my long service in the ranks.' He did not attempt to explain or excuse this. 'But that's not till the end of the month,' he said. 'We'll be seeing a bit of one another until then.'

Questioned, later, about what sort of fag-master Brewster had been, Jerry was loyal but vague.

'I can't seem to remember anything about him,' Jerry said. 'He never beat me, I do remember that. In fact it's what he *didn't* do that is clearest. You know, I don't think he *actually* did anything at all. Oh yes: he insisted on a decent shine on his shoes.'

Further enquiry elicited, after long pauses for thought by Jerry, that Brewster had been in the 3rd XI at cricket, the Under VIth for science and had become a house prefect (never a school one) because his record was so blameless that it was impossible to neglect his claim (however negative) any longer.

'A good man,' said Jerry dubiously 'Rather embarrassing all this – I mean, me being a cadet and him just a serjeant. I must say, he doesn't seem to bear a grudge or anything like that.'

Nor did he. On parade he treated Jerry like any other cadet, i.e. dully but correctly. Off parade they occasionally had a meal together at Ley Wong's Chinese restaurant, until Brewster announced, to Jerry's politely concealed relief, that the RSM had counselled him that it was ill-advised for instructors to consort with cadets, whatever their former relation.

'So this is our last little forgathering,' said Bruce Brewster. 'Anyway, I hope I shan't be here much longer. In three days I'm off for my board and I rather expect' – this with entire lack of velleity or presumption – 'that they'll be arranging something else for me.'

So off went Brewster for his board in Mysore, which was to take ten days. Normal boards took only three. The official explanation of this expansion in the case of Serjeant Brewster was that since he was being considered for an immediate commission more complicated analysis than usual would be required.

'Or that's what he told me,' said Jerry. 'Ten days. It's nice to have poor old Bruce out of the way for a bit. His presence was – well – rather repressive: it made me feel as if I was still a study fag and had better behave or else... Now,' he said with a spirited glint, 'I can be myself.'

And he went that very night to the Soldiers Three Tavern (a place of entertainment for Other Ranks only and so barred to cadets), where he picked up a chi-chi girl (our regrettable expression, in those days, for an Anglo–Indian in the sense of Eurasian).

'She's called Rosalie,' said Jerry. 'She's a stunner.'

'How much?' said Barry Barnes (a notable boxer).

'Nothing like that about Rosalie. She thinks I'm going to marry her and take her home with me. She calls

England "home", you know – all these half-caste girls do, because their fathers were mostly Englishmen or Scotsmen in the railways. It's rather touching.'

'It'll be more than touching if she takes you at your word,' said Giles Benson.

'I didn't give my word. She thought the whole thing up herself.'

'Stay away from the Soldiers Three Tavern,' said James Prior.

'But I've promised Rosalie to meet her there tonight.'

'Then on your head be it,' said Giles.

'I hope,' said James, 'that you haven't given her your name.

'Only Jerry.'

'Then keep the rest of it to yourself, if you don't want her mother up here, complaining to the Brigadier.'

'Right you be,' Jerry said.

So that night and many nights (so he informed us) Jerry held tryst with Rosalie, deserting her only once, to attend a celebration given by Bruce Brewster. For the board at Mysore had smiled upon Bruce at last and he had returned to Bangalore only to collect his stuff before proceeding to the OTS at Dehra Dun, where he was to attend a short course of six weeks for senior NCOs and warrant officers before becoming a full lieutenant.

'It couldn't have happened to a better man,' said Jerry luxuriantly to Bruce at Bruce's party and rendered the last verse of the Cranford School Song:

'Floreant Cranfordiani
Qua sunt loci tropicani,
Qua sunt milites Reginae,
Quorum Enses et Vaginae
   Procul lucent, procul vincunt,
   Nunquam Ius et Fas relinquunt.'

'*Vaginae?*' questioned James Prior.

'*Sheathes,*' said Bruce, a trifle crossly – 'Whose Swords and Sheathes shine afar, conquer afar, never desert the Just and the Right.'

'Bravo,' said James. 'That song might have been written for you.'

'Thank you,' said Bruce sincerely, without arrogance or false modesty. 'I do try, you know. The last three or four years have been very trying. Thank God it's all over now—Dehra Dun next week, then commissioned as lieutenant a few weeks later. I shall put myself up for a regular commission next summer or autumn. There's no life really like it.'

'Shush,' I said. 'Never let the gods know that you are happy. The gods, on the whole, are not in favour of human happiness.'

'*We* have a Christian God,' sniffed Giles.

'I dare say the same applies to Him,' remarked James; and shortly afterwards, after 'Three times three for Bruce Brewster' and 'He's a jolly good fellow', the party ended.

'Pity you can't behave with some of Bruce's responsibility,' said Giles to Jerry on the way back to our quarters.

'Bruce Brewster,' said Jerry, 'is the sort of chap that has his shower in his underpants in case someone else comes in and sees his cock. If that's being responsible, then you can keep it. And stuff it. But Bruce is a great chap and Cranford was a great school – '*Floreant Cranfordiani,*' he bawled, '*Qua sunt loci tropicani*—'

'Now, now,' said James. 'Most people are asleep and tomorrow will be a long day.'

It was. Even at Bangalore there was a pretence of work,

reluctantly introduced out of respect for the war and still lingering. So the days were long, yet not really very arduous (as an elaborate but in part fictitious timetable allowed many plausible hiatuses and camouflaged much opportunity for lolling about), certainly not arduous enough to keep Jerry away from Rosalie.

At first no harm came of this: The days went placidly on. In place of Bruce Brewster we were given a mild, undemanding serjeant of fusiliers as an instructor in small arms. When the time came for the selection of cadet NCOs and under officers (about eight weeks after our arrival, with Christmas now long behind us) James Prior was appointed a junior under officer and therefore the leading man in our platoon, and Giles Benson was made a cadet serjeant. James wore his new rank lightly; Giles continued censorious, but though he now had official sanction to promulgate and enforce his judgments, he forbore, being a gentleman, to exact penalty and confined himself, like a Greek chorus, to moral complaint and foreboding.

'Jerry Stanley will come to no good,' he kept saying. 'That half-caste girl...'

'How often do I have to tell you,' said James, 'that Jerry is the Devil's Cadet? So he will be well taken care of. As for that girl, we only have his word for it that he is seeing her – indeed that she exists at all. He may be making the whole thing up to entertain us. He is very generous in that way.'

'He certainly goes to that tavern place,' said Giles, 'although it's out of bounds to cadets. I just happened to spot him as he went in there last Saturday.'

'Snooping, Giles?' I said.

'Don't worry, I shan't do anything about it. I just like to know what's going on, that's all.'

'But you don't,' said Barry the Boxer, 'know anything much at all. You didn't follow him in to check on that chichi girl? You didn't see him come out with her?'

'I've better things to do than hang around places like that. I came back to quarters to brush up on my military law and then went to bed.

'So for all you know, it could be as James says? The girl may not even exist?'

But she existed all right. Oh dear, yes. And one day, Jerry told us, she announced (a) that she was pregnant and (b) that her old mother insisted on marriage.

Giles moaned and quivered, as if about to launch into a dithyramb of invective against human folly and lust.

'But she can't be pregnant,' Jerry insisted. 'I always used a thing.'

'They're not infallible,' said Morgan Grenfell. 'What are you going to do?'

'I've got a plan.'

'I yearn to hear it,' said James.

'Bruce Brewster is coming through in a day or two, *en route* for the Nilgeris. Lieutenant Bruce Brewster on his commissioning furlough. I'm going to give a little dinner party at Ley Wong's, to which I am now cordially inviting you all, get Bruce drunk (with your help) and afterwards introduce him to Rosalie. She will be impressed by a real officer – much swisher than a cadet. A full lieutenant at that. So I think I can simply leave the matter to her. Poor old Bruce is a bundle of frustrations and just now, flushed with success at last, he'll be off his guard.'

'But what on earth,' said Morgan Grenfell, 'do you think is going to happen?'

'God knows. But look at it like this. Bruce is a man totally without personality or attraction. In his whole life not a single woman, except possibly his mother, has even looked at him. Now if Rosalie takes an interest... encouraged by the thought that he's a millionaire...'

'You're going to lie to her?'

'Tit for tat. Anyway, Bruce could have become a millionaire for all I know. I remember, at school, hearing about some sort of uncle he had in the City. I shall simply pass that on to Rosalie. These girls are very greedy and very simple minded. They'll try anything on. Well, let her try something on Bruce.'

'Perfidy,' snorted Giles.

'Rather caddish, I must say,' said Morgan Grenfell.

'I don't know,' I contributed. 'Bruce may well get a bit of pleasure out of life at last.'

'And pay rather dear for it,' said James. 'Shall you ask Rosalie to the dinner?'

'No. I rely on you chaps to help me get Bruce nicely plastered and then I'll take him off to a special rendezous.'

'Not at the Three Soldiers Tavern?'

'Bruce would never go into a place that was out of bounds, however drunk he was.'

'But he might let himself fall into the hands of Rosalie?'

'If given a little push...'

Jerry's dinner for Lieutenant Bruce Brewster got off to a bad start when Bruce revealed that during the course at Dehra Dun he had been converted to total abstinence from both sex and drink. Always a moderate man (Bruce told us) he had decided to enter into his life as a commissioned officer as spare and chaste in habit as a mediaeval knight, whose dedication to duty and contempt of carnality all officers of the King should wish to emulate.

When we pointed out that most knights, however dedicated, had seen no need to go to quite such extremes of asceticism, he replied that he himself was taking the Knights Templar and the Knights Hospitaller as his examples, and that these had been renowned for their abstemious regime and regimen. The Knights Templar, we said, were also renowned for coming to a very sticky end. No doubt the penalty, he rejoined, of their later falling-off from grace.

And so with his plan, such as it was, already in tatters, Jerry led Bruce away to 'meet a special friend of mine', begging the question of why the rest of us were to stay behind with some feeble evasion about lack of space in the tonga which he had hired for the evening.

'The whole scheme was ridiculous anyway,' said Morgan Grenfell. 'What on earth did he hope was going to happen? That Bruce should be so smitten with this girl that he would instantly abandon himself to lust and then take responsibility for the pregnancy?'

'Something of the kind,' said James. 'He was just setting up a situation and hoping the Devil would lend a helping hand.'

'But the old Bruce would never have fallen for that trick,' I said, 'a moderate man in every sense, as he himself has just been telling us. And as for the new teetotal Bruce, the *sans peur* and *sans reproche* Bruce... What in heaven's name does he think he's letting himself in for anyhow? Where does he think he's going?'

'He's fond of Jerry,' said Giles, 'though God knows why. He wants to see what he's getting up to and then weigh in with some advice. Not before time.'

'It'll take more than advice to sort this Rosalie thing out – whether she's in the club or whether she's not.'

Jerry re-entered Ley Wong's Restaurant.

'I thought you'd still be here,' he said.

'You've only been gone half an hour. What have you done with Bruce?'

'I left him with Rosalie – both of them on their knees, side by side, fervently praying, indeed howling, for God's mercy on the fallen girl. You remember what he said about wanting to be a Knight Templar or something similar?'

'Vividly,' said James.

'Well, the moment he saw Rosalie he started his act. He was her holy knight, he told her, who had come to save her from the Devil and everlasting torment. Could she not see that her whoredoms would soon deliver her to Hell? Let her kneel with him and repent. And she was so impressed, or terrified, or astonished, or spiritually uplifted, that she did just that.'

'Where was all this going on?' said Morgan Grenfell.

'In the lounge bar of the Hotel Maharani.'

'The what?'

'The Hotel Maharani. A rather dubious establishment that admits Eurasians and which for some reason the authorities have not put out of bounds.'

'They went down on their knees in the lounge bar?'

'So did a lot of others who were there. It seems that Bruce, whom we always thought the most ordinary man in the world, has got some gift. Like that absurd Semphill Macpherson woman.'

'Like Christ Himself,' murmured James. 'Why didn't he try it on us? Or on you, Jerry, in the tonga?'

'Just a guess,' said Morgan Grenfell. 'It could be that he is only inspired to preach his mission by and to women. It's a sort of sexual sublimation. When he sees an attractive woman, he doesn't want to have her in the usual way, he wants to strive for and win her soul.'

'Come to think of it,' said Jerry, 'it was only the women there that responded.'

'There you are, you see. It's a sexual deviation on both sides. Rather like Gladstone and the prostitutes. He got his thrills out of discussing their trade and trying to reform them. It seems that although some of them just charged him so much an hour for answering his questions and pretending to listen to his sermons, others really got a big bang out of making their confession.'

'Doesn't this sort of thing sometimes end in mystic copulation?' asked Barry the Boxer. 'You know, like those monks and nuns in the *Thebaid*, who tempted each other and then succumbed, but were raised to holiness again by the fervour of their repentence?'

'I didn't stay to see,' said Jerry. 'I should say that the probability is that they'll all be themselves tomorrow, after Bruce has gone his way. But the useful thing is that when they reached the peak of hysteria they all started rending their garments – quite an amusing sight – and confessing their sins. Rosalie confessed, in front of many witnesses quite apart from me and Bruce, that she had lied about being pregnant. She asked my forgiveness, which she can have with all my heart. And that, you see, is now that.'

'Funny,' said James. 'It was God Who came to save you when you were counting on the Devil.'

And if Rosalie hadn't been bad enough, Jerry then became infatuated with a polo pony. Or rather, with the idea of a polo pony. Or rather, with the idea of owning and riding a polo pony. Which first had to be bought.

He borrowed the money, 1,500 rupees, from Ley Wong, who acted as private banker to many cadets on a principle of no–interest–but–you–and–your–friends–give–

your-parties-at-my-bloody-damn-fine-restaurant. And he bought the pony. And he even played polo (rather well), until it broke its neck in a gymkhana in which it was being ridden, on loan, by our company commander's wife, who refused, being a bitch, to pay up. 'Badly schooled, that pony of yours, young man; wrong footed itself; no fault of mine.' Well, possibly not. No particular worry either, not yet. Jerry was already sick of polo, and as for Ley Wong's Rs 1,500 – well, Ley Wong could wait.

But not forever.

The custom was to pay Ley Wong what one owed by way of restaurant bills and personal loans from the handsome 'pre-commissioning' pay-out which one received about a fortnight before one was actually commissioned. One could then, the official theory was, buy necessary uniforms in preparation and set up funds and arrangements for one's furlough, of which three weeks were due to each newly created second lieutenant. Well and good. But when one had Rs 1,500 to pay for a dead polo pony, the thing was not so easily done. Jerry, of all people, had need of well-cut uniforms (to be had, at a price, in the bazaar of the military cantonment) and had planned a lavish leave. It was going to be a tight fit. Ley Wong must go on waiting. But until when? Until Jerry returned to Bangalore, in transit and awaiting posting, after his leave. Time to worry about this dreary debt then, thought Jerry. No, said Ley Wong: 'Ley Wong must be paid before cadet Jelly Stanrey receive pletty pip on thoulder.'

'Come, come, man: don't take that disobliging tone with me.'

'Ley Wong must be paid thix days before cadet Jelly Stanrey have paththing-out palade; else Ley Wong must talk with Bligadier Commandant.'

And that was that. Ley Wong's terms were generous but they were absolute: final settlement (the date for which was always made clearly known to all cadets who dealt with him) was not to be fudged or postponed. Since Jerry, in hope of just such a fudge or postponement, had already paid substantial cash deposits from his pre-commissioning money towards his clobber and his hols, there was currently nothing for Ley Wong at all. Yet 'talk with Bligadier Commandant' must be avoided at all costs, as it now appeared (on the authority of a friendly staff-serjeant instructor) that debt, that old abominable scourge of the Raj, was reckoned by the authorities to disqualify a cadet from being commissioned quite as surely as lunacy or death.

'Five things only cause a cadet to fail here,' the staff-serjeant said. 'Demise, irremediable pottiness, pox the third time round and debt.'

'That's only four,' Morgan Grenfell said.

'The other thing is...hard to define. It can be trivial, on the face of it, or evidently damnable. There was an instance, when I first came here, but I was too new to the place to appreciate what was going on. I *do* remember that the cadet concerned was instantly disgraced and sent, as a private soldier, to the nearest battalion of infantry.'

'Yet you can't remember what he'd done, Staff?'

'No.'

'Trivial...or damnable?'

'Depends how you look at it.'

'Surely, in this unique case...however strange you were to the OTS...you must remember what the chap had done.'

'It was an infringement...of security. In general, a pretty obvious crime, you may think. Yet this case might be seen as so petty, until you think about it carefully, that you wouldn't guess in a millennium what that wretched cadet had done, that whatever it was…could conceivably have brought about his dismissal.'

'Come on, Staff. Tell us. We'd be grateful,' said Giles, 'for the warning.'

'That's just why I'm not allowed to tell you. They don't want you to be warned, you see. They consider it is something which a cadet should think of for himself, something a proper potential officer should not need warning about. It is all to do with having unceasing care for the details of discipline, particularly those aspects of discipline that affect security. You have to remember that India always was, and definitely still is, a hostile country in many, perhaps most ways. So have a care for detail, young gentlemen, right up to the time you march past the Commandant on the very last lap.'

There was a long and gloomy silence.

'Why can't you be more concrete?' said Giles.

'I've told you. But we have got one immediate and concrete matter to hand, to which we must now revert. Cadet Stanley's debt to Ley Wong. Somehow or other you must prevent Ley Wong from taking a complaint to the Commandant. If he reports Mr Stanley for not paying up, then it's all UP for Mr Stanley. Abuse of trust…not to be confused with what I've just been talking about, gentlemen. That is all…slightly chancy, like an ambush where you least expect it, though expect it you should. This business of Mr Stanley's, on the other hand, is perfectly straightforward: gentlemen must keep their word over money.'

'I have a plan,' Jerry said.

'Oh good,' said James.

'May we know what?' pouted Giles.

'At Bangalore Races this weekend there is a scurry for polo ponies. During my recent polo days, I got to know quite a lot of the local ponies – and their riders. Now, there's a pony called Lars Porsena, ridden by Captain Piers Longshaft of the Mysore Lancers…'

'Gambling,' jeered Giles. 'It will never work.'

'It has been known to,' said Morgan Grenfell.

'*Informed* gambling,' said Barry the Boxer. 'Inside knowledge makes a lot of difference.'

'I need a small loan,' said Jerry '150 rupees.'

'Let me oblige,' said Morgan Grenfell. 'It runs in the family.'

'What is the exact plan?' asked James.

'Yes,' I repeated. 'What is the *exact* plan?'

'Call it a plan?' quacked Giles. 'He'll just put the money on and hope for the best. I imagine this thing is an outsider,' he said to Jerry, 'or you couldn't win enough to pay Ley Wong.'

'Oh yes,' said Jerry. 'I've already agreed the price with Mr K. Veeraswami, turf accountant, of the bazaar. One hundred to six for cash.' He waved Morgan Grenfell's loan in the air. 'So thank you very much for this,' he said. 'How kind. I'll take it along to Veeraswami this evening.'

'I shall expect a commission of ten per cent in case of success,' said Morgan Grenfell. 'That also runs in the family.'

'But your plan can't be as simple as that,' said James. 'Just a straight gamble at long odds?'

'It isn't,' said Jerry. 'The whole point of my plan is that this pony will lose.'

'Yet you'll still put your money on?'

'My money,' said Morgan Grenfell.

'Oh yes,' said Jerry. '150 rupees at 100 to six, call it sixteen to one, makes a nice little win of 2,400…so I shall have a good bit over after I've paid Ley Wong—'

'—and returned my loan with commission—'

'—to deal with all other possible embarrassments.'

'But you said,' nagged Giles, 'that this pony will lose.
So how can you win 2,400 rupees on it?'

'It's got to lose before it can win. It can never beat the
favourite...which is the fastest job between here and the
Malabar Coast, except by coming second and objecting
on grounds of having been fouled.'

'Rather difficult to arrange?'

'But not impossible. The thing is, you see, that Piers
Longshaft, who owns and rides Lars Porsena, is, as I told
you, in the Mysore Lancers. Now, the Mysore Lancers
aren't a regular Indian regiment but troops raised by the
Maharajah of Mysore. Most of the officers are natives,
and both they and the few white officers, like Piers, hold
the Maharajah's Commission; not the King Emperor's
Commission, nor the Viceroy's, but the Maharajah's.'

'And so?' said Morgan Grenfell.

'They are appointed and dismissed at the Maharajah's
pleasure, not subject to British or Indian Military Law, or
King's Regulations, or to the Army Council.'

'And so?' said James.

'Wait and see,' said Jerry Stanley.

The favourite for the polo scurry, Wee Willie Winkie, was
ridden by its owner, Lieutenant-Colonel Mordaunt
Jackson, Commanding Officer of the Third (TA)
Battalion of the Pembrokeshire Regiment, which was at
that time stationed at Napier Camp, near Bangalore, and
employed in support of the Civil Power. A cramped,
shrivelled man, Mordaunt Jackson seemed to claw his
way on to his pony in the paddock rather than mount it
and then chivvy it into a series of crablike, sideways

movements to get it on to the sand path which led to the course. Piers Longshaft, on the other hand, mounted with aplomb and rode bravely out like a banneret at the head of his squadron.

'Why is Wee Willie Winkie the favourite?' said Barry the Boxer, 'and Lars Porsena one of the outsiders?'

'Because Lars Porsena is all show,' said Jerry, 'and Wee Willie Winkie is as fast as the Four Horses of the Apocalypse.'

'They're yards apart in the line-up.'

'No draw for a polo scurry.'

'Then why doesn't Lars Porsena get closer to Wee Willie Winkie if it's going to stage a foul?'

'Wait and see.'

Wee Willie Winkie won by a street. Lars Porsena was second, as Jerry's plan required, but at no stage during the race did it come anywhere near Wee Willie Winkie, let alone get in any way impeded or fouled by it.

Colonel Mordaunt Jackson rode into the winner's stall. Captain Longshaft rode up behind him, dismounted, removed one glove, flapped it across the cheek of the Colonel as he walked out of the stall and said, 'My second will wait on yours, Colonel, if you will kindly name him, and they can agree a suitable place. As I am the challenger, you will have choice of weapon.'

What's this tomfoolery all about?' said Colonel Mordaunt Jackson.

'Nothing more serious, Colonel, I do assure you. I am challenging you to a duel on the ground that you deliberately fouled my pony during the race.'

'Then object to the stewards. I was nowhere near your damn pony.'

'So now you give me the lie. Another cause for a challenge.'

'Officers of His Majesty the King are forbidden to engage in duels of any kind.'

'Officers of His Highness the Maharajah of Mysore are not forbidden. We can fight on neutral territory, where you are not subject to arrest. HH will gladly lend us a corner of his gardens. Or we can fight here on the course, all of which belongs to him.'

'What are you trying to start?' said Jackson. 'You know the form as well as any man in the Indian Peninsula. If you think you've been cheated in this race, you object to the stewards. You don't start waving sabres around.'

Piers Longshaft leaned forward and spoke in Mordaunt Jackson's ear. Jackson stiffened, then nodded. They conferred very briefly, then went off with their saddles and gear to the weighing room. A few minutes later Captain Piers Longshaft's Lars Porsena was announced and posted as the winner. Wee Willie Winkie, it appeared, had weighed in at five pounds under.

'Well, well, well,' said James, 'and what was all that about?'

'Plan B,' said Jerry. 'Plan A, as you know, was that Longshaft should get himself fouled or bumped and claim the race on an objection. That didn't work. Piers couldn't get himself close enough to Jackson in the scrimmage. So then Plan B came into operation. Piers Longshaft issues a public challenge to Mordaunt Jackson to fight a duel with weapons of the latter's choosing. Longshaft can do this with impunity as there is nothing against it in the Maharajah's regulations for the conduct of his officers and the racecourse is the Maharajah's property – his ground. But of course, no matter whose ground it is, Jackson, as a King's officer, cannot accept the challenge. Longshaft knows this very well. He also knows, because I have told him, that Rosalie's mother was employed in the Jackson house, into which she introduced the eleven-year-old Rosalie. Enough said.'

'Blackmail,' said Giles with disgust.

'A gentlemen's agreement: you, Jackson, get rid of some of your weights, say this occurred by accident during racing and honourably cede the race; I, Longshaft, shall say nothing about dear little Rosalie... who is now, incidentally, in an Anglican Convent in Kodykanal, repenting her former sins but still with a very sharp tongue in her head if someone should make trouble and Rosalie be called as a witness.'

'And all that stuff about a duel?' said Morgan Grenfell. 'Why bother with that?'

'A red herring. A false scent to obscure the true one. For public consumption, the story is that Piers knew, or thought he knew, that he had been cheated by Jackson's riding under weight and became so angry when Jackson won that he challenged him. Jackson admits that he has lost some weights but assures Longshaft that this was due to a nasty jolt in riding. The rumour that he intended to ride under weight has been put about by a disaffected syce, who has now (rather conveniently) disappeared. Anyway, Jackson gives his word as an officer and a gentleman that the weights were shifted by accident, whereupon the whole thing is amicably settled in the weighing room and Piers gets the race. All plain sailing; a bit of understandably hot temper, but no harm done; no farther explanation needed and absolutely no talk of eleven-year-old Rosalie (which nobody concerned really wants) or of anything as horrendous as blackmail. Thus an amusing tale is put about in the clubs and messes instead of the unsavoury truth.'

'Rough on Jackson?' said James. 'Losing his prize.'

'Not really. The prize for that scurry was piffling. And

once he is in friendly agreement with Piers Longshaft, Longshaft is happy to give him a few tips (also originating from me) about some unreformed young, very young, friends of Rosalie's who will be happy to meet the distinguished Colonel Mordaunt Jackson. A much nicer prize than a cheque for a hundred chips and a cheap trophy. And I collect my 2,400 from Veeraswami. Something for everybody.'

'Surely not much for Longshaft,' I said. 'As you observed, the race itself is almost worthless.'

'He had a nice big bet on himself. The Maharajah, loyal to one of his officers, had a much bigger bet. The Maharajah will be very pleased with Captain Piers Longshaft. Cheerio for now, chums. I'm off to the bazaar to lift my loot from that old crocodile, Veeraswami.'

'You settle with Ley Wong before you go anywhere to celebrate,' said James.

'I shall go straight to him from Veeraswami's snakepit. Where else should I celebrate but in Ley Wong's restaurant?'

'I think I'll come along,' said Morgan Grenfell, 'to secure my investment. Plus ten per cent of the profit, if I remember aright. But I thought I might waive some of that if we just happened to meet one of Rosalie's little sisters and you were kindly to introduce me...'

'No more of that,' said Jerry. 'We're now into the last furlong and I'm going to take no more risks before we get our commissions.'

'The Devil a saint would be,' scoffed Giles.

'Will *nothing* please you, Giles?' said James. 'Bravo, Jerry. Straight running now till you're past the post.'

On the night before our passing-out parade everyone stayed sober, including Jerry Stanley. We all dined early in the officer cadets' mess, including Jerry Stanley. Virtue was not rewarded. At three in the morning half of us were woken by violent enteritis, in no case more violent than that of Jerry Stanley.

The next morning about a third of those due to pass out that day were excused the actual parade, being afflicted by continuous flux. Among those excused was, of course, Jerry Stanley.

'Don't forget,' said James, who was unaffected by the pest, 'to hand your rifles in.'

As junior under officer of our platoon, he was quite properly reminding us of the last procedure we must complete as cadets. Our rifles, which were kept in a guarded arms kote for reasons of security, must be taken out, cleaned and formally presented to the kote orderly (a senior Indian NCO) who would certify the weapons as being in the correct condition and then strike them off our personal charge. Normally this would be done immediately after the passing-out parade; but those who were not to appear on the POP because of illness were commanded, by standing orders of the OTS, to attend the arms kote for the handing in procedure during the parade itself, thus reducing the stampede at its conclusion.

A simple task, cleaning one's weapon and handing it over a counter to be checked and signed for by a responsible Indian orderly; not so simple, however, if one had diarrhoea like Vindaloo curry.

True to his resolution to run straight until the end, Jerry Stanley cleaned his rifle with care and accuracy, down to the last finicking notch of the foresight. Then, 'Christ,' he said to me as we stood in the queue to hand our arms over, 'I've got to trot. Hold my rifle for me just a mo.'

Jerry trotted. I held his rifle for him, along with my own. Giles, who had been ahead of us in the queue and had now completed the formalities, passed me on his way out.

'Two rifles?' he said. 'What's the trouble?'

Here I should explain that the rifles at Bangalore were old and faulty, and that very often cadets had to be issued with a second while the first was kept permanently in the kote awaiting repair by the armourer, who sometimes took weeks before he got round to it. When this occurred, one would have two rifles on one's charge and it was one's duty, if this was still the case at the time of passing out, to clean and hand back both to the orderly, who would then strike both off one's charge. Clearly, this was what Giles thought was happening here and it was the merest whim that had prompted his question.

'Which one is out of order,' he said now, 'and why? Someone really ought to make a report,' he continued pompously, 'about the poor state of the weaponry at this OTS.'

Bored with this inconsequent silliness, nerves fluttering and bowels simmering, I said, 'For Christ's sake, Giles, buzz off.'

'As cadet platoon Serjeant, I'm only taking a proper interest in the state of the platoon's rifles.'

'There's nothing wrong with either of these,' I said. 'One of them is Jerry Stanley's.'

'And where is Stanley?'

'In the bog just over there.'

'Leaving his rifle unguarded.' Giles took a deep breath. His face began to swell like a balloon.

'Not unguarded,' I said. 'With me.'

'You know the regulations in this country. Except when a man's rifle is locked away in the arms kote, he is

119

responsible for keeping it with him at all times. It is not a responsibility that can be delegated.'

'For Christ's sake, Giles.'

Jerry appeared.

'I'm afraid some got away before I got there,' he said. 'I'll have to go back to the basha [quarters] and change my knickers. I suppose I'd better take my rifle in case you get to the counter before I'm back.'

'Officer Cadet Stanley,' said Giles. 'It is my duty to inform you that I am now placing you under close arrest for failing to keep your personal weapon under proper surveillance.'

'It's like I said the other day, gentlemen,' said the friendly Staff-Serjeant instructor at the passing-out party. 'There's certain breaches of discipline or security that they never forgive out here. Little things, you might think; but things that have so often cost good men's lives. You're on the Frontier, right? You leave your rifle with a mate for two ticks while you go for a crap. You're caught by Fuzzi Khan with your trousers down, you can't defend yourself or give warning, the whole company is butchered by Fuzzi and his pals...'

'But Staff,' said James. 'This business of Jerry Stanley's occurred in peace time, in the secure arms kote of a secure barracks in a secure garrison town—'

'— The point about a rule, sir, is that you obey it all the time. Even when it doesn't matter, in case you start getting careless and forget it when it does.'

'Then you see no hope that they might let Jerry Stanley off and allow him to take up his commission?'

'None at all, sir. And in my view, rightly not.'

'Did Giles do it out of spite?' said James to me as we

walked back to our basha from the party. 'Or did he think, like that Staff-Serjeant, that a drill must be a drill forever and in all circumstances?'

'Giles did not approve of Jerry. He did not think that he should be allowed to get away with things. Jerry has got away with rather a lot during this course.'

'The worst problem, now,' said James, 'is that they are not sending Jerry away to another unit as a private soldier. He's to stay with us. Come on commissioning leave with us. Still as a cadet.'

'But—'

'—Clement Attlee is keeping his promise and bringing the boys home. We are *all* going home when we've been on leave, as are all the battalions out here to which we might have been posted. So it is administratively convenient, the company commander told me, to send Jerry back with us. He wants us to take care of him.'

'What do we do about Giles? We must keep them apart.'

'Mercifully, Giles is going to spend his furlough with grand cousins, near Madras. So Jerry can come with us to Outy.'

'Hadn't he made plans of his own?'

'He won't have the money to follow them up. Now he's not to be commissioned, they'll be screwing him to pay the advances and allowances back.'

'Then he can't even afford Outy.'

'That will be seen to,' said munificent James.

'So all will be well – during our leave?'

'Yes.'

'But then…?'

'Then we shall all have to report to the transit camp at Deolali, to await passage home. A draft of 299 newly commissioned second lieutenants, and the one failure, Officer Cadet (for that is to be his style until further notice) Jerry Constant Stanley.'

Officer Cadet Jerry Constant Stanley was subdued and agreeable while we were on leave. Since we did not wear uniform, he did not stand out as the odd man. He didn't seem to resent his calamity. He never referred to the absent Giles.

'I don't like it,' said Morgan Grenfell, who was helping James to see that there was ample and tactful management in the matter of Jerry's expenses. 'Why should he be so calm when he's been served a dirty turn like that? One would have expected him to be raging and shouting all day long.'

'That would not be dignified. He always had an odd sense of his dignity, whatever he was up to. And it would not be polite to his hosts. Although flamboyant and flashy, he always had considerate manners. It explains much of his success.'

'It did,' said Barry the Boxer.

'I hope he's all right at Deolali,' said Morgan Grenfell. 'You know there's a thing called Deolali Tap? It's a sort of madness people get when they're kept there too long without a passage and without any orders. They begin to feel they don't exist. They think they have to do something – anything – in order to draw attention to themselves before they finally vanish into thin air.'

'So long as we are with Jerry, and treat him just like one of ourselves, he will be all right,' James said. 'He will be with us in Deolali and then on the boat. After that we really cannot be answerable.'

It had all been my fault. If I had only, when Giles asked

about the two rifles I was holding, just agreed that they were both in my charge for a perfectly commonplace and respectable reason, then all would have been well. But no. I wasn't well and I wasn't thinking straight that morning. I was sick and tired of Giles. I wanted peace. So I told him what appeared at the time to be a perfectly harmless truth – that I was looking after Jerry's rifle for him while he went to the loo, which was ten yards away, just over the floor of the rifle kote.

What had got into Giles? He'd barely been seen since the day of our commissioning. He had attended the party, been treated with suspicion and reserve (but not incivility) by all present, and had then left to join his smart connections on the coast south of Madras. He had said nothing to his friends before leaving, had indeed said nothing to anybody, save for his oral report while delivering Jerry to the guard house, since Jerry's arrest. He had no need even to give evidence, for Jerry was never formally charged. Neither he nor anyone else could deny what had happened; rather than get up a court martial with all the fuss and pain of it, the Commandant had simply pronounced, as he was fully entitled to (back in 1947) without giving any particular reason, that Officer Cadet Stanley, J. C., was unfit to become an officer and that was that. The authorities did not like cadets being failed at Bangalore after the expense (as we have seen) of getting them there, but one cadet out of 300, for there was no other, was an acceptable ratio. The whole affair was therefore being very coolly passed off.

'Firm but not vindictive,' was James' judgement of the authorities' behaviour (though not of Giles'), 'yet obviously obsessive. You,' he said to me, 'are not to blame. How could you know that Giles would turn Judas or that the army in India is still living in the era of the

Mutiny?'

So although it had all been my fault for saying what I did, morally, it appeared, it was not my fault at all. James' word, in such matters, was conclusive. But what was to happen next? Not culpable though I might be, I must surely, like everyone else, take an interest in the outcome. Neither the absent Giles nor the taciturn Jerry had given any indication of personal feeling and intention, but feeling and intention, on both sides, there must be, and surely no longer to be disguised when Second Lieutenant Giles Benson was confronted by Officer Cadet Jerry Stanley in the officers' mess (which Jerry, under the present dispensation, would be allowed to use) in the transit camp at Deolali, celebrated for Deolali Tap.

But in the event there was no confrontation, or not of the kind we expected. James, Morgan Grenfell, Barry the Boxer, Jerry and I returned from our furlough in the Nilgeri Hills to the OTS at Bangalore. There we were given documents and orders, and after two days took the train for Deolali. Giles, we had heard from the friendly Staff-Serjeant instructor, who made it his business to know such things, had been taken ill at the home of his influential relatives. These telephoned the Commandant of the OTS to seek an extension of leave for Giles, who was reputedly too ill to telephone for himself.

So what was the matter with Giles? we enquired.

Well, according to the ORQMS, who had overheard the Commandant's end of the telephone call, Giles had dysentery, not just the sporadic and annoying diarrhoea (Bangalore belly) common among all British troops in the garrison, but real, red-hot dysentery that went through a man like a ray gun. Then the situation was as follows, the Commandant had instructed Giles' host:

Giles was due to return to the OTS, to collect his documents and then proceed to Deolali, not later than three days hence; if, therefore, he was still unfit to travel by then, Giles must be placed in the military hospital in Madras and he (the Commandant) must be notified that this had been done. In this way the whole matter would be put on an official basis, and responsibility for Giles would have been correctly and satisfactorily shifted. Thus the business stood when we boarded the train for Deolali; and when we arrived there three days later we heard from the head clerk in Postings that Giles had indeed been moved into the military hospital at Madras and was not expected to reach Deolali in time to catch the troopship on which the rest of us were to embark for England, home and beauty from nearby Bombay.

'Well,' said Morgan Grenfell in the ramshackle junior officers' mess, 'that's one embarrassment out of the way.'

Jerry came in.

'Can't come in here, boy,' said the mess Serjeant. 'Only officers in here. Hop it.'

James tactfully explained what had been decreed about Jerry and his status. The mess Serjeant listened crossly but condescended to serve Jerry.

'I've had a letter,' Jerry said. 'From those relatives of Giles Benson's who had him to spend his leave with them. They say he wanted to write to me but was much too weak. He wanted to write and say he was sorry for sneaking on me. It's been troubling him. He now thinks (according to these people at Madras) that he acted out of spite, impulsive spite. He was jealous about my way of enjoying life and avoiding the consequences. He wanted to give me a lesson. *Et cetera*. So now he's ill and he's sorry, and he wants to be forgiven. I must write, say these friends of his, to Giles at the British military hospital,

Madras and say I forgive him everything.'

'Who exactly are these "friends" or "relatives"?'

'Distant cousins, I gather,' said Jerry, 'a husband and wife and their daughter, to whom Giles was apparently going to be engaged. Later, when they were both a little older. They'd known each other before the war, in the nursery, while they were growing up. *Et cetera*. The man wrote the letter, and his wife and daughter added postscripts. The daughter's was particularly affecting. "This guilt about what he has done to you is making Giles far worse," she writes. "Please save him for me. I feel he may die unless you write. He gets weaker every day. All he talks of when we go to see him is his wickedness to you. He is obsessed. Only you can cure him of his obsession." '

'What are you going to do?' asked James.

'I shall write. Of course I must.'

'Good man.'

'But I shall not write at once,' said Jerry. 'Clearly it is a letter that will have to be composed very carefully.'

But before he could write, the daughter, Giles' fiancée to be, arrived, to intercede with Jerry personally. He was given leave to go and meet her in the Taj-Mahal Hotel in Bombay.

'She helped me to compose the letter,' said Jerry, when he got back to Deolali the next day. 'Marjorie – that's her name – will go straight back to Madras and deliver it to Giles in person. Can't think what he sees in her: stupid, dumpy, snobby little bitch. Fell into my arms. Hot for anything I'd give her – though she wouldn't allow *it*. Says she's keeping herself pure for her husband.'

'For Giles?'

'No. For me. I've got to take care of my future, chums.

126

I'm sailing home with no commission, no prospects inside the army or out. I can do with a really influential father-in-law. He'll be back in England almost as soon as we shall be—he's only here on a three-month tour of duty for his firm. Marjorie says he can get me out of the army early—industrial priority of some kind. You see what sort of post-war world it's going to be, if bloody rubbish of that sort is going to take precedence over the service. Ah, well. The job he'll find me will be desperately boring but exceedingly well paid.'

'What about Marjorie?' Morgan Grenfell said.

'What about her?'

' "Stupid, dumpy, snobby…" '

'She'll be a loyal wife and a good mother. She's randy but she means what she says about purity. I don't object to that…in a wife.'

'What shall you tell Giles?'

'It's all in the letter which Marjorie's taking to him. Oh yes, I forgive him all right. He's fucked up my commission, he's reduced me to the ranks, once we get home, for the rest of my National Service, sentenced me to subordination and misery and discomfort. But I've forgiven him, I've written, because he's brought me and Marjorie together: Marjorie will make up for everything. I haven't spelt it out – I couldn't, of course, with her breathing over my shoulder – but he'll know what I mean.'

'Mightn't this kill him?'

'Oh no. They all said he was dying of weakness made worse by remorse, that he was dying of guilt because of the way he's treated me. Now that things have turned out so well for me after all, he can hardly feel remorse or guilt any more; so he can throw off his weakness and live. Not many people die of dysentery these days. Let him pull himself together: it was what he was always recommending to others.'

Giles died in the military hospital at Madras from amoebic dysentery, probably exacerbated by outrage and loss of face. This would not have occurred, for Jerry would never have met Marjorie and there would have been no shock to render Giles' illness fatal, had not he committed a mean and treacherous act of delation; so justice of a kind was done.

Jerry, the freebooter, married squat Marjorie, was placed in dull but opulent circumstances and fell ill of a cancer. He would have been dead within months, but Marjorie, who loved him, used her money on treatments to keep him alive, until he was pleading for death and her entire portion was spent.

Much of all this, and that the worst of it, would never have happened if only I'd behaved sensibly when Giles Benson commented on my having two rifles in my care and if only I'd gone along with the plausible explanation which he himself suggested, instead of insisting on telling the truth. I can't even claim I did this out of habit, as I more often than not told lies – one is apt to, in the army. Perhaps I wanted to kill a few moments of waiting in a boring queue (desiring not peace, as I once thought, but distraction) or perhaps I wanted to remind Giles that even he did not know everything. In any case, I said what I said without thinking or noticing or caring—so utterly trivial was the whole affair—and thereby set in train a sequence of events that ended in protracted agony for Jerry Stanley (instead of the quick and early death that would normally have been his lot) and an unhallowed decease for Giles Benson.

Sneak House

from
Boys Will be Boys

There is a widespread illusion that 'sneaking', or the bearing of tales to those in authority, is unheard of in British public schools. This was certainly true in Tom Brown's day and was more or less true as recently as twenty years ago. It was true because the British were still a robust and independent race with their proper sense of *laisserfaire* as yet unspoiled. The advent of notions about Welfare and Social Responsibility has settled that—and settled it as surely in the adolescent world of the public school as it has everywhere else. To mind one's own business and leave others to mind theirs, formerly a simple matter of good manners, something any gentleman in school or out did without thinking, is quite definitely no longer the fashion; and it is interesting to note that it had already ceased to be so, at any rate at my own school, as early as the 1940s, although at this time the social virtue of prodnosing, while rapidly gaining recognition in the favourable conditions of war, was still at a fairly harmless stage of development. But of course even the most reactionary of educational institutions are more sensitive to social climate than is commonly allowed, and it is possible that the boys were almost unconsciously adopting the habit of talebearing as a preparation for and a protection against the new world into which they would emerge.

In any event, I reckon that I must have been at school at the very time when the traditional and honourable schoolboy custom of holding one's peace about the affairs of others was finally thrown on to the ethical scrap-heap. There is additional interest, for me, in the passing of this custom, since the school at which I was educated and so observed its passing is one of those mentioned, though without enthusiasm, as being conceivably suitable for the Prince of Wales. This school, I should add, is neither at Windsor nor in Scotland. It is one of the 'big six', it had a fine reputation for classical scholarship in the nineteenth century (a reputation which, on the whole, it retains), but in general it is remarkable chiefly for solid adherence to the more Arnoldian of the middle-class virtues. It encourages the idea of service rather than that of intellect on the one hand or money-grubbing on the other: and indeed it might be taken as truly representative of the better-found schools which cater for the most reputable sections of the professional classes. I find it significant that it was such a school which first taught me that it was no longer thought dishonourable to carry tales. What follows is the manner of that teaching.

To start with, my House at this school was 'keen' House. We liked to win the House Football Cup and the Shield for efficiency at P.T. We even took seriously the annual J.T.C. competitions for drill and such like. Most Houses (credit where credit is due) were pretty cynical about the annual drill competition, but not (alas) my own. Now, the one thing you obviously can't have in a 'keen' House is 'slackness'. Everyone is meant to do P.T., and a small caucus of people observed being slack at it can ruin your chances of winning the P.T. efficiency shield. And if you can't have slackness, neither can you have people making jokes or remarks which, even by implication, make light of the sterner virtues. Hence, towards the end of my second term, came my first reckonable lesson in the new values which the times were incubating. Having remarked to a friend at tea that the Chinese had once been a civilized people with a low opinion of military qualities, I was summoned, later in the evening, by the Head of the House. It seemed that my remark had been overheard by a boy called Cave-Watkins who was my senior by just two terms. He had immediately reported this instance of my 'unsatisfactory' attitude. The Head of the House did not take the line, which at that time (1942) would have been reasonable enough, that small boys enjoying a first-class education in the middle of a world war would do well not to belittle their protectors: he insisted, instead, that the tone of my remark was unsuitable for a House which, by its spirit of conformity, co-operation and enthusiasm, had won the distinction of amassing more cups and having a more healthy atmosphere than any other House in the school.

'Remember, Raven,' he said, 'that such an atmosphere is easily poisoned by the least hint of disaffection or cynicism. If you must pick up unhealthy ideas, then keep them to yourself.'

I found this point of view both juvenile and yet obscurely frightening, but at least it was consistent with the character and aims of the Head Monitor. What was still a mystery, however, was the point of view of the boy who had actually reported me. As I say, he was only two

terms senior to myself and held no official position
whatever.

'What do you mean, Cave-Watkins,' I said when I
found him, 'by going off and sneaking like that? Why
couldn't you mind your own business?'

'We don't use the word "sneaking",' Cave-Watkins
said, 'we talk about "showing up". And it was my business.
The good of the House is everybody's business.'

And he then began to explain the new philosophy.
Showing up, he said, was a permissible practice, much
encouraged by masters and older boys, when there was
any question at all of it being one's duty or responsibility
to speak out. In the bad old days, nothing short of
murder would have elicited a word from anyone. And just
look at all the bullying and 'immorality' and slacking
there had been. But nowadays everyone knew better.
Anything said or done that raised a moral issue, however
piddling or remote, or that touched upon the tone or
efficiency of the House, was suitable material for retailing
to the authorities. This applied, he went on, not only to
bad things but to good ones: evidence of the proper spirit
was conveyed, no less surely (though perhaps with less
immediacy) than news of slackness or moral decay, to the
ever-open ears of the Head Monitor. A good Head
Monitor, he explained, had no time even to do his school
work, because he devoted his entire evenings to listening
to the endless reports of boys like Cave-Watkins about
the characters of their contemporaries. This happened at
every stage of seniority; and even Monitors would drop
into the Head Monitor's study for three hours or so to
complain about the other Monitors. Every member of
the House was expected to do his duty in this way. If I
myself, for example, was 'to get anywhere at all' in the
local hierarchy, I must soon start taking in my own

reports. I need not wait to be summoned. I should just go along and knock on the Head Monitor's door and announce that I would like 'to talk to him' for a while. In the unlikely event of no one else being there and talking already, I should be welcomed—particularly so if I brought news of disloyalty to the House or some sexual irregularity.

As far as I could make out, even failure on someone's part to wash in the morning should be reported instantly. Anything should be retailed which related to the moral state of the House—and that, by current standards, seemed to mean anything at all. The whole place was a midden of priggishness and betrayal. Incredulous and appalled, I retired to think the position over. It simply could not be true. This wasn't the Vatican. Cave-Watkins must surely be exaggerating: he was saying that such behaviour was general in order to excuse his own brand of ambitious malice. Or again, this was the end of the term: perhaps he was overwrought by excitement at the prospect of the holidays, or was suffering under the strain of a strenuous term; for life in our House was nothing if not intense, and very apt to induce an occasional sense of nightmare. By the end of the holidays, I thought, both Cave-Watkins and myself would have forgotten his every word.

But the truth of what had been told me was made only too plain by two incidents which occurred the following summer. Both incidents involved exact contemporaries of my own: both clearly indicated that these boys, likeable, I had thought, and intelligent, were already firmly committed to the course of life which Cave-Watkins had described, with such vile relish, as normal.

Chancing one day to be watching a cricket match, I was approached by a boy called Fisch:

'Matron,' said Fisch, 'has asked me to tell you that your hair is too long and you must get it cut.'

'Tell Matron,' I said, 'that I like it long and she can mind her own bloody business.'

And that, apparently, was what he did tell Matron—verbatim. A summons from the Head Monitor followed fast.

'What's this about you telling Matron to mind her own bloody business? She's complained.'

I explained the circumstances.

'It never occurred to me,' I said, 'that Fisch would even dream of reporting my remark back to Matron.'

'But,' said the Head Monitor, 'he was very properly showing you up to Matron for taking an insolent tone behind her back.'

'I suppose you could look at it like that.'

'Any responsible person looks at it like that...I shall beat you this evening.'

So I received four strokes of the cane, which I didn't care for, and a severe reminder, which I cared for even less, of what Cave-Watkins had told me the previous term. This reminder was the more sharp as Fisch was shortly afterwards appointed to some rudimentary office which carried authority over the first-year boys. He had scored some valuable points by reporting me and was now getting his reward.

The second incident was, if anything, even more distasteful. There was that term a school production of *As You Like It*. I myself and some contemporaries were in the cast, which was taken to see the play performed by professionals in a town some forty miles away. After the performance we were allowed to go off on our own for tea, being firmly bidden to reassemble at the station by six. With Murray and Sale, two boys of my own standing,

I went off to a café in the town.

'A good opportunity,' said Sale, 'now we're this far from school, if anyone wants to smoke.'

Whereupon Murray produced a packet of cigarettes. Sale declined the offer of one: Murray and I lit up.

The moment we got home, Sale rushed to tell the Head Monitor what had occurred. Murray and I were roundly dressed down for abusing the privilege of being allowed away for the day, and then of course beaten. Sale was commended, and more or less overtly assured of future favour. Once again, good points had been scored by somebody who was, this time, not only an informer but also an *agent provocateur*. I recall with pleasure that later on Murray and I, bowling in a net where Sale was batting, sent down fast bumpers at his legs for a quarter of an hour on end. Since even he could scarcely report this, we were well revenged by the terror and pain we caused him. But that was not the point. The point was that a fourteen-year-old contemporary had deliberately reported us for the foolish but harmless activity of smoking, urging responsibility as his official motive, receiving approbation for his undoubted treachery.

So there it is. It is not my intention to explain in detail how such phenomena came to be possible in circumstances in which, even five years previously, they would have excited unmixed loathing. I can only observe, as I did at the beginning of this lament, that all this was probably the instinctive response of schoolboys to an outer world in which motives of envy, interference and self-righteousness were becoming daily more rancorous and dominant. However this may be, the plain truth is that what I have here described is the system which, I am most definitely assured, still does obtain. The old Tom Merry standards of rough and ready honour, shallow and vulnerable as they might have been, left no one in doubt where he stood. He could do more or less what he wanted so long as he didn't start whining about the wickedness of others. But the code of Tom Merry is as dead as the laws of Solon; and school life is ever more insistently punctuated by the self-congratulatory whimpers of morally outraged pubescence.

Of course, I may be exaggerating. I doubt it. For take heed of this. There was a custom, tolerated even in my time, whereby Monitors of the various Houses would visit each other, on the last night of the school year, to drink and smoke together, a pleasing celebration for those who would return, a poignant yet gay occasion for those who would not. A touching little custom? Generous and appropriate? So it was thought in my time, and for a long time afterwards. But I am told that a young and progressive Headmaster now details several ushers, at the end of the school year, to patrol the grounds and Houses, to interrupt and report any festivities they may uncover. How enthusiastic they are in their task, I do not know; but their mere appointment to so dismal an errand says all that is needed. No, they don't call it 'sneaking' any more: they 'show each other up'.

He Knew He Was Right

from
Bird of Ill Omen

'Colonel Smith, Sir?' said the Serjeant-Major (a very senior man in his grade). 'Colonel Smith?' he said, and thought carefully for a while. 'A gentleman, unlike some we needn't mention at that level or near it. Slow. Steady. Not over bright. Easy in many ways but impatient of contradiction. Why they chose him instead of Major Max, God alone knows.'

'Quite simple. The present CO detests Major Max because Major Max is charming, handsome and popular, and has a brilliant record. DSO and Bar. Commanded a brigade during the war – commanded a division, very briefly, while the GOC was ill. But since Colonel Smith is senior to Major Max, if only by a few days, and since for some reason he holds a Brevet Lieutenant-Colonelcy, the present CO has the chance to put Max down. And he has taken it. The rules say that the senior available officer, of field rank and under that of full colonel, must be chosen to command the battalion unless there is a very good reason why not.'

'Major Max is a very good reason why not.

Lieutenant-Colonel Smith is possibly another.'

Warrant officers in our regiment were free with their opinions if they knew one.

'As bad as that?'

'There are many good things about him as I say, sir. But every now and then, not always, but every now and then he is determined to have his own way. He becomes …obsessed.'

The take-over happened at Lichfield, in the barracks of one of the Staffordshire regiments, where we were waiting to take ship for Kenya. Our former CO had long since taken his *congé*. Lieutenant-Colonel Smith arrived unannounced and without fuss in the empty barracks one Sunday afternoon, thus sparing us the trouble of mounting special guards and putting on tedious ceremonies. A good start, it was felt. Smith would live in the officers' mess until we embarked at Liverpool for Mombasa. His own house in Shropshire, where he would leave his family during our tour of duty in Kenya, was too far from Lichfield for convenience – no bad thing, from our point of view, as we should now have an excellent and immediate chance to observe the man, his habits and his foibles.

The man was ordinary enough. His habits and manners were orderly and acceptable. His only foibles (as it appeared in those early days) were quite common in a married infantry officer of little or no private means: firstly, a pretence that not only himself but all other members of the mess lived on the border of extreme poverty and ought to be ashamed of themselves if they didn't; and secondly, a tendency to disapprove of officers who preferred to remain single rather than equip themselves with dowdy and pleasure-inhibiting wives.

Smith had a tiresome way of enquiring how soon one was thinking of joining 'the married fraternity'. I myself at that time belonged, in theory, to the 'married fraternity' already; and although Smith was deeply suspicious, because he very soon learned that my wife had not once been seen during the two years odd I had been with the regiment, he could hardly question me as to whether and when I proposed to get myself one. My friend O., when approached in the matter, earned low marks by quoting Shakespeare to the effect that 'a soldier is better accommodated than with a wife'; and a well-known point-to-point rider in the battalion was imprudent enough to observe that he was already married to his favourite mare, and in any case could not afford fodder and stabling for another on two legs.

People forgave Smith for his enquiries on the topic because in most other ways he was undemanding, because he was probably acting on the instructions of the Colonel of the regiment (a well-known hater of bachelors) and because, in any case, since there was nothing whatever either Smith or his superior could do about the matter, his interference was otiose. What we did not forgive Smith quite so easily was his habit of raising his eyebrows whenever anybody ordered a bottle of wine and pointedly calling for beer for himself. This, of course, was part of the poverty act, in which we were all meant to share; but as O. observed, if no one had ordered wine the CO would have had nothing to raise his eyebrows about, so we were probably doing him a good turn. Very likely, said the point-to-point rider, but he wasn't doing us one, looking at our wine like a warlock who wished he knew the spell to turn it sour. Never mind, said O.: so long as he never *did* turn it sour...For myself, I said, I didn't like to feel that I was being grudged any of my enjoyments and there could be no doubt that Smith grudged us this one. However, since in all other things, both on and off parade, he behaved with civil good sense and apparently had no quirks of zealotry, he was rated as harmless enough. Of course, said O., he had rather a lean look; a cosy, pear-shaped colonel would have been more reassuring. Not to worry, said our amateur jockey; Smith's was the rather flabby leanness of the sparse-living desk officer (as he had been for some years), not the black and savage gauntness of the martinet; we could depend on two years' peace and quiet during Smith's incumbency; being asked occasional silly questions about a fellow's (non-existent) marital intentions was a low price to pay.

It was 'Benghazi' Malcolm, our Adjutant, who first alerted me to unsuspected dangers. We were visiting Hereford Cathedral together in order to plan the troop movements at a forthcoming farewell service; A and B companies would enter in single file and sit to the left (north) of the nave, C and D ditto and to the right (south), and so on and so on…

'Hymns?' said a cleric.

' "I Vow to Thee my Country"?' I suggested.

'Not in *A & M*,' said the cleric, 'but in the *Clarendon Hymn Book*. Not popular with the ecclesiastical policy-makers these days, because of imperialist and bellicose tendencies. Still, I can arrange to have it printed in the order of service, at the risk of a row I shall very much enjoy.'

'I'm afraid I must deny you the pleasure,' said Malcolm. 'The CO has given me a list of hymns for this service: "All Things Bright and Beautiful", "For All the Saints" and "O God our Help in Ages Past".'

'Appropriate,' said the cleric, 'except possibly for the

first, but that's quite inoffensive. By the way, these days we do not sing the verse,

> 'The rich man in his castle,
> The poor man at his gate,
> He made them high or lowly,
> And ordered their estate.'

'Why not?' I enquired.

'It is considered to be undemocratic.'

'Who ever supposed God was a democrat?'

The cleric chuckled. 'The Church is encouraging Him to take populist views,' he said.

'The CO,' said Malcolm, rather wearily, 'does not take populist views. He said he hoped that we should be singing the entire hymn, including the verse you would like to exclude.'

'We *shall* exclude it,' said the cleric.

'Oh dear. My CO says that they always sung that verse when he was at school, that he has cherished memories. Surely, if you could have smuggled in "I Vow to Thee my Country" in the face of official disapprobation, you could manage "The rich man in his castle"?'

' "I Vow to Thee" is mistrusted but not yet forbidden. The verse, "The rich man in his castle" – though the rest of the hymn is of course all right – is definitely forbidden. We have our orders. Lieutenant-Colonel Smith will understand that, I dare say.'

'And I dare say he won't,' said Malcolm to me, as we walked across the cathedral close to his shagged-out Austin. 'He regards this as our service and therefore to be arranged to his liking.'

'It is somebody else's cathedral.'

'Not when *our* service is going on inside it.'

'Oh, come, come. Anyway, I should have thought he would be only too pleased to have those verses left out. He's always complaining about being poor.'

'It comforts him to think that his poverty is ordained. That way he needn't feel inferior.'

'Benghazi' Malcolm (so called because he had won a Military Cross there, leading his platoon into the attack with his bottom bare, during a bad bout of enteritis) now lowered his celebrated bum into the driving seat and opened the passenger door, in a shower of rust and splinters, for me.

'He has nothing much to feel inferior about,' I said. 'Many men are poor, whether or not it is ordained by God.'

'He needs constant assurances on the point – which he doesn't always get. He likes to think that all his officers are poor. But some of them aren't and few of you behave as if you were. Of course, he's much too sensible to try to enforce his views in the mess. But that wouldn't stop him from enforcing them, by way of compensation, elsewhere. This hymn business. Yes, it's someone else's cathedral but it's our recruiting area (that's why we're having the service here) and the occasion is in our honour.'

'Oh God. Poor Malcolm. What shall you do?'

'Tell him that the Bishop has asked him, as a special favour, to allow that verse to be omitted. The idea that his authority is recognised and his permission is being sought will probably render him amenable.'

And so it did. Things did not go so smoothly in the matter of the boots.

I should explain that our troopship was about the last to sail. Air transport was now generally used: it got everyone there much quicker and so did not allow whole divisions of men to hang around doing nothing but sun themselves, for weeks on end, at Her Majesty's expense. But for whatever reasons, nobody was in much hurry to get us to Kenya; HMT *Kitchener of Khartoum* was scheduled to make one more voyage to Mombasa and back before being scrapped, and we were to travel on it. All the officers were delighted and purchased much superior fiction to beguile the journey. The CO alone was furious.

'He has developed a minor frenzy,' Malcolm told me, 'for what he calls "getting on with the job". I'm rather worried about it – it's a phrase which has only come up during the last few days. I think the Colonel of the regiment has been nagging at him.'

'Oh dear.'

'It's all the fault of people like you. You all *enjoyed* yourselves too much in Germany. Now, the Colonel of the regiment rather approves of enjoyment – *his* kind of enjoyment, polo and hunting and trekking and the rest. He does not approve of your sort of enjoyment, long weekends at Baden-Baden or Bad Homburg. Since he cannot actually rebuke you for this, he's invented a complaint that "the officers in BAOR did not get on with the job". And now he's using it to torture our new CO.'

'Poor Cuth.'

'The immediate point is that lounging around for four weeks on the *Kitchener of Khartoum* is certainly not "getting on with the job" and the CO is desperate to find ways of using the time to good purpose. The first bother is going to be the matter of ammunition boots.'

The poor bloody infantry wear, or then wore, heavy 'ammunition boots' with blancoed gaiters. Everyone hated this style of dress and wore shoes instead whenever possible. On troopships shoes were always worn in order not to ruin the wooden decks or damage delicate fittings.

'Colonel Cuth,' said Malcolm, 'thinks that if none of the troops wear boots for a month, their feet will get soft. That, you will readily understand, is not "getting on with the job". He intends that all ranks of our battalion shall wear ammunition boots for at least two hours every day... and this despite the copy of standing orders which we have already received from the OC troops of the *Kitchener*. These state, unequivocally, that although troops can embark and disembark in boots, as they must, they will not wear them at any other time for the entire duration of the voyage. There is also another item, stating that there is a compulsory siesta for all ranks on board every afternoon between 1400 and 1600 hours.'

'Siestas are very slack indeed. They even stopped having them in India. Someone said they were an insult to the war effort.'

'That chasm I shall cross,' said our gallant Adjutant, 'when we arrive at it. The CO has not yet noticed the order about siestas; he is still stuck at the paragraph about not wearing ammunition boots. He is determined to appeal against it – has already done so, although there are still several days before we embark. The OC troops has simply written a one-line letter which refers Cuth to the standing orders in force on the matter.'

'From what I remember, the OC troops will only be a lieutenant-colonel, like Cuth.'

'He is vastly senior. The OC troops is like a master of a college used to be. He only gives up when he is carried off. And apart from being senior, the OC troops is paramount on board his ship. If he says no boots, it means *no boots*.'

'Thank God for that.'

'So you may say. But think of me. I shall have to

handle the rumpus, which is going to begin the minute we have sailed out of Liverpool. I shall be go-between. I shall have to find some compromise, otherwise Cuth will fret himself to death.'

'What is the OC troops like?'

'He is an extremely amiable old gentleman – so it is reported to me – who lives entirely for his stamp collection. He deprecates any avoidable noise or activity on board his troopship. He loathes any kind of enthusiasm, military or other.'

'What a blissful man. If only *he* could be our CO.'

'Let's have a little loyalty. There's nothing much the matter with Cuth.'

'Probably not. Hymns are a harmless field of obsession. Boots are just that much more damaging, as boots are hard and heavy and disturb the peace. What we have to watch out for,' I said, 'is an ascending scale of unpleasantness. If each obsession is less sympathetic than the last…'

'The next one will probably be the siesta. I don't think that can be too disagreeable.'

'No? Suppose he commands the whole battalion to stay awake?'

'It is time you went back,' said the Adjutant, 'to supervising the packing of your company stores. That is what the Second-in-Command of a company is for. Not for hanging about and making subversive remarks.'

'Had we better take some empty hay boxes?'

'What for?'

'For packing the company's boots in. You know – Not Wanted on Voyage.'

'Piss off,' said Malcolm.

My hero.

My hero was a worried man when I saw him six days

later, on a rough morning on the *Kitchener of Khartoum*, twenty-four hours out of Liverpool.

'Colonel Cuth is driving the OC troops crazy,' he told me. 'He won't give the old man any peace to sort out the new stamps he's just bought in London. Cuth says to his face that if our feet grow soft and give out in the jungle, it's going to be his fault.'

'Surely,' I said, 'the whole point is that we don't wear ammunition boots in the jungle. We wear jungle boots, which are soft boots with rubber soles. It's those the men have got to get their feet used to. Now I'm absolutely sure that the OC troops will not mind our chaps' going round in canvas boots with rubber soles.'

'*Christ*,' yelled Malcolm. 'Why has no one thought of that?'

When I saw him next, at lunch, he was looking like one of the Eumenides.

'Something wrong?'

'Yes. Cuth says that the men's feet have got to remain used to ammunition boots because they'll be wearing them for routine parades in Nairobi. They may even, says Cuth, be needed for a bit of a show in Mombasa.'

'Obsessions are not to be dispelled by reason,' said O., joining the conversation unasked. 'However, Raven tells me you got over that difficulty about the hymn at Hereford by making it *appear* that Cuth was absolutely entitled to his own way but would give great pleasure if he graciously abrogated his right. Same technique possible here?'

'No. He knows, this time, that he is not entitled to his own way,' Malcolm said. 'He knows that the OC troops outranks him and that the standing orders are exactly what one would expect to find on any troopship. He also knows that he, Cuth Smith, is *right*. The men's feet must be kept hard by constant wearing of ammunition boots, whatever standing orders may say to the contrary and no matter how much trouble may be caused. There'll be no soft-soaping him as there was about that hymn.'

'Surely,' said our point-to-point rider, who had drifted up, 'the men could carry their boots up to one of the higher decks, thus making no noise and causing no damage, put down blankets when they get there, and then put on their boots and sit in them, presumably keeping their feet hard.'

'Cuth wants them to move about in their boots. Feet don't keep hard just with sitting in them.'

'I know,' said O. 'They could do exercises in their boots – exercises in which their feet did not touch the deck. Lying on their backs "bicycling", that kind of thing.'

'It's an idea,' said Malcolm. 'Thank you all for taking such an interest. I'll put it to the CO after lunch.'

The weather worsened and everyone except the sailors and the OC troops (seasoned) was sick. Cuth was sick but would not lie down, which meant that Malcolm couldn't lie down either. At the high point of his queasiness he was informed that the OC troops could not approve O.'s idea about exercises, as the booted feet might accidentally strike the deck and so do it damage.

'I said they would strike the blankets on the deck,' said Malcolm, reporting the conference later that evening when the wind had dropped. 'The OC troops said that a lot of harm could be done to a deck with the heel of an ammunition boot, even through an army blanket. But at last they've agreed something. Cuth said that if they built up piles of their kit – shirts, pants and so on – on their blankets, then their boots would strike a good foot of soft material and couldn't possibly damage anything. The OC troops was compelled to agree. So tomorrow the men will proceed, by shifts, to the stern deck, carrying their boots, and will put down their blankets and protective piles of clothes, don their boots, and exercise their legs and feet in the air and over the piles. Brilliant.'

Well, yes. Foolproof, one would have thought, had it not been that, of the first squad that exercised on the stern deck, five men impaled their lower legs on needles in their 'housewives' (repair kits), which had been included in their heaps of clothes to build them up higher, while seven toppled over while 'bicycling', in two cases inflicting huge scars on the deck, in two more cases savagely kicking the skulls of comrades in front or behind and in three cases nearly emasculating personnel sideways adjacent. The damage to the deck was somehow disguised from the ship's crew by our battalion carpenter (summoned in secret), but the damage to skulls and groins could not be disguised from our medical officer, a jolly, gambly, foul-mouthed Liverpudlian lieutenant, who had joined us in Lichfield.

'Mary, Jesus and Joseph,' said the Liverpudlian lieutenant, 'what sort of a loony outfit are you running here?'

'The CO,' I said, gritting my teeth, 'is determined that the men should wear their boots during the voyage and move their feet about inside them. Hence these exercises on the stern deck. *Please* don't try to get it changed. Someone will only think of something even sillier.'

'Could they not be less crowded?'

'No. There would not be time to get through the whole battalion daily.'

'Well,' said the doctor cheerfully, 'if they go on injuring themselves at this rate, it should clear the deck for you very nicely. You do realise,' he went on, 'that

148

when we get to the Red Sea we can't have them lying out there? The sun would kill them.'

'That,' I said, 'would solve a lot of problems.'

The doctor chuckled.

'I'm sorry to disappoint you,' he said, 'but my professional conscience will come into play in their protection somewhere about Suez. Someone had better warn the CO.'

'You'll have *his* professional conscience to cope with.'

'You'd better remind him,' said the doctor, looking very Liverpudlian, 'that in such cases the MO's recommendation is final.'

'Oh, yes. It's just that you may be surprised by the quality and obduracy of the CO's resistance if he doesn't like your recommendation.'

'Why shouldn't he like it? He wouldn't want his men to get heat stroke.'

'No. But he may persuade himself that they need training in how to endure extreme heat.'

'He must understand common sense.'

'He's full of common sense over most things. With a bit of luck he will be over this. We've got a good ten days to Suez. Let's just wait and see.'

'Let's do that,' said the Lieutenant. 'Are you on for a game of backgammon?'

'At 1100 hours?'

'You're in here consulting with me. No one will come in. Lance-Corporal Beatty,' he called. 'You there, Flossie?'

'Thir?' said a voice from an outer office or waiting room.

'I'm not to be disturbed for half an hour. If anybody calls, say I'm busy designing St. Paul's.'

'*Thir?*'

'Famous clerihew, you illiterate slut.'

'All right, thir. That'th what I'll thay. It will be interethting to thee what happenth next.'

'Only a joke, Flossie. Just say I'm on my rounds.'

'On your roundth where…thir?'

'Ship's hygiene.'

'That'th for the ship'th MO.'

'Say I've gone with him, under instruction.'

'And if anyone checkth up?'

'He won't let me down. He owes me a fiver which he hasn't paid. Silly arse,' he said to me as he produced an expensive travelling backgammon set and a bottle of Irish whiskey from a drawer. 'He bet me five quid that Labour would win the general election.' (This was the summer of 1955.) 'Said the people were sound at heart. Couldn't understand that one dose of socialist humbuggery and busybodying puts everyone off for a good ten years. Ten shillings a point, right?'

The CO was not very pleased about the large number of soldiers declared unfit for further 'deck exercise', but like many men of obsession he was prepared to relax slightly in practice once he had vanquished in principle and been given his way, or a good part of it. Anyhow, by now he had a new craze to occupy him. As Malcolm and I had surmised, he most strongly deprecated the ship's regulation which enjoined on all a two-hour siesta between 1400 and 1600 hours. He therefore started badgering the OC troops for permission to conduct special officers' seminars in the ship's library during those hours. There would be no noise, he said: nobody would be disturbed.

'Except,' said the OC troops (Malcolm reporting), 'for your officers. I dare say they like a siesta as well as anybody.'

'My officers,' said Cuth, 'are my concern. They all

know they've got to get on with the job.'

'What particular job had you in mind?'

'Beating the Mau Mau.'

'The Mau Mau,' said the OC troops, 'are already beaten. Do for God's sake get the thing right. You are not going to war against an enemy; you are going to Kenya to help clean the place up. You are going to collect out of the forest a few hundred starving and syphilitic wrecks armed with catapults and put them in detention camps until the administration decides on the most humane way of treating them.'

'I won't argue with you, Colonel,' said Cuth, 'though some might put the matter in a different perspective. Whatever we are doing in the forest, we shall need certain basic skills.'

'Not the sort you can learn in the ship's library.'

'I beg your pardon, Colonel,' said the courteous Cuth. 'We can learn Swahili in your library. Surely a useful asset?'

Game, set and match to Colonel Cuth, as Malcolm told us later. Further objections from the OC troops would have been merely perverse.

However, Colonel Cuth now proceeded to overdo it. Narked, if not very much, by the numbers of soldiers excused from taking part in deck exercises with ammunition boots, he decided on a little compensation. All officers, he promulgated, besides wearing boots when on the stern deck with their men (and thus being compelled to keep order from a squatting or at best sitting position), would also bring their boots with them to the ship's library every day and wear them during the Swahili lessons from 1400 to 1600 hours. In order to prevent their damaging the library floor, subalterns would bring piles of clobber of the kind they took on deck, while captains and above (whose dignity would suffer if they were seen to be toting laundry about) would use books from the library shelves to put their booted feet on.

Before the first day of the Swahili lessons, it had become apparent that there was only one Swahili book on the ship, an out-of-date concordance which belonged to the senior steward. A list of suitable words was copied out of this on to a worm-eaten blackboard by the officers i/c Swahili (O., and a rather precious but very intelligent National Service second lieutenant who had just come down from Oxford); the arrangement was approved (there being no better) by the Colonel; and after everyone had put on boots and, in the case of captain and above, rested his feet on volumes from the shelves, O. requested the CO's permission to begin.

'One moment,' said the CO, surveying the class. 'I see that the medical officer is not present.'

'The custom is, sir,' said Malcolm carefully, 'that the MO does not attend parades of regimental officers unless specifically requested to do so.'

'Why not?'

'He has private studies to attend to, sir. We are asked to take note that a medical officer, like any doctor in practice, has to keep up with current trends in medicine and important new theories, forensic and pathological. He therefore has a lot of reading to do, sir—'

'—And plenty of time in which to do it. He spent three hours yesterday after dinner, playing bridge, so no doubt he is not pressed, at the moment, for leisure in which to pursue his studies. Will the orderly officer of the day kindly find Lieutenant Wosking and request his presence here?'

After about ten minutes, a very cross Dr Wosking,

who had been hauled out of his bunk, reported to the ship's library, was sent back to his quarters to get his boots and also, as he ranked only as a lieutenant, a suitable pile of shirts to rest his feet on. As the Colonel pointed out, when Wosking was finally settled, he would need to know Swahili as well as the rest of us.

The plain fact remained that his legitimate, or at least his customary, prerogative had been denied. A medical officer does not wear boots, not even, unless he chooses to, in the field. The medical officer does not attend officers' parades, for P.T., say, or instruction, unless there is a very special reason and he is warned well in advance.

'The CO was out of order,' said our point-to-point rider that evening.

'He's been well paid out,' said Malcolm. 'After the Swahili lesson, Wosking went straight to the ship's librarian and told him of the use his books were being put to by captains and above. The librarian (a steward of long standing) has complained (a) that this is vandalism and (b) that damage has already been done, to covers and bindings, to the extent of £57 17s 9 ³/₄d. The OC troops has directed Colonel Cuth to find the money, not out of any regimental fund, but out of his own pocket. Now, before you all start chortling yourselves sick, please remember that Lieutenant-Colonel Cuth Smith is indeed a poor man, with two growing boys to educate; also that he genuinely and conscientiously believes that he has the battalion's interest and honour at heart. Remember, too, that it is your duty, and should be your pleasure, to support your commanding officer with all the loyalty you can muster. In short,' said Malcolm rather splendidly, 'I expect to see more willingness, keenness and co-operation, and less scrimshanking and girlish giggling, from all of you. Colonel Cuth is a very good-natured and well-intentioned officer; and if he is, on occasion, rather misguided in his enthusiasms, you will not stop him by thwarting or opposing him, you will merely make him unhappy and very possibly bloody-minded.'

'Which is all very well,' said O. after Malcolm had moved heavily away, 'provided Colonel Cuth confines his compulsive hankerings to trivial matters. What happens if something really serious crops up and he starts riding his romping hobby-horse then?'

'Malcolm will manage him,' I said. 'As I understand it, the technique with Cuth is now to give way over things that don't matter in order to keep him in his normal good temper. The more he thinks we're on his side, the less he'll push his luck when he knows we're against him.'

'Wrong,' said the point-to-point rider. 'He does not acknowledge opposition when he gets carried away. As we know, every now and then something carries him away Most things he will discuss as calmly and as rationally as you please. He made excellent sense the other day when he sent for me to talk about the regimental saddle club he wants to establish in Nairobi. Very slow he was, but also friendly and amenable to argument. But there are some things about which he knows that, whatever anyone else may know, he knows best. So far, thank God, these have only been trifling things like ammunition boots and siestas. But when such things appear on the agenda, as we have all observed, he is simply non-negotiable…as the moneylender said of the cheque which came back marked "no account".'

'I'd still back Malcolm to negotiate with him over anything that really mattered.'

'Perhaps,' said O. 'The trouble is that Malcolm is getting no practice.'

'I should have thought,' I said, 'that he was getting plenty.'

'Only,' insisted our amateur jockey, 'about small things. He will need lots of special practice before he can cope with the Queen of Spades.'

'Do you remember that absurd but endearing film?' I said. 'A Russian officer of engineers made a huge sum playing cards with some guardees by naming the Queen of Spades as next card to turn up. He'd been tipped off by a ghost played by Edith Evans.'

'There'll come no ghost played by Edith Evans to tip Malcolm off in time,' said O.

'In the film the face of the card suddenly changes in front of them all—so the engineer hadn't won after all and went mad as a result. The card changes back again, just as they're all putting him in the loony van, so nobody sees it.'

'That's another thing,' said our horseman. 'Serious matters are apt to go into flux under your eyes. Which is no help at all.'

'Everything is in flux, according to Heraclitus,' I said, 'and in that case nothing can matter at all.'

'That's the same as saying that in the long run we'll all be dead,' said O. 'In the army it's the short run we have to deal with – the here and now.'

'Here and now,' said Malcolm, who was very restless that evening and had just rejoined us, 'there is another cauldron about to bubble.'

'So long as it doesn't set the house on fire.'

'One or two people may be scalded. The CO has caused continuing schedules to be published in tomorrow's orders about the use of the stern deck for boot exercises. This schedule takes us all the way to Mombasa. I have just whispered in his ear that it might be ill advised to have men on the stern deck at noon when, say, we were stuck in the Suez Canal. He says that they must learn to get on with the job no matter what the weather.'

'You'd better watch out for the MO,' I said. 'He's worried about that too.'

'How do we get the MO on our side?' said Malcolm. 'I mean, make a chum of him? We're going to need his help.'

'First, you apologise to him for what happened the other day about that Swahili lesson.'

'If I do, I shall have to tell him that he needn't attend any more. Cuth insists that he should.'

'Invent a man who's ill enough to require constant attention. That'll cover it.'

'If one of our men were that ill,' said Malcolm, 'Cuth would be the first in the sickbay – even if the man had bubonic plague – to wish him well and ask what he could do for him. We'd look pretty silly inventing a sick man and then being unable to produce him.'

'Take the doctor into your confidence,' said O., characteristically at his most sensible when others were at their silliest. 'Explain about Cuth's little urges. Make the doctor feel like one of the club. He'll be your man then.'

And so he was. He settled the matter of the stern deck quite simply by asking Cuth to let him cover his own professional reputation by persuading the ship's crew to put up awnings in the Suez Canal and the Red Sea. Cuth magnanimously consented. The doctor was liked by the crew, because he had run a starting-price book on the Derby a few days before and manfully paid out despite some very stiff wagers on a popular winner. Awnings? they said. Of course. Much easier than a boxing ring, which was rather a finicking affair.

Boxing ring?

On the bow deck, under the bridge. It had to be there because that's where the necessary brackets and fittings were.

Yes, yes, said Lieutenant Wosking. He understood all that. But who had ordered the boxing competition?

Lieutenant-Colonel Smith, they said, for his battalion. And who was the boxing officer? Wosking enquired. Someone called Raven, they said: he'd been round to inspect the ropes for the ring.

'Yes, yes,' I said, when Wosking collared me about this. 'I am indeed the battalion boxing officer. And I have a darling little certificate of proficiency on the strength of a course I was sent on.'

'What sort of course?'

'Four days at Hamelin. The Pied Piper place. Charming town.'

'And on the strength of four days' instruction there you propose to run a battalion boxing competition?'

'Why not? I did it in Germany.'

'Didn't your MO get into a state?'

'He did rather. There have been a number of nasty accidents lately.'

'Some of them fatal. More in the last two months before we left England. I do read some of the literature which comes round for army doctors. If there are any accidents on board this ship, I shall be in for it. So will you.'

'And so will the Colonel,' I said. 'Shall we suggest that the competition be scrapped? We can say there is all the more chance of an accident on a ship. A sudden lurch, anything like that…A boxer slips and hits his head on a coil of steel cable…Do they still have burials at sea, or would they freeze the chap till Mombasa?'

'Take care you're not laughing on the other side of your face,' said Wosking.

'Well,' I said, 'we'd better go to the CO and warn him – if you think we ought.'

'I do.'

But Colonel Cuth was going to have his boxing. No problem about heat, he said. The best time for the boxing was the early evening and since the boat would be going West the bow would be out of the sun. Accidents? Of course there had been accidents and would be again. One couldn't spend one's life cancelling things because of the possibility of accidents. Since this was a proposition with which, though I should have been happy to escape the trouble of the thing, I very much agreed, I couldn't fault him there. I could only remind him, as did Wosking, that we must take very careful precautions and that I would be needing a lot of responsible officers and NCOs as umpires and seconds and assistants to ensure nothing went wrong. Quite right, Colonel Cuth said. The doctor still regarded it as not right at all, but he too acknowledged that one could not put off what might be a highly entertaining event (by that stage of the voyage we all needed entertainment) just in case something went wrong.

'Have you got the OC troops' permission, Colonel?' the doctor said.

Colonels of infantry battalions like to be called 'sir'. They regard 'Colonel' as casual, cavalry usage. Cuth Smith was no exception.

'Call me "sir",' he said sharply. (A mistake, thought I.) 'The OC troops is agreeable providing no applause is allowed during the rounds. Standard practice, I believe.'

I nodded.

'And no women are allowed as spectators. Also

standard practice?'

'Not any more, sir, I'm sorry to say, Women have been allowed as spectators since last autumn. And a very improper audience they sometimes make.'

The Colonel, as a matter of chivalry, now changed his ground.

'On board this ship,' he said, 'the only ladies are four wives of senior officers.'

'None of them officers of our regiment, sir. There is no reason why their wom – their wives should wish to attend.'

'I can think of several,' said the MO, and grinned louchely.

'That's enough from both of you,' said Colonel Smith. 'It is all quite clear. If army boxing regulations allow the presence of females, then the ladies aboard should be invited to attend, if only out of courtesy to their husbands. They are not of a class who will applaud in a vulgar fashion...nor of a type' – he looked at the doctor – 'who will take an unwholesome delight in the proceedings. This said, I shall take it, Mr Raven, that you have no objection to their being present.'

'None, sir. So long as they clearly understand that no noise may be made while a round is being fought. Women...even ladies...are apt to be carried away. You are familiar, sir, with what Martial and others have to say about their behaviour in the Colosseum?'

'You know very well that I have not had your advantages at Cambridge and elsewhere. Do not patronise me, Mr Raven. Simply get on with the job.'

So I did. Together with the battalion carpenter I checked the ring and its fittings—five times. I chose a cadre of officers and senior NCOs to act as judges

(I myself, as boxing officer, would have to be referee), timekeepers, marshals of the audience, administrators of first aid, cleaners and keepers of the ring. Suitable contestants were chosen, weighed, medically examined, dentally inspected, and given brief refresher courses in the noble art by P.T. instructors and myself. The contestants in each weight were numbered, their names drawn, the lists made, duplicated in the orderly room, despatched to all officials and displayed in public places.

So far, so good.

And then came a summons to the Adjutant's office.

'The CO wants to know,' said Malcolm, 'why no officers are taking part in the boxing.'

'They are taking a huge part. They are judging, timing, organising, seconding—'

'—The CO wants to know why none of them is actually boxing.'

Count up to ten.

'It never occurred to me that any of them should. Officers do not normally take part because any of them with any knowledge of the sport are needed to judge and so on. Those with no knowledge are needed to organise and arrange. Apart from that,' I said, 'you know as well as I do that to put officers in the ring against Other Ranks is asking for every kind of trouble in the book.'

'The CO does not think so.'

'The last CO did. We never had officers boxing in Göttingen and he raised no objection.'

'We are talking about the present CO. Lieutenant-Colonel Smith. He wants to see at least four junior officers in the ring – boxing.'

'Then perhaps he would care to run the competition himself.'

'Don't be insolent.'

'Malcolm. When officers box with Other Ranks, one of three things happens. Either there is a fair and sporting bout, at which everyone is delighted – though even then, if the officer is awarded the match by the judges, there is often grizzling about favouritism. *Or* the officer wins hands down, in which case it is said that a weak opponent was deliberately drawn against him. *Or* the Other Rank wins hands down, sometimes humiliating the officer, in which case there is a lot of ugly glee. In any case whatever, class prejudice and hatred, never far below the surface even in the best of battalions, are awakened and sometimes dangerously roused. Am I right?'

'The CO is asking nothing unusual – a lot of officers box in the Welsh regiments – and certainly nothing contrary to declared policy or existing regulations. Am I right?'

I nodded reluctantly.

'Then kindly go away, Simon, and arrange that a minimum of four subalterns should take part in the boxing.'

'Very well, sir. It will mean scrapping and redrafting these lists, which have taken time to prepare. It will mean selecting four willing and suitable officers, which may not be easy. It will mean finding and briefing new and obviously less adequate people to take on many of the offices on which the success of the thing depends. It could mean, in one word, disaster. I wish to go on record, *now*, as saying so.'

'Please don't make difficulties, Simon. I have rather more than I can easily bear.'

'Oh. I see. I'm sorry, Malcolm. I've been self-important and silly about this whole thing. I'll do what is asked and bother you no more. Cubs' honour.'

'That's my good boy.'
My hero.

Soon afterwards, I reported to O. and the jockey what Malcolm had said about having more difficulties than he could easily bear.

'It can't all be Cuth's doing,' I said.

'It isn't,' said O. 'It's the instructions which keep coming in on the ship's radio from the GOC-in-C's headquarters. It seems that the minute we arrive we're to be pitched straight into some major operation.'

'I thought,' said the point-to-point man, 'that we were simply waiting for the Mau Mau to come out of the jungle and then intern them.'

'They're not coming out quick enough,' said O., who always knew about that kind of thing. 'Too many of our troops tied down and doing nothing but waiting. They want to flush out all the remaining Mau Mau from the Aberdare Forest in one final operation and then run down the number of units in Kenya. The Government is keen on saving money.'

'But what form,' I enquired, 'is this operation to take? They can't expect us to disembark and plunge straight into the jungle without some preliminary training.'

'The talk is,' said O., 'that we shall only be required to provide ambushes. Heavy guns and bombers will plaster the Aberdare Forest; out will come the Mau Mau; and our ambushes will capture them.'

'Capture?'

'The policy is that from now on Mau Mau terrorists are to be fired on only if they resist arrest.'

'But what happens if they fire first? They have still got a few pukka firearms left, or so I'm told.'

'If they fire first,' said O., 'that's just too bad.

Politicians require that we set a humanitarian example.'

'So prudence dictates,' I said, 'unless one wishes to risk perishing for the humanitarian ideals of politicians, that the minute one sees a Mau Mau contingent one shoots the lot. One can then say, without risk of refutation, that they were either about to fire or to resist with other weapons. They have a lot of things called pangas, which resemble very sharp and nasty short-swords.'

'There is now a new and special kind of magistrate,' said O., 'recruited in England, that goes round investigating the deaths of terrorists. If they can prove we have killed a Mau Mau without provocation, we're in real trouble.'

'But if the Mau Mau in question is already dead,' I insisted, our story is the only one and the magistrate has to believe it.'

'Presumably.'

'If everyone's getting so humane all of a sudden,' the jockey said, 'why are they allowing the jungle to be strafed and bombed?'

'It has been conceded by the politicians, with their fingers no doubt crossed behind their backs, that the Mau Mau still in the forest are in such miserable case that we are doing them a good turn by forcing them out, even if one or two are killed in the process. But once they are out, it's got to be, "Dear Mr Mau Man, kindly come this way." '

'That's what our ambushes will be doing?' I said.

'Right,' said O.

'Then no wonder Malcolm is in a state. The idea of sending untrained men to set up ambushes in a totally strange and very formidable environment... and telling them that they must not fire unless fired upon...it's an absurdity. What does the CO think?'

'He thinks we must get on with the job,' said O. 'I don't think he's really taken it in, about not killing "the enemy", as he sees them. He thinks we're going into old-fashioned action. Which is one more worry for Malcolm.'

'Of course, what nobody seems to understand,' said O., who had fought with some distinction in Korea a few years before, 'is that bombing forests and so on never brings out the people you want. They go to ground, quite easily. You get a few animals coming out in a panic – but not many even of them, unless the bombardment is very intensive. The Aberdare Forest is too large for intensive bombardment and I suspect that our resources are pretty meagre. So the odds are that nothing and nobody will come out at all.'

'Tell Malcolm that. It might cheer him up.'

'I have. But he's got another horrid worry. The VD returns.'

'VD is always with us.'

'Precisely. Some six cases have been diagnosed since we've been at sea,' said O. 'Four of clap and two of the great pox. Clearly they were picked up in England before we sailed.'

'Quite a virtuous statistic. I remember,' said the amateur rider, 'when we had thirty-three cases, in Göttingen, in a single month.'

'*Thirty-three?*'

'Yes. I've always remembered it, because thirty-three is my favourite number at roulette. Compared with that, six cases since we've sailed is, as Ronald Searle would say, a Kredit to the Skol.'

'They take,' said O., 'a very strict view of VD in Kenya. It is assumed, if you catch it, that you have been out of bounds to a brothel area.'

'Why shouldn't you have caught it from a settler's beautiful daughter?'

'White women in Kenya don't have VD.'

'Baroness Blixen did.'

'She'd have been far too grand to give it to a common soldier. No. If one of our soldiers has the pox or the clap, he's had it from a black when out of bounds. That is axiomatic, as far as the authorities are concerned, the absolute truth that needs no proving. It follows that he must be court-martialled, found guilty and sentenced to a month or more in a military prison.'

'A month in the slammer for a dose of clap. *Not* very humane.'

'That,' said O., 'is what is worrying Malcolm. He says that when our six cases get to Kenya, they'll be court-martialled as a matter of course.'

'Surely not – if they caught what they caught in England.'

'Malcolm has been advised, by a senior officer on this boat, that that will not be taken into account. It is a matter of handing out "deterrent sentences". Soldiers in Kenya with VD must be given "deterrent sentences" to discourage the rest. If you make an exception, for whatever reason, the exception will be known about but probably not the reason. Other soldiers may conclude that a reign of clemency is coming in, which may make for lax behaviour, and then for bloody-mindedness when that behaviour is punished as brutally as ever. So our six wretches can expect no mercy. Malcolm is a just man and is badly bothered.'

'By the time we get to Kenya,' said our jockey, 'they should have been cured…if Doctor Wosking knows what he's at.'

'He does. And he's very much an ally. But the records are there. They will be inspected by some senior medic shortly after our arrival.'

'Oh, no, they won't,' said Doctor Wosking, who had just turned up with his backgammon set. 'Dear little Flossie got up an accidental fire and it just so happened that some of the records were burnt. Since we're at sea, no one else has yet had a copy. However, there isn't much gratitude in the world. One of your men has complained that Flossie has been carrying on in the lay. Your man is called Stevens, J. H.'

'Mine,' said O. 'I'll settle him. He's a thief. It's always men like that who get righteous about club members.'

'Club members?'

'Boys like your Flossie.'

'Not Flossie, for Christ's sake.'

'Your Lance-Corporal Clerk.'

'That's better.'

'Have you,' I said, 'told the Adjutant the good news—about the files going up in smoke?'

'Yes. I've just seen him. He says that that's one problem out of the way. And would I ask Simon Raven to step into his office as soon as he's finished his mid-morning coffee? Boxing, he says.'

'But we've settled all that,' I said. 'I've agreed to do everything the CO wants and I'm doing it— though not for the CO's sake but for Malcolm's. I'll pop along and reassure the old thing. He needs all the reassurance he can get.'

'Second Lieutnant Richard Legh,' Malcolm said. 'What do you know about him?'

'He came down from Oxford last year with a First in Greats. He received a National Service commission in the usual way, though his training was shortened because he'd been in some university cadet set-up at Oxford. He joined us soon after we went into barracks at Lichfield, i.e., about five weeks before we sailed. He seems an agreeable and highly intelligent fellow, and he is helping O. with the Swahili.'

'A little bit affected?'

'Not bad as Oxonians go.'

'A little bit conceited?'

'Not everyone gets a First in Greats.'

'And of course far too privileged a young gentleman to be made to box in your competition?'

'What on earth do you mean? He's wholly unsuitable. He has legs like the stems of hock glasses and a chest like the handle of a broomstick.'

'He was found fit for active service in the infantry. The CO thinks he is fit enough to box and does not see that an Oxford degree excuses him.'

'Nor does it. But I've already put five young officers into the new lists. Surely enough?'

'The CO is very keen that Richard Legh should box.'

'I suppose he wants Richard Legh brought down a peg?'

'He didn't say so. He just said that he could not understand why he had been left out of the boxing.'

'Because he has a lot to do preparing the Swahili lessons. Because he has never boxed in his life. Because he would be an embarrassment in the ring. Because no decent man could bear to hit such an obvious muff. Look, Malcolm. When we did our course at Hamelin, they said it was important to use judgement and instinct to make sure that certain soldiers did not get into the boxing ring. You'll know them when you see them, the senior instructor said: just don't let them box. And another thing he said, very emphatically, Malcolm, was: "Always remember, the final decision is yours. If you are required to organise a boxing competition, you are responsible for seeing that the wrong people don't get mixed up in it. *You*, the organiser, have the last word."

'So this time I'm having the last word, Malcolm. No Richard Legh in my boxing ring.'

'The CO won't like it.'

'Legh is like…a brittle beanpole. As I just said, no decent man could bear to hit him. If through bad luck he drew another kind of man, he'd be half killed. I'd almost certainly have to stop the fight. Fiasco or carnage: is that really what the CO wants?'

'He wants Richard Legh in the ring. In this regiment, he says, no one is too dainty or distinguished to join in with the men. It's part of getting on with the job.'

'Malcolm…can't you get round him?'

'No. I've tried. He is determined. If you stand on your rights as boxing officer, he will either overrule you—'

'—He can't—'

'—or he will make very nasty trouble for you. There are some subtle ways of punishing officers who stand on their technical rights and give offence to their CO. No one comes forward to help them: they are seen as barrack-room lawyers —subversive and disloyal.'

'What shall I do, Malcolm?'

'What you are told. You can't come to any harm.'

'Richard Legh can. And so can I, whatever you say I am responsible. If something goes wrong, they'll be down on me like a road drill. *They* won't say, he was being loyal to his CO and respecting his wishes. *They* will say, he should have stopped it before it started and he had, as he well knew, every right to do so. Cleft stick. Knight's fork at chess: if I save one piece I lose the other.'

'Simon. You are being very obtuse this morning. Before Legh can box, he must be passed fit by the MO. Do I make myself plain?'

'Right,' said Wosking. 'We should be able to find something wrong with him. Please ask him to come in.'

As boxing officer I had to be present when any boxer was medically examined.

'I'm sorry,' I apologised to Richard Legh. 'Regulations compel me to be here.'

'Why should I mind?'

With that he stripped the khaki shirt off his narrow torso, eased his slacks over his skeletal knees to his ankles and shoved down his pants to reveal a surprisingly stalwart groin.

'You know,' he said, 'I'm a fitter man than you might think. Otherwise I should hardly have been passed fit to serve abroad with this battalion. I'll tell you another thing. I came fifteenth out of 350 odd in the spring cross country steeplechase at Mons OCTU. So you don't need to worry about me.'

'The question is,' I said, 'whether you're fit to box.'

At a sign from the MO Legh pulled up his pants with huge hands that dangled from arms like twigs.

'I am fit to do anything, within reason, that I am required to do. If you want another officer for your boxing, here am I, take me.

'I don't want another officer for my boxing. I shall only have to change the draw, for your weight, for the second time. The CO wants you to box. He has an old-fashioned army prejudice about graduates: he thinks we're soft.'

'Funny,' reflected Richard Legh. 'In the old days the army took a great many regular officers from the universities. What has Colonel Smith got against them?'

'He was a poor boy, relatively speaking, who came to the army straight from school. He thinks that people who spend three or four years reading Latin and Greek are pampered.'

'Then it's up to me to show him he's wrong.'

'Richard,' I said. 'You know nothing about boxing. You're the wrong build and wrong physique. Wosking here can get you out of it by finding something wrong with you. Even a loose tooth would be enough.'

'I had a dental check before coming to Lichfield. If the Colonel wants to see me box,' said Richard Legh, 'I shall be happy to oblige him. You read your Plato, I know – I spotted you with a Loeb edition of *The Republic* the other day.'

'What's Plato got to do with it?'

'You may recall Socrates' views about obedience to the state and those in authority under the state. Such obedience is obligatory.'

'Obedience to their legitimate orders or requests. Not to their whims.'

'If a whim is expressed as an order, then it is so. He who indulges his whim will be answerable to the gods: so will he be who refuses to obey an order. I am, as it happens, a Christian: the same sort of reasoning applies. *Mutatis mutandis*, of course.'

You, I thought, are an insufferable prig. If you get hurt, it serves you right.

'Then I prick you – thus,' I said, sticking my pencil into his name, which was entered under 'ineligible'. 'Your weight makes you light welter. Luckily, I now see that I shall have no need to make another draw if I give you a bye in the first round.'

'Is that fair?'

'Someone has got to have a bloody bye,' I grated. 'Why not you? Please don't make any more trouble.'

'Trouble is just what I'm trying not to make.'

'I'm sorry, Richard. It's just that life would have been much simpler for all of us if you'd allowed the doctor here to find a sprain in your little finger or an itch in one of your ears.'

'I dare say. And if I'd had any such affliction I should have been the first to tell you. I haven't and that's all there is to it.'

'So there it is,' I said to Malcolm. 'Just for once we have an honest and an honourable man in our midst. Quite pleased with himself for being so.'

'Over the years,' said Malcolm, 'I have come to dread one thing more than any other.'

'Honest men?'

'No. Honest intellectuals. Why couldn't he be a conscientious objector and skip the army altogether? It's quite easy these days. You just fill in a form when you get your call-up papers.'

'He's not that type. He prides himself on his manliness and normality. He sees nothing wrong in the use of force to defend the state. Boxing, he would probably tell you, is part of the necessary training in quick thinking and agile moving. He's thought about it all and he has come to his conclusions.'

'Intellectually. Which I suppose has made him smug?'

'Almost unbearable.'

'You see what I mean about honest – and honourable – intellectuals. They can't just do something, like anybody else, because it is the done thing. They think it out, they watch themselves thinking it out and give themselves maddening airs when they finally condescend to agree with the rest of us.'

'What is to be done?'

'Nothing. He's had his chance. Now he must take what's coming to him.'

'If he's pummelled to pieces, it may not be good for discipline. People will despise him.'

'Only if you stop the fight. If,' said Malcolm, 'you make him go the full distance, people will admire his courage.'

'Suppose he's knocked out?'

'That wouldn't be too bad. Provided he lasted for a round or two. Who's he up against?'

'The winner of Matthews v. Tarlin. Which has to be Tarlin. He's one of those chunky numbers, short and vibrant. You remember what Byron's boxing coach advised—"Mill to the left and mill to the right"? That's Tarlin.'

'Oh, God. Fur flying everywhere. Like a dog fight.'

'Precisely.'

'I must count my blessings,' said Malcolm. 'Dr Wosking and his clerk have got our VD cases off the hook. As for the CO, his immediate obsession is about Richard Legh and the boxing. Surely, with just a tiny bit of luck it can't turn out too badly?'

It turned out worse than anyone could possibly have imagined. As I had predicted, Tarlin beat Matthews; I had to stop the fight after the first ten seconds of the second round. This meant that Richard Legh must fight Tarlin. 'Mill to the left and mill to the right.' I thought I knew exactly what would happen. Stocky Tarlin would mill at beanpole Legh's midriff; Legh would at first flail ineffectively back, then gradually droop as he was forced nearer and nearer to the ropes, until as Legh sagged, Tarlin's whirling fists went banging like pistons on his jaw, his mouth, his nose. Very soon Legh would be cruelly scuffed in the cheeks and welling with blood from all orifices. I should have to stop the fight after about half a minute, the men would jeer as the humiliated Legh was manoeuvred out of the ring like a wrecked bicycle, Tarlin would preen and prance, the image of the gloating prole in victory, and would bounce away towards the contestants' entrance/exit while his besotted comrades banged and stamped and (so to speak) threw their sweaty nightcaps in the air. That was my vision and quite nasty enough. The reality, colourless and noiseless, was a monster of horror.

What I should have remembered about Richard Legh was that he was an exceedingly intelligent man who had a very long reach from a very great height. When Tarlin rushed milling left and right towards him, Legh simply stuck out his left arm and stopped Tarlin dead with a straight punch on the nose. Tarlin next attacked with his head down. This time he was stopped by a flimsy but painful (on Tarlin's nose again) uppercut. Tarlin retreated once more, clearly angered, eyes watering. He bent himself nearly double this time, his face and torso far too low for lanky Legh to reach down and administer another uppercut, and simply ran at Legh, still milling, and with his head butting straight towards Legh's parts. Being, as I have explained, too tall in this predicament to uppercut, Legh punched down with his right and landed a foul (rabbit) blow to the back of the neck, not harmful (though it might have been) to the top of the spine, where it struck, but lethal nonetheless, in that it levelled Tarlin very hard on to the deck. This occurred quite silently, as I have written above, because Tarlin's head hit the boards, not with the boney forehead, but with the soft nose (rather prominent on Tarlin's face) which was crushed against and almost right into the wooden surface. Again, the scene was colourless, or almost: white boxing vests and shorts against scrubbed deck; and, to my amazement, no blood.

The first thing to do was to count Tarlin out, which, with the assistance of the timekeeper, I now did. The next thing, as Tarlin showed no sign of stirring, was to call for a stretcher. A rather puzzled Legh, who was leaning over Tarlin to peer at him, was now escorted to his corner by his seconds (two National Service second lieutenants). Three orderlies came into the ring and handled Tarlin through the ropes to the stretcher bearers. An ugly susurration began to rise above the audience, while two bright-eyed women who were sitting with the CO began a fierce and clearly audible argument across his chest about the rights and wrongs of the matter. These were desperately confusing; as referee, I was required to resolve them and give a decision in a matter of little more than moments. Grim and sweaty, I stood in a vacant corner and tried to sort the thing out.

In the first place, there was no question whatever but that Richard Legh had delivered a foul blow. He had more or less thumped down with his fist on to the nape of Tarlin's neck and fouler than that you could not get. And yet it was difficult to see how he could have defended himself otherwise. Tarlin's butting was also foul; it was aimed at Legh's fork, which made it doubly foul; but it had not actually made contact. Had it done so, Tarlin would have been disqualified out of hand, but his head had been a good nine inches short of Legh's *membrum virile* when Legh struck in defence, side-stepping as he did so and thus moving out of the line of the butt. Would he have escaped it altogether if he had not made his downward blow? Could this blow fairly be said to have been aimed at the top of the head (a legitimate target if the head was bowed) and to have missed it through no fault of Legh's? The answer to the first question was that Tarlin's head, had it continued in a right line, would almost certainly have struck Legh's thigh very dangerously on the joint between the limb and the pelvis, for Legh, though side-stepping, was too cumbrous to have escaped altogether. The answer to the second question was that, yes, Legh had punched at such of the legitimate target as was visible and could hardly have been expected to submit to probable and violent injury from an opponent who was in a definitely foul posture and making a deliberately foul attempt.

Another question: why had Tarlin, who knew the rules perfectly well, made this disgraceful sortie? Had he forgotten Legh's height and thought that he was aiming at his opponent's upper belly and not his *privata*? Answer one: Legh's straight left followed by his uppercut must have riled Tarlin beyond bearing—though more because of the loss of face, I thought, than because of the actual pain inflicted. Answer two: even had Tarlin thought that he was butting at Legh's solar plexus and not his *pubes*, he was still totally out of order. Final question: did Tarlin hope to raise his head before reaching Legh and confront him without butting him? Answer: if so, he had left it too late; for had Tarlin raised his head at the time he was struck, he would have been in danger of striking Legh viciously in the midriff (or lower) with his crown; and if he was imagining his opponent as being shorter than Legh, he must have known that he might have savaged that opponent (again with his crown) with the most appalling blow to the face.

And now it was time to pronounce. I looked at the CO, who did not look back. I looked at the chattering women

175

and resolved to have them banned from the next session on the ground of shameless behaviour. I looked at Malcolm, who raised his eyes to Heaven. I saw the absolutely motionless Tarlin disappear on his stretcher through the entrance/exit; I turned my glance to Legh, no longer puzzled but apparently indifferent, who was now sitting on a stool in his corner showing what seemed like five yards of boney thigh, the least lust-making I have ever inspected in my whole life. I listened briefly to the hornet-buzz of the audience. I announced:

'Private Tarlin is disqualified from the bout for a deliberate and very dangerous foul.'

The audience melted away from the bow deck, muttering. Although there were still two bouts to be fought that evening, the only spectators that remained were sergeants, warrant officers, officers and the CO's two female guests. Even a small group of ship's officers, who had been watching with some enjoyment, swiftly dispersed. The verdict of the majority was obvious: Second Lieutenant Legh, being an officer, had been given the fight, though he was more fouling than fouled.

Nor did the MO's verdict improve matters: 'Tarlin is badly shocked; he will have to have surgery on his nose as soon as we reach Mombasa.'

And of course there was another factor in the situation, perhaps the most hellish of all: Richard Legh, having won his bout, would go through to fight another.

The cognoscenti, my own assistants, that is to say, and the better informed PTIs, thought I had been right in my decision. Those concerned more with politics than with boxing took a different view. The Colonel himself did not comment, just went around the ship looking rather hurt, as though somebody had forgotten his birthday. Both O. and the jockey thought that I had had good enough ground to disqualify Legh and should indeed have done so in order to get a dangerous joker out of the game. Malcolm said the whole affair had been brutally difficult, but also opined that a decision in favour of Tarlin would have been well received by the rank and file, though not nearly as well received as the decision in favour of Legh had been badly received.

'In my worst nightmares,' I said, 'I did not envisage Legh's going on to fight a second match.'

'What line does Legh take?' Malcolm said.

'He says he did his best in very troublesome circumstances. I agree. I did not and do not see that he could have done anything else, given that low charge of Tarlin's. That's why I called him as winner.'

'Do you think that Wosking could now find something wrong with him? Couldn't he have hurt his hand giving that punch?'

'I've thought of that – and a great many other things. Legh is firm. He didn't much want to fight in the beginning. He was ordered to and of course consented. Once having consented, however, he will proceed by the law. It is a brave and unexceptionable attitude. I hope the Colonel has taken notice of this instance of "pampered" university behaviour. Not many Sandhurst men would have conducted themselves so well.'

'The Colonel thinks his win was a fluke. He thinks you found in favour of Legh because you are another university man.'

'What do the men think? The RSM will have told you.'

'Much the same – with a stronger ingredient of class.'

'They don't think that Tarlin lost his head?'

'You'd better talk to the RSM yourself. He may be able to advise you about the continuation of the business.'

The RSM was a good-spirited father of his flock, a little apt to get flustered and to fluster everyone else, a decent and an upright man, prone, like all decent men, to doubt, striving to be impartial, finding, in the end, with his heart.

'That Tarlin has always been a troublemaker, sir. Lucky he's flat on his back and in the sick bay, and can't make trouble now. But he's already sending messages out to his friends and of course we can't stop him having visitors. He thinks he was cheated. He thinks he has been savagely injured by a foul blow.'

'In a way he's quite right. Does he think his own boxing above reproach?'

'He's contrived a new picture of it all, sir. His head was slightly tilted forward, he says, not in a butting position at all. Mr Legh, he says, deliberately reached too far to deliver that rabbit punch.'

'How does he explain that he was parallel to the ground as he fell?'

'He just says that a punch from behind would make a man fall flat on his face in the way he did.'

'And all his cronies believe him?'

'Never mind, sir. We'll drop him at the military hospital at Mombasa. It'll be a long time before he appears again. He'll soon be forgotten.'

'Not on this ship. Can't we keep people away from him?'

'He's been very nastily hurt, sir, however it all came about and by the fault of whomsoever. You would not grudge him a few friends for his comfort—trouble-stirrer as he is?'

'I suppose not. Can you make sure that the men do not...get over-excited—when Mr Legh appears in the ring tomorrow evening?'

'Mr Legh, as you know, sir, is to fight Corporal Lendrick. Corporal Lendrick is a graceful boxer and a fair man ... in every way. Corporal Lendrick will commit no fouls. There must be none coming from Mr Legh, for all his inexperience.'

'I realise that. All I ask is that the audience shall give him a proper chance, let him start again from scratch.'

'I'll do my best, sir.'

'Thank you, RSM.'

The RSM had always loved his men and served them well, and they knew it. When he put it about that Legh was a tyro who had meant no harm to Tarlin, and that he was to be given a straight chance to re-establish himself as a sportsman and a gentleman, his word was regarded. Even the Tarlin faction was prepared to watch and wait, uneasily aware that their principal's case was not as clean as he urged.

The only people who misbehaved when Legh stepped into the ring to fight Corporal Lendrick were the two senior wives, who had again come to watch with Colonel Cuth. They cackled and jabbered, these respectable upper-middle-class women, as I knew they would if they were allowed to come. I had asked Malcolm to ask the Colonel not to bring them; surely they had been conspicuous enough for their noisy antics on the occasion of Legh's first fight, I said; let them not come again. Malcolm had agreed and made a hint to the Colonel, which had been ill received. They were merely interested, the Colonel had told Malcolm, very interested; surely nobody could object to that. Clearly their husbands were embarrassed, I thought now; otherwise they too would have come. But there was no helping the matter at this stage. Richard Legh and Corporal Lendrick sat in their corners; the two women squawked, the bell rang, the boxers came out and shook hands. The women made elaborate shushing noises and gestured at each other like a Punch and Judy show, then turned their eyes to devour gaunt, gangling Richard and beautiful Lendrick, who was as perfect as a fifth-century statue of Hermes, except for a very slightly snub nose.

If anyone had been expecting the kind of action we'd had in the Legh-Tarlin encounter, then he was to be disappointed. Connoisseurs of human oddity, however, had a banquet. Neither man even attempted to hit the other. They sparred gently round the ring, exchanging little pats on each other's gloves, sometimes feinting, to no purpose, sometimes even aiming a blow, but a blow that always stopped short or landed harmlessly on the other's open glove, which was waiting to receive it long before it arrived.

At the end of the round, the Colonel rose from his place and beckoned me to an empty corner of the ring.

'They're not trying, either of them,' he said. 'They're playing with each other. It's a disgrace.'

'Legh is nervous, sir. You will remember he injured Tarlin very seriously in his last bout.'

'Looks like a put-up job to me. I want to see some proper boxing; tell them.'

So I went first to Legh.

'The Colonel thinks you're not in earnest.'

'He's right. How could I strike a face as beautiful as that?'

Then I went to Lendrick.

'The CO thinks you're playing pit-a-pat.'

'It's clear that Mr Legh is not going to hit me, sir. How can I hit him?'

'Hit him once – over the eye,' I said.

'Sir?'

'Please do as I ask.'

The bell rang for the second round. The wives uncrossed their legs, leant forward and splayed. Lendrick, a good boxer, hit Legh sharply above the left eye.

'That's better,' the Colonel observed aloud, breaking the rule of silence.

'Stop,' I called.

Both boxers stood back. I examined Legh's left eye and made a sign to the doctor. He too examined Legh's eye.

'A gash,' I said. 'Skin broken. Not bleeding yet.'

All this quite loudly, for the Colonel to hear.

'Slow bleeding,' said Wosking. 'It'll start gushing if it's hit again. I'd advise you to stop the thing.'

The MO left the ring.

'Mr Legh retires with injuries to the eye,' I announced. 'Corporal Lendrick is the winner.'

Legh and Lendrick shook hands and smiled at each other. One of the women let out her breath with a slight but unmistakable hiss. Never mind her, I thought: thank God we've got Richard out of this quite plausibly and without more trouble.

'And now about that farce with Legh and Lendrick,' the Colonel said. 'I'll admit you covered up quite neatly for them. But why wouldn't they box properly?'

'I told you at the time, sir. Legh was nervous because he'd hurt Tarlin so badly.'

'Accident.'

'Accident or no, he didn't want another.'

'You're saying he's soft.'

'Civilised, sir.'

'And Lendrick? He made one proper punch, but did

nothing at all for the whole of the first round.'

'Chivalry, sir. He understood Legh's problem and would not take advantage.'

'That's not how wars are won. We are going to a war, you know.'

Malcolm, sitting behind the CO, raised the fingers of one hand very slightly. 'Don't get into a quarrel about *that*,' the gesture said.

'What jobs do they do, Legh and Lendrick?' said the CO over his shoulder to Malcolm.

'Lendrick is in the bugle platoon, sir. Routine administrative duties when not playing with the bugles or the band.'

'And Legh?'

'Liaison, sir. Or so I thought. He teaches Swahili, as you know.'

'He's not going to liaise with blacks, is he? Only with their white officers.'

'Correct, sir.'

'Then what has teaching Swahili to do with his possible appointment as liaison officer?'

'Nothing in particular, sir. But it does indicate a certain dexterity of mind' – for a second Malcolm's face was impish – 'a quality somewhat rare among your officers.'

'What else makes him suitable?'

'He has the manners of a gentleman, and is lucid and accurate in his speech. He will do us credit with other regiments.'

'He is also,' said the Colonel, 'mealy-mouthed and longwinded. You are obviously in his favour, Raven. But would you not admit that he is mealy-mouthed and verbose?'

'He tries to see things from every possible point of

view, sir. This makes for complication and qualification.'

'And his unction? His air of moral self-congratulation?'

'The fault of his college, sir. Corpus Christi, Oxford. A very high-minded and sanctimonious institution.'

God knows why I should have dragged Corpus Christi into it. No reason at all, of course. I just spoke off the top of my head.

'Corpus Christi, Oxford?' said the CO. 'My grandfather's college. He was a fine man and a dedicated – and distinguished – Schoolmaster.'

This was new to me and, to judge from his face, to Malcolm.

'He too,' said Colonel Smith, 'tended to be what you call sanctimonious. But that was not the only attribute he brought away from Corpus Christi. There were honour and truth, to name two more. I think I must get to know Mr Legh rather better. Mark him down as intelligence officer, Malcolm, for the time being. That way he'll be in battalion HQ and always available for liaison if needed. Thank you, Simon,' the CO said, using my Christian name for the first time, 'I'm very glad to know that Richard Legh was at Corpus Christi.'

'So all's well that ends well,' I said to Malcolm.

'No, it's not. Just for a start…why do you think Colonel Cuth didn't know that Richard Legh was at Corpus – before you told him?'

'Colonel Cuth is not interested in universities in the usual way. He heard Richard was from Oxford and that was enough – more than enough, it seemed at the time. He's the kind of man – Colonel Cuth – who's more interested in people's schools than their colleges.'

'More or less right. But it was, of course, recorded in

Richard's file when he arrived...some time before Colonel Cuth. So far, then, Colonel Cuth has not got round to the personal files of very junior officers – he's had enough to read through without that. Sooner or later – much sooner, now that he's taking this sudden interest – he's going to read Richard's file, the one that came with him from OCTU, and what do you think he is going to find?'

'It can't be anything very dreadful.'

'He's going to find that Richard's father and mother were prominent members of the Peace Pledge Union in the Thirties. They actually campaigned against the waging of the 39–45 war and for a time they were put in a detention camp—from 1941 to 1943.'

'But so long as none of this was concealed when Richard joined the army, or when he was later interviewed by the Colonel of the regiment, there is nothing to be said about it.'

'Colonel Cuth won't like it.'

'He didn't like Richard before. Now, it seems, he does. When he finds out about his parents, perhaps he won't. So sodding what?'

'Because of *your* remark about Corpus,' said Malcolm, 'Richard Legh is to be intelligence officer. What happens to him when the Colonel reads that file?'

'If Cuth has got any sense at all, he keeps him as intelligence officer. The point about Richard is that he believes, on intellectual grounds, in obedience to the state and those in authority under it.'

'The Colonel believes in heredity. He believes his grandparents and his parents made him what he is. Because his grandfather was at Corpus, Corpus is a good thing (no matter that Cuth distrusts graduates as a rule) and because Richard was at Corpus, Richard becomes a good thing despite having displeased the Colonel till now. But when Cuth finds out that Richard's father and mother were pacifists, he will cease to trust him (heredity again). So either he will sack Richard from the post of IO, which will be a very bad thing for confidence and discipline in the battalion as a whole, or he will keep Richard as IO but continue to mistrust him, which will be a very bad thing for the Colonel's work and Richard's, and for the efficiency of battalion HQ.

'And what will make it all one hundred times worse,' continued Malcolm, 'is that gallant Colonel Cuth thinks that we are riding to war, when we are going to Kenya only in an administrative role, to help clean things up. What is even worse is that our arrival is going to coincide with the last remotely warlike operation that will be staged – i.e. the bombing of the Aberdare Forest – and this, although it is only intended to bring the Mau Mau out of the forest for beneficent detention, will confirm Cuth in thinking we are at war and in behaving accordingly. Last and worst of all is the apparent determination of the GOC-in-C to send us into the forest to provide ambushes to net the terrorists before we have had any training in any jungle role whatever. What we now need, therefore, like we need an outbreak of bubonic plague, is an internal crisis in battalion HQ which brings Cuth into unfounded and emotional mistrust of his intelligence officer.'

'Lose the file. Make out a temporary one which does not go into detail about Richard's parents.'

'Unfortunately my ORQMS is neither as biddable nor as versatile as the doctor's Flossie. Oh, for more Flossies in this world,' Malcolm wailed. 'But I have removed Richard's file from the orderly room for "Adjutant's perusal" and I think I can keep it away from Cuth for a very long time – if only he doesn't call for it before we reach Mombasa. Once we're there he's going to be much too busy to start fussing about personal files.'

When we reached Mombasa, we were met by the GOC-in-C, who took Colonel Cuth in his helicopter to Nairobi, thus leaving Malcolm and the second-in-command of the battalion (an amiable and bibulous cricketer, who did precisely what Malcolm told him) to bring the rest of us up by train.

'Thank God,' said Malcolm disloyally, 'that the General has taken You Know Who. I think we were in for an obsession about train discipline – sitting to attention in full battle order in case we were attacked. I do hope the General can make Cuth understand that all that is over. The truth is, Cuth enjoys that sort of thing so much. He's the kind of man who reads *Boys' Own* until he's forty.'

The men travelled third class, in exactly the same way as African Askaris (soldiers): hard seats with haversack rations. Warrant officers and sergeants went second class, with their own egg-and-chippy restaurant. Officers rode first class, with a deluxe restaurant (Portuguese oysters and game).

'It's nice to know,' said O., 'that Kenyans still have a correct social perspective.'

'I'm told,' said our point-to-point rider, 'that flat racing in Nairobi is lively but corrupt and there is quite a good steeplechase course near Naivasha, where they run the Kenya Grand National. This will be the second year they've held it since the Mau Mau rebellion ceased.'

'Ah,' said Malcolm, 'will you please tell that to the Colonel 500 times. "Sir," you must say, "can I have leave to ride in the Kenya Grand National, which has been running again for several years now that the emergency is well and truly over?" I shall see that you get the leave if only you will apply for it often enough. I cannot emphasise too much to you all,' he said, 'that only romantics like Colonel Cuth and a few careerist last ditchers still conceive that there is a war here. I rely on you Richard,' he said to Legh, 'to discountenance any tendency towards belligerence or competition.'

'Competition?'

'Yes. As you know, even now there are occasional circumstances in which the Mau Mau have to be shot. Certain officers, who should know better, keep a tally of killings and circulate their scores. Some of these think that their enthusiasm will be rewarded by promotion. Some of them are just haters of blacks. In either case they are very bad news.'

'In other words,' said O., 'you are counselling us not to get on with the job?'

O. was always bating his seniors; one sees why he never became a general or even a brigadier.

'I am counselling you,' said Malcolm through his teeth, 'to be quite sure what the job is before getting on with it.'

'And what form will it take during the forthcoming operation in the Aberdare Forest?'

'We shall be told soon enough,' said Malcolm, and ground his molars.

Once in Nairobi, we settled into a tented camp in the suburbs, near a luxurious country club of which all officers were made honorary members. The men were less fortunate; their canteens were fly-blown and ill provided.

'The sooner we get out of here and into the forest, the better,' said O., as we stood by the barrack square,

187

waiting for nothing to happen. 'It will take just three days more for the men to find out how to get to the brothel area; and then watch out.'

'This operation in the Aberdares may be a blessing in disguise then? Even if we haven't been trained for the jungle.'

'Anything must be better than rotting away in this horrible suburb.'

'We've got the Muthaiga Club.'

'*You and I* have got the Muthaiga Club.'

'And that Swiss restaurant. They somehow get marvellous veal.'

'Such a consolation to Corporal Lendrick and his chums, to know that you're dining off tender veal.'

Our amateur race-rider sauntered up.

'The Colonel's got a new fixation,' he said 'ABCA: The Army Bureau of Current Affairs.'

'Does it still exist?'

'If it doesn't he's going to revive it. All platoon commanders must be prepared to give daily lectures on European and African matters, if possible relating them. Weather, geography, trade, ethnic composition, language; anything except politics.'

'All the platoon commanders,' I gloated. 'That lets me out.'

'No, it doesn't. Officers second-in-command of companies will lecture the personnel of company headquarters.'

'That's the company commanders' job.'

'They're going to be too busy making a recce of their companies' positions for Operation Exlax.'

'Operation *what*?'

'The idea is,' said O., 'that the jungle will be opening its bowels to void all the remaining Mau Mau…into our ambushes.'

'They'd better hurry,' said the jockey, 'or there'll be no ambushes left. Four of my chaps have already reported with clap.'

'They've found their way to the brothels already?'

'The whole place is a brothel. You've only got to take one step out of the camp. That's why we're going to have all this ABCA. The chaps will be set homework in the evenings so that they won't have time to go out.'

'A little training might be a good thing,' said O.

'Unfortunately,' I said, 'they've just withdrawn all our jungle boots. Defective issue, it seems. The new lot was due in this morning, but all that arrived was ping-pong tables.'

'Pingers,' said O., 'just the thing to take their minds off zigzag.'

'There are neither nets, balls nor bats. Just tables.'

'I must be off,' said the point-to-point rider, 'to give my ABCA lecture to my platoon. I've got just the job for today. I'm calling it, "The Manners and Morals of Happy Valley – about the settlers.'

'The Muthaiga Club has a cricket ground,' I said to O. 'We might get up a match.'

'No kit, old bean. Except for ten pairs of bails.'

My company serjeant-major came up. 'Ten cases of clap for orders, sir,' he said.

'The company commander is going to love that,' I said.

The RSM came up.

'Morning, gentlemen,' he said. 'Preliminary warning. The CO is going to call a curfew. No personnel allowed out of camp after 1800 hours except on duty.'

'Not even for dinner, RSM?'

'*No* personnel, sir, not even for dinner.'

189

'ABCA,' said O. as the two warrant officers departed, 'was bliss compared with this.'

'We'd better go into Nairobi,' I said, 'to stock up with caviar and stuff.'

'Won't keep long out here.'

'There is a refrigerator in the cookhouse.'

'Not for storing officers' caviar,' said Malcolm, who was looking very regimental in khaki shorts (cut just above the knee) with boots and puttees, and carrying an ebony light infantry cane with a silver knob.

'I'm on my way to commanding officer's orders,' he said, 'where the curfew is to be announced.'

'Why didn't you warn us?'

'I didn't know until a few minutes ago. The idea is that if they're not allowed out the men will pay more attention to their evening homework for their ABCA studies. And you lot will be able to prepare your lectures more carefully.'

Malcolm marched off, swinging his cane parallel to the ground, like a guardsman walking out in Windsor Park before the war.

Richard Legh came up.

'Heard about the curfew?' he said. 'Well, I've arranged to be liaising with other liaisers from all units in the Muthaiga Club every night this week. Duty, you see.'

'For a Corpus Christi man, you're getting very smooth and worldly.'

'I have arranged with the CO that I can take two friends with me every evening to help me liaise. Want to come, boys?'

'Yes,' we said. Richard passed on as if wearing seven-league boots.

'Success has changed him,' said O. 'Three weeks ago he wouldn't have called us "boys" to save his life.'

'Success has improved him,' I said. 'He's no longer a howling prig. And it was kind of him to remember us in his scheme for curfew-dodging. There's many as wouldn't.'

Lieutenant (Doctor) Wosking stumped past.

'There's a medical officers' conference at the Muthaiga Club,' Lieutenant Wosking said, 'every evening for the next fortnight. I'm allowed to take two officers from the battalion to put their problems to the learned doctors assembled. Strictly duty, of course, but we shall adjourn after half an hour for dinner. Any use to you two?'

'Thanks. But we're already fixed up.'

The second-in-command of B Company came up.

'Ah, Simon,' he said. 'There's a special committee of seconds-in-command, to discuss the problems raised for us by Operation Exlax. To last ten days, or until Exlax actually begins. Every evening from 1830 hours.'

'At the Muthaiga Club?'

'No. All the special rooms there are already booked. We've taken the banqueting room in the Swiss restaurant, pro tem, but we've got first option on a cancellation at the New Stanley Hotel.'

'Which is the better for dinner,' I said to O., 'the Muthaiga or the New Stanley? Or the Swiss restaurant?'

'The Muthaiga do those giant prawns, flown up iced from the coast. The New Stanley has a good line in snails cooked in Burgundy. But as you yourself say, there's nothing to beat the veal at the Swiss place.'

'What an agonising decision. I'll tell you what,' I said to my brother second-in-command, 'I'm booked for the liaison officers' *soirée*, but I might switch to the second-in-commands' committee in a few days.'

'We'd be honoured, I'm sure.'

The Quartermaster Major, a dour Methodist killjoy,

came past.

'I hear the CO has put a spoke in the wheel of pleasure,' he said with relish. 'A curfew from now on.'

'Yes, Q.,' we said demurely. 'Very sensible. We must get on with getting on with the job, must we not?'

'Rotten dinner in the mess last night,' said Malcolm at midmorning break next day.

'Oh yes?'

'Tinned stew. Only the Colonel and me and the QM eating it. Even the padre was out...at a prayer meeting in the Muthaiga Club.'

'You know how important all this liaison and... er...er...the rest of it is?' said O. 'They say the GOC-in-C is tremendously in favour of it.'

'There will have to be a rota,' said Malcolm. 'One volunteer every evening to keep the Colonel company.'

'He's got the QM.'

'The QM has gone on a fortnight's course, on the maintenance of stores in the tropics.'

'I'll tell you what,' O. said. 'We'll all chip in with five bob an evening and draw lots. The lucky man wins about ten quid and gets the Colonel for dinner.'

'He might smell a rat fairly soon,' I said.

'He's already smelling it,' said Malcolm.

'Another suggestion,' said O. 'Send him off to inspect the company commanders who are inspecting their positions for Exlax. All four rifle companies are on the perimeter of the forest covering the arc from Fort Hall to Naivasha. It'll take him some days to move round that lot.'

'Then there'd be no officers in camp at night at all.'

'Yes there would,' said O., 'the orderly officer. Why

didn't we think of that before? Where was he last night, by the way?'

'I agreed to stand in for him,' said Malcolm, 'but it's rather *infra dig* and I shan't do it again.'

'The Muthaiga is not good for you,' said O to Malcolm. 'You're altogether too plump and sweaty already. You'd do yourself a good turn by having a few more nights in the mess with the Colonel and tinned stew.'

'Thank you. I feel as if I were developing duodenal ulcers. That being the case, I must have a lot of soothing cream in my food. The only place I shall get that will be in the Muthaiga Club. So be it – and the orderly officer, as you very sensibly suggest, can dine in every night, with or without the CO. I wish to God they'd give the order to take up positions for Exlax.'

'On the boat you said you were dreading it.'

'I was. But not so much as I am now dreading the Brigadier's reaction to today's VD returns: we have the worst record of any battalion ever to have been in Kenya.'

'Oh dear. Obviously we need even more ABCA… Have they sent the new jungle boots yet?'

'No. A consignment of dartboards without any darts.'

'Clearly,' said O., 'in the absence of other entertainments for the troops, VD is the only alternative to having a mutiny. So let's settle for VD. But if you're really bothered, can't the padre do anything?'

'He is at least clean,' I ventured.

That evening, Richard Legh and I walked back together after the liaison officers' jamboree at the Muthaiga Club. (O. had decided to spend the night there, in anticipation of crapula.)

'As intelligence officer of this battalion,' said Richard, 'I must read all official handouts and computations. As liaison officer among others of that ilk I discover just what rubbish the handouts and computations are. Take these ambushes we are going to provide for Exlax. As you know, the policy is that any Mau Mau who come out of the Aberdare Forest should be captured, not killed. All very proper and humane. There is just one teeny weeny snag, as Wigmore of the rifles was pointing out this evening. As a matter of statistics most of the Mau Mau are diseased. Each group of them is allotted a couple of whores from Nairobi, who are smuggled into their area—and then pox the lot.'

'Just like our battalion,' I said.

'You've put your finger on the problem. There is only a certain amount of penicillin available to the army and for other official purposes. What with our own patients – and though our battalion may be worst, the others are neck and neck for close second – and what with the supplies that are "lost"– i.e. sold to the madams and the black market – there is not very much left over for Mau Mau captives. Now, if the army captures as many live Mau Mau during Exlax as theory declares possible and if they are all sent to internment camps, there simply will not be enough penicillin in the whole of Kenya to cure a quarter of them.'

'Send for more penicillin.'

'Wigmore says that such a request would give the show away. There'd be a tremendous row about the amount needed by the army and somebody would prod his pointed nose into the scandal of the supplies that have gone missing. Bad trouble for everybody – not just the bootleggers.'

'So what are we going to do? Shoot the Mau Mau as they come out of the jungle instead of capturing them?'

'Either that, or have thousands of them sitting round in internment camps slowly decaying at the taxpayers' expense.'

'I wonder they're going to have the operation at all,' I said.

'They can't cancel it, because too many distinguished people are coming out to watch.'

'There won't be anything to watch. You can't have distinguished spectators hanging around with the ambushes. The marquees for their meals would give the game away. What else is there for them to see?'

'Bombers taking off. Guns firing. Anyway, that's GHQ's business. To revert to ours. The official instruction will still be to capture the Mau Mau, but in the case of inexperienced troops, like our own, who cannot be expected to handle live and hostile blacks, the order will be to shoot when in doubt—i.e., unless the enemy comes forward peacefully and gives himself up immediately.'

'And who will take the responsibility for this order? The official policy is capture and arrest, but in practice our boys are to be told to shoot. At which…descending stage in the hierarchy…is the doctrine to be subtly transformed? And what line are these pestering magistrates going to take?'

Richard and I waited by the barrier at the camp entrance. We were challenged ('Get you the sons your fathers got') and gave the answer, 'And God will save the Queen'. A sullen lance-corporal lifted the barrier, while a dopey sentry wrongly presented arms, on the off-chance we were somebody more important.

'That your idea?' I said. 'Housman for the password?'

'It seemed appropriate. The poet of Shropshire and Hereford.'

'I wonder what he would have made of all this?

> "The files move slowly past," ' Richard quoted,
> ' "Towards the hollow;
> The bugles sound again;
> The soldiers follow."

'That says it all in the end.'*

'What it does not say,' I said, 'is that they may be charged with murder by some malign little pinko prick with a temporary magistracy, if they panic and shoot in their own protection.'

'Oh no,' said Richard. 'Wigmore has told me what to do. As intelligence officer, I shall be first on the scene after any killing, and I have a number of captured Mau Mun weapons, supplied by Wigmore and others, with which to rig the tableau if necessary. Remember, proven self-defence is an absolute get out in this game, even with pinko magistrates umpiring. And now you're going to ask what they'd say about *that* in Corpus Christi, Oxford?'

'I was rather wondering.'

'My parents were pacifists, you know.'

'So I believe.'

'Friends of Aldous Huxley and Gerald Heard. They died not long after the war. They left some reputation behind them and this was one of the reasons why Corpus Christi was happy to accept me.'

'Ironic. The Colonel first took to you because his grandfather was at Corpus. And now we learn that Corpus welcomed you for your pacifist connections.'

'But the point I wish to make is that neither my

---

* It was only many years later that I realised that Richard Legh was misquoting or improvising on this – to me at least – memorable occasion. In fact there is a Housman poem that ends, 'The soldiers follow'; but the rest of Richard's quotation is corrupt.

parents nor the high-minded dons of Corpus understood a necessity which they had never been required to face. Plato, echoed by Marcus Aurelius, tells us that it is one's duty to stay at one's post until one is ordered to retire or killed by the enemy; that it is one's duty to carry out one's orders but also to survive if possible. If you do not meet violence with violence, very often you cannot survive.'

'But we were talking about rigging the truth in order to avoid charges of murder.'

'In order to help others avoid charges of murder. My conscience is quite clear, Simon. Our soldiers are very young and frightened men far from home and far from Jerusalem. They are going to be pitched into the jungle without training or preparation and told to stop any black man that tries to come out of it. They must therefore be given absolutely clear orders and be defended by us if they get into trouble while obeying them. So that it is, after all, just as well that Colonel Cuthbert thinks this is a war. He is going to address each platoon in the next few days, and tell them that it is their right and their duty, if in any doubt whatever, to fire on any Mau Mau that come their way.'

'Thus to the great but concealed joy of the authorities diminishing the numbers that require penicillin.'

'There is so much hypocrisy going about that it is a pleasure to work with Colonel Cuth Smith. It's a pity about these obsessive hankerings of his, but if it hadn't been for them I don't suppose I'd have come to his attention. In most matters he is admirably honest and direct: they need a breath of him to blow through the senior common room in Corpus Christi.'

One week later, all our companies were in position

between Fort Hall and Naivasha. Each company would send into the forest, and then from time to time relieve, eight ambushes of five men. The distances between the company encampment and the ambush positions would vary from a mile to a mile and a half, a march just tolerable in the men's new and badly fitting jungle boots.

Battalion field headquarters was in a farmhouse about twenty miles from Fort Hall, a few hundred yards from the main road, or rather the main track, that led from Fort Hall along the edge of the forest to the escarpment. Hardly had Cuth arrived there with Malcolm as Adjutant, Richard Legh as intelligence (liaison) officer, the RSM and other attendant personnel, when there was a very annoying scene.

The settler who owned the farmhouse did not live in it (he had several more) but nevertheless conceived that his ownership gave him the right to enter at will and hobnob with Colonel Cuthbert. By way of initial introduction, he arrived drunk and demanding more drink. He was told that the field HQ mess was not yet established; if he would care to come back tomorrow evening...Bugger tomorrow evening, he wanted a drink and don't try to fob him off or he'd have the battalion HQ evicted from his property.

Since Richard was the youngest and (he supposed) the most vulnerable officer present, he concentrated his demands and his threats on him. Finally Richard simply ordered him to go, was threatened with violence, called in a corporal and two men of the regimental police, and instructed them to lock the settler in an outhouse until he was sober...unless he consented to leave at once. The settler went roaring off in his Land Rover, toppled off the track a few miles down it and broke his neck.

This meant that Richard, who had seen him off in

every sense and was the last person (together with the regimental policemen) to see him alive, had to answer a number of questions from the Kenya police. They settled into the farmhouse to make a real meal of it; among other things, they demanded to see Richard's army documents, were taken down by Malcolm to Nairobi, where Richard's file now was (having long since been replaced by Malcolm in its correct place in the orderly room cabinets), and were invited to inspect it. Now, although the regular Kenya police were not a bad lot, the temporary officers, who had been recruited for the emergency, were muck...and, since they knew that their employment was about to end as the emergency finally dwindled to nothing, poisonous muck for ill measure. Although it had nothing to do with the case in hand, they became hostile and suspicious on learning that Richard was an Oxford graduate, and additionally so when they had read what the records said of his parents. The line they began to take was that Richard had been high-handed and inhospitable to the settler, had forcibly expelled him from his own territory, well knowing that he was in no fit state to drive, and had thus indirectly but culpably brought about a fatal accident. They attempted to arrest Richard on trumped-up charges of manslaughter, were themselves arrested for threatening a commissioned officer of Her Majesty while he was performing his duties on active service and were taken away to the police station at Fort Hall, where the superintendent, an old-time police officer, suspended and confined them, and ultimately had them dismissed. But in the course of all this Colonel Cuth called for the file that had provoked their hostility and zeal, and now discovered that his intelligence (liaison) officer was the son of militant pacifists.

As Malcolm had apprehended, Cuth did not like it

at all. All his former prejudice against Richard was now renewed; his earlier enthusiasm for the products of Corpus Christi was most damnably vitiated by his recalling that that 'fine man', his grandfather, had intervened in some quarrel between the Senate House of Oxford and the War Office, a quarrel to do with the status of officers sent by the War Office to study the natural sciences. Since such officers were normally mature men, the War Office requested that they should not be subjected to the puerile regulations then imposed on ordinary commoners but should be invited to dine at High Table and, in general, treated as gentlemen commoners. When informed that the rank of gentleman commoner no longer existed, the War Office suggested a special grade, carrying special privileges, for all officers of more than five years' service, a suggestion that was peremptorily rejected. Cuth now remembered that his grandfather had been prominent among the anti-military group in this fracas, and his former suspicions of Richard were revived and magnified.

'I have persuaded the Colonel to keep him on as IO until this operation is over,' said Malcolm, while pausing one afternoon at my company encampment. 'Richard has studied the territory with great care, and it would be both unfair and injurious to send him packing just as the circus is coming to town.'

'And when Operation Exlax is over?'

'We shall see. If only it hadn't been for those accursed brutes of temporary policemen, I think I could have kept that file away from Cuth forever.'

'He must see that Richard is still the same man he was getting on so well with?'

'Yes. The same man, but now flawed with an

hereditary infirmity; latent at the moment, but which may at any second start discharging the pus of disaffection.'

'He thinks that Richard may turn on him and denounce the army and all its works?'

'That kind of a thing,' Malcolm said.

A few days later, Richard himself appeared and told the following story:

'The bombardment was stiffened up a bit a short while after the operation began, but nothing much came out of the jungle except a pregnant cow-elephant and no Mau Mau at all. The Colonel became very restless.

' "The boys in the ambushes will be getting pretty bored," he said, "bored and damp. How can we encourage them?"

' "We can't," I said. "Ambushing is a thankless task. You have to stay still, without food or rest or movement, for hours on end. If you want to pee, you have to piddle where you sit." I turned from my desk to the Colonel. "I've been talking, sir, to Captain Kitson of the rifles. You know he used to specialise, before the emergency was over, in cloak and dagger operations?"

' "And so?" said the Colonel peevishly.

' "Kitson says that one of our handicaps in the jungle was that we smelt too clean. If we'd made the men go without baths and without shaving, we'd have had a better chance. As it was ... the hygienic smell of the white men radiated hundreds of yards before and behind them. We'd have done much better, Kitson says, to stink like the Mau Mau."

' "And so?" the Colonel said again.

' "Have I your permission, sir, to request company commanders to send out their ambushes unwashed? So that they can't give themselves away by their cleanliness?"

' "And what would that do for morale?" said a company commander, who had dropped in on battalion HQ to make a nil return.

' "If it were explained to the men, they would understand why they were doing it and, however repugnant they found it," I said, "they would do it without complaint."

'But the CO wasn't listening.

' "I've got an idea," he said. "Where's Malcolm?"

' "He had to go to Nairobi, sir. With the second-in-command. Corporal Lendrick's court martial, if you remember."

'For Lendrick, as you may have heard, caught the first pox in the bugle platoon since we came to Kenya.

' "In the middle of a major operation," the Colonel said, "they have to waste time and energy on court martials."

' "Courts martial," I corrected, stupidly and officiously, doing nothing to mend matters.

' "Since Malcolm isn't here," said the CO with distaste, "you had better come with me. You and the RSM," he called.

' "Sir?"

' "We are going to go round some of the ambushes, to cheer the boys up and put them on their mettle, now that the bombardment is being stepped up."

' "We are going where, sir?"

' "Round some of the ambushes. Your company is the nearest," he said to the company commander who was there. "You can guide us out to your ambushes."

'The Company Commander [Richard told us now] opened his mouth and shut it.

' "We don't need any guides," I told the Colonel. "I have an exact chart of all ambushes. In any case, sir, it is impossible that we should go to them."

' "Oh? Why? Oblige us with your superior wisdom."

' "Ambushes are not to be disturbed, sir. It gives away the position. Besides…as I said just now, they are meant to sit and wait. They are also meant…to apprehend or to shoot anyone who approaches them."

' "They'll recognise us," said the CO.

' "With the greatest respect, sir," said the RSM, "I think that Mr Legh may be right. It is difficult to recognise people through thick forest."

' "Mr Legh," said the company commander, "is an Oxford man. He likes to keep his hands nice and clean. He doesn't want to go into the horrid jungle."

' "I didn't notice, Major Lambert," said I, "that you were any too forward in the matter yourself. However, I shall be happy to accompany the commanding officer if that is what he wishes. But I should be rather happier if he would wait for the return and advice of his Adjutant."

' "I respectfully agree, gentlemen," said the RSM.

' "You are against this, Legh," the Colonel said.

' "I am, sir."

' "I might have known you would be. I've been expecting something of the kind for days." And to the RSM, "We shall be needing a party of four askaris* to accompany us. To assist us if we meet any of the enemy."

' "We have the bugle platoon here, sir. Some of them—'

' "—No, RSM. We need Africans. They understand the jungle better than we do. How soon can you collect them?"

* Loyal black troops.

203

'As you know [Richard told us at my company encampment] O. is in charge of the Africans. I prayed he would back me up and help stop this idiocy. But when the RSM and I came to their quarters, O. wasn't there. He was away in Naivasha, consulting with officers of the African rifles about the best methods of handling black soldiers. There was only an African serjeant there, who at once picked and paraded a detail of his men.'

'Oh Richard. What happened next?

'What happened next was that the company commander who had been on a visit to battalion HQ slunk away when nobody was looking. The CO's servant appeared with a sack of goods – Coca-Cola, chocolate, NAAFI wodges [cakes or buns].

' "Father Christmas," the CO joked. "You carry the sack, Legh. You're the junior man."

'The RSM cleared his throat.

' "Senior warrant officers don't carry sacks," said the CO. "There's no reason why very junior National Service officers shouldn't."

' "The Africans are outside, sir. Perhaps one of them—'

' "The Africans have their own duties. Among them to sniff out possible danger from the Mau Mau." And to his servant, "Give the sack to Mr Legh."

'So off we went [Richard told us], two Africans in the lead, to spot rhino or buffalo, and Africans also in the rear. Colonel Cuth led the whites; the RSM was still, for some reason, carrying his pace stick; and I carried the sack of goodies to cheer up the ambushes and a map. I know what I'll do, I thought. I'll guide them between two of the ambushes—make us miss them all.

' "I'd better get up front, sir," I said, "in order to direct us."

' "No need, sir," said the good old RSM, too thick to see what I was at. "Some of these Africans went out when the ambushes was put into position. They know exactly which way to go."

'And so we wagged along through the forest ... until a rifle cracked to front right of us, and the Colonel staggered and fell. One of the ambush told me afterwards that he had fired at a black face. Not one of the blacks was scratched. Our rifleman had missed the Africans and shot the Colonel. Who shall say that justice was not done?

'One of the Africans in the rear was fitted with an RT set. The RSM tried to reach HQ. I attended to Cuth. It seemed more sensible to let him lie, from what little First Aid I knew, rather than to prop him up. Always leave them where they are until the doctor comes, I'd been told. So I left the Colonel where he was on the ground. I wondered what to do about his wound – wherever it was. I could see the blood in his throat when he spoke.

' "What happened?" he said.

' "You've been shot, sir."

' "You were right, Richard, weren't you? One shouldn't disturb an ambush. What was I thinking of?"

' "Don't talk, sir, please don't talk. The RSM is sending for the MO."

' "He will need a guide. It will take time."

' "*Don't talk, sir.*"

' "Prop me up."

' "It is better you lie flat."

' "I'm choking, Richard."

'So I propped him up. Although a little blood spilled from his mouth, he seemed better for a while. I held my handkerchief against the wound which, I now saw; was high in his chest.

' "The doctor is on his way, sir," said the RSM. "He says we're not to move the Colonel at all."

' "Mr Legh has his orders," said the CO. "He is to prop me up."

'The RSM turned away and muttered, "God have mercy. Christ have mercy. God have mercy. What a fuck-up."

' "Come," said Colonel Cuth. "I hope we need not talk of God just yet."

' "Please, my Colonel, don't talk."

' "There is something that must be said. Tell the boys from the ambush to come here."

'The RSM fetched the five men of the ambush.

' "It wasn't your fault," the Colonel said to them. "Never, in all your lives, feel guilty. You were doing your duty and did it well. *It wasn't your fault.* Now resume your positions."

'He seemed to faint then and when the MO came, three-quarters of an hour later, he was dead. I don't know how long he had been dead. He said nothing more after he'd spoken to the men of the ambush. A good death. I thought of Falstaff babbling of green fields. I don't know why. Cuth didn't babble at all, and there was never a man less like Falstaff. I suppose ... green fields seemed right for him. Cuthbert, the country boy. The Shropshire lad.'

'The Serpent in Happy Valley'

plus coda

from *Boys Will be Boys*

Many qualities are commonly imputed to colonial settlers, among them industry, greed, courage and obstinacy; but during the ten months odd which I spent as a soldier in Kenya I found that by far the most interesting was *guilt*. Guilt of a specialized and oddly slanted kind, certainly, but all the more fascinating for that. My own dealings with settlers were mostly social, so that it was on a social level—a level of eating and drinking—that I observed this phenomenon. But a man's attitudes in his pleasures are, if anything, more revealing than those he displays in business or official functions, and I therefore make no apology for treating the matter against a background of frivolity.

Let us, then, consider that most significant of Kenyan institutions, the Muthaiga Club. Situated in a wealthy suburb of Nairobi, the Muthaiga Club is the summit of the settlers' social aspiration. As a serving British officer, I was automatically an honorary member and was therefore inclined to treat the privilege lightly; but I soon discovered that the waiting list for membership proper was almost endless, that fees and subscriptions were portentous, that the process of election was grudging to the point of inquisition. To admit junior British officers to the club was, in truth, a notable act of hospitality, for colonial officials, and locally-born young bucks of comparable standing would not be elected for many years, not until they became formidable in rank or estate. To belong to the Muthaiga, to sleep there when you visited Nairobi for a weekend, was to have obtained, as it were, the letters patent of Kenyan nobility. And for this reason men who seldom came to Nairobi more than once a year, men from the coastal plains or the distant borderlands of Uganda, jostled and intrigued and paid heavy sums in money for a place. Nor, having done so, were they denied amenity: the bar, the longest in the colony, was stocked to meet the most *outré* or extravagant request; the service, provided by squads of white-robed Africans, was immaculate; the rooms, public or private, were comfortable, spacious; even, if you discounted the ubiquitous trophies of the chase, elegant; and the food was various and exquisitely prepared.

All of which was balm to the souls and bodies of exiled Europeans, such as I counted myself. One could eat, drink, sleep as civilized men understood the functions. But here lies the point. Most of the Kenyan members, the farmers and settlers, did not care for these refinements; having paid enormous fees to belong and being on one of his rare visits to Nairobi, the average settler misused this magnificent place of entertainment in order to do just what he did every day at home—to drink gin or whisky from six till ten p.m., and then to go drunk to a plain dinner accompanied by water ('No oysters or fal-de-rols for me, old man; just steak and veg.'). Every effort had been made by the committee to provide a club that would have done credit to London itself: and no pains were spared by the members to assert themselves, constantly and aggressively, as simple men of pioneering tastes who would have none of such decadence.

And yet they were proud of the Muthaiga and wished it to remain exactly as it was. The elaborate dishes and fine wines were untouched save by 'foreigners' (e.g., visiting Englishmen) and the soft-living city-dwellers of Nairobi itself, nevertheless the whisky-swilling 'pioneer' contingent, wholly contemptuous of such luxury, boasted of it all over East Africa ('Why, man, some of them even eat snails'). Nor is the clue to such equivocation far to seek. For on the one hand the settlers were terrified of being looked down on as 'colonials', as ignorant, unmannered bumpkins who knew nothing of the world, and they were therefore anxious to exhibit luxuries and refinements to match any in the West: but on the other hand they despised those who valued such delicacies.

The whole affair finally resolved itself into four simple propositions. First, a settler was as good as any of your Europeans and could meet them on their own ground (i.e., the Muthaiga Club). Second, a settler was much better than any of your Europeans, because he was con-temptuous (though not ignorant) of their effete habits and cultures, and preferred a rough, tough, adventurous life and a cuisine consisting of convenient essentials, such as whisky followed by tinned luncheon meat. Third, he was fortified by such customs and sustenance to maintain a firm and unsentimental attitude toward the native African, who was himself a simple man and respected unsophisticated usage. Last, it was the European's over-elaborate and over-leisured habits of entertainment and, by extension, of thought that led them to take up uncalled-for liberal attitudes toward African questions.

A compact view, one might think, and consistent after its fashion. But the essential flaw in these propositions reveals the curious brand of 'settler' guilt. For if pioneer ways were the purest and the best, then why erect—*and covet*—the ultra-smart Muthaiga Club in direct contradiction of those ways? Clearly, there was a guilty doubt lest the 'European' might, after all, be right—and right about African questions as well as about food and drink. And equally clearly, guilt might be temporarily and in part assuaged by entering the halls of luxury and false enlightenment and there defying the tutelary Lares —by wearing tattered drill trousers and insisting on raw spirit and coarse food.

One inevitable result of the Mau Mau emergency in Kenya was an increase in government organizations of every kind, some of which did an excellent job. But all of these still centred round the two oldest—the Colonial Service and the Kenya Police.

Before the emergency, both bodies had been held in esteem; but by the time the Mau Mau revolt was running down, while the Colonial Service remained more or less reputable, the Police had attracted odium and contempt. It was all a matter of recruitment. The Colonial Service, compelled by ever-increasing commitments to make temporary appointments and to advertise short-term contracts, was nevertheless careful to offer these either to old 'Africa hands' or the more presentable of their sons; with the result that their new auxiliaries had some knowledge of Africa and were disposed, provided their authority went unquestioned, to treat Africans fairly. The

Police bestowed their contracts altogether less discriminately and attracted some of the riffraff of England and the Colony. Young men turned up as 'Inspectors' (to receive generous salaries and to command large bodies of native policemen) who had often never been out of England—and, what was far worse, the sort of young men who had been kicked out of their university for drunken driving or were in trouble in their home town for cashing bad cheques. In common with 'white trash' everywhere, they were eager to find someone—anyone—over whom they could claim superiority. The native African was the ideal victim for this purpose. Africans were wrongfully arrested, prisoners and suspects were beaten up.

In 1956 I was attached to a company of English soldiers which was stationed near a village in the foothills of the Aberdare Mountains. It was an important village, the seat both of the local District Officer, an old and emergency Colonial appointment, and of the local Chief Inspector of Police, an Irishman called Lynn Flynn, who was of the 'old' and regular school of policeman and was liked by us well enough. I should explain that 'Chief Inspector was the lowest rank in the Kenya Police. 'Inspectors', of whom Lynn Flynn had several under him (all of them 'short contract' men) scattered round the locality, were considered as being on probation; as Lynn Flynn made very plain, to be reckoned only as the equals of our own sergeants. He therefore suggested that any of his Inspectors who had business with us (information about Mau Mau and the like) should be entertained, if at all, in the sergeants' mess. This did not at all suit the temporary Inspectors' *amour propre*. In their dealings with other units of the army they had often contrived to bluff their way into officers' messes and they did not like being excluded here.

Now, the pride of our officers' mess at this time was an African cook, whom we paid out of our own pockets and who had once cooked in Government House itself. Thence he had been dismissed by some busybody for being discovered drunk; but we had argued that any good cook must be expected to drink, and since he carried the recommendation and the security clearance of our own District Officer, we had engaged him. And had no cause to regret it. He could improvise a *bouillabaisse* out of the dreariest tins, he knew all about the use of cream, brandy and wine, and he had a knack of making even the skinny local chickens seem plump and tender. True, he not only got drunk at night but also behaved louchely with the village women; but artists of his calibre, we said, must be allowed some moral licence—and in any case (this rather inconsequentially) he was a great favourite with the men, who called him 'Randy Dad'.

So no one was at all pleased when Lynn Flynn went off on a course and the morning after his departure an Inspector—his stand-in—drew up in a Land-Rover and said that he had come to arrest our African cook. On what charges? we asked. Charges, he said, need not be specified—under Emergency Regulation So-and-So. What about a warrant? Not needed—under Emergency Regulation So-and-So. But—this was Army ground, W.D. property, and unless he could show a warrant authorizing him to enter and make his arrest, then he should now leave at once before he was thrown off....First round to us. The Inspector drove away radiating high-frequency malevolence, while Randy Dad beamed and started to prepare an extra-special lunch.

The next day the Inspector was back, armed with a warrant apparently signed by everyone from the

Provincial Commissioner downward; and Randy Dad was taken away, a sad little figure in the back of the police Land-Rover, to be charged, so the Inspector in his triumph was indiscreet enough to tell us, with raping a girl in the village.

That night the District Officer was to come to dinner. He had especially asked for Randy Dad's Supreme of Chicken cooked in *pâté de foie* and was vexed when given a corn-beef hash. We explained what had happened, but he sulkily refused bridge and left at once. The next morning he reappeared: he had been questioning the local men and women, it seemed, and discovered that the Inspector had been badgering them for any information such as would make our poor old cook suspect of complicity with the Mau Mau. They hadn't given it, for they had none; after the fashion of Africans being questioned by a white man they had politely agreed that the Bwana was no doubt right. This had given the Inspector his excuse for his first attempt at arrest. Thwarted, he had then used bribes and threats to induce a black girl who was known to have granted her favours to Randy Dad to say that she had in fact been raped: hence the high-powered warrant.

What the Inspector did not know, and what could hardly have occurred to anyone so ignorant and so base, was that the local Africans held their District Officer in some reverence and affection, if only because he spoke their language fluently, and fell over themselves to tell him any news they thought he would be grateful to hear. So the Inspector's attempt to revenge himself on us through our stomachs was speedily squashed. What became of him I have no idea, as I left the district a few days later. But it was just this combination of malice, stupidity and bad dealing on the part of 'short-contract men' which afflicted the Kenya Police throughout the Emergency.

The 'new' racecourse in Nairobi is some two miles out of the city proper, up the Ngong Road and beyond the cemetery. The surroundings are attractive, the course itself is well laid out, and the arrangements for eating and drinking compare more than favourably with those at the Ally Pally or Hurst Park. The racing itself, however, gives less cause for satisfaction. Despite a positively Augean clean-up in 1954, despite the unquestionable integrity of the stewards, there remains an impression, so strong as almost to amount to physical presence, that there is something about Nairobi races incurably and inalienably *wrong*.

There could, of course, be several very simple reasons for this. The horses are none of the finest and African stable boys are no more scrupulous than any other kind. The wealthy settlers who predominate among the owners, having spent their youth and maturity in a rough and ready 'frontier' atmosphere inimical to moral or financial refinement, are often less delicate in their 'arrangements' than the stewards might wish. And then there is the matter of the jockeys. For professional jockeys, Kenya can be very near the end of the line; they may have been warned off in England, Australia, India and Hong Kong before arrival, and be somewhat less than predictable. But none of this entirely accounts for the leprous state of racing in Nairobi.

Late in the summer of 1955 I attended Nairobi races with an advertising manager from the city, famous for his poker and his knowledge of form. But the form, as always in Nairobi, was totally unreliable, and so, being heavily down after the first five of the seven races, I selected a horse for the sixth by the ancient pagan method of waiting to see which was the last to defecate before they left the paddock. This animal duly obliged at long odds, cleared my previous losses, and left me a nice sum of 'up-money', all of which I decided to risk on the last race. Feeling that the old gods, by so kindly arranging the omen for me, had done all that could be expected of them for one day, I reverted to the Christian faith and chose a horse called Holy Roller. My advertising chum was sceptical and remarked that Holy Roller's jockey, whom I'll call Addy Bates, had only just recovered from a terrific bout of D.T.'s. Not to mention, he added, that he was thought to be wanted on charges of fraud and bigamy in Lourenço Marques.

From the start of the race a horse called Naivasha Boy took up and maintained a lead of some five lengths; Holy Roller never got within three lengths of him and at the post he was a clear second to Naivasha Boy—who was cheered in with some enthusiasm since his jockey, a cheeky little African, was a favourite with spectators both black and white.

'Well,' I said, 'it was worth a try.' And started towards the car park.

'I shouldn't go just yet,' my chum said. 'There might be an objection. Addy Bates is a great one for objecting.'

'He can't object,' I said, 'the black boy went right ahead at the start and neither Addy nor anyone else got within a mile of him.'

'All the same…' my friend said. And at that moment the loudspeaker announced an objection.

'They won't allow it,' I said. 'They can't. Addy must be warming up for another go of D.T.s.'

'He could always say something happened at the start,' my friend said. 'It was a bit of a mess. And in any case I rather *think* you'll find that Addy will now get the race.'

And so it was. Naivasha Boy was disqualified (the alleged reason for this being obscured by a sharp cackle from the loudspeaker), Holy Roller was declared the winner and I had picked up a very pleasing sum.

'And now,' I said, 'perhaps you'll explain?'

'People here are rather keen on keeping the blacks in their place.'

'Meaning no black jockey can ever win a race?'

'Oh no. It's quite all right for black jockeys to beat white ones. But if a white one raises an objection...that means a white man is accusing a black of cheating. And if a white man does that, he *must* be upheld as a mere matter of face. In this case, I expect Addy cooked up some story about the start of the race–and he just had to be believed. There's still a few jockeys, mostly amateurs of course, who are too sporting....But with a man like Addy Bates, to object is standard procedure—unless he'd happened to back the African himself....But what the hell are you moaning about? You won money, didn't you?'

And there was a lot, of course, in that.

This piece caused a mild rumpus. There is, as the elder Goncourt wrote, an agreeable truth about most things under the sun and also a disagreeable truth; but no amount of emphasis on the former will entitle one, in the eyes of those concerned, even to hint at the latter—which indeed they are *biologically* unable to recognize, let alone to acknowledge. To ourselves, our own activities and motives must always appear immaculate. Since the Stewards of the Nairobi Race Club were no exceptions to this rule, there was indignant talk of lawyers and writs; but it was wisely decided not to put the purity of Nairobi

Races to a legal test, and after a few letters of bluster no more was heard.

I mention this circumstance because I am increasingly irritated by the modern tendency, in all quarters, to have recourse to law the moment anything unflattering appears in print. The libel lawyers are much to blame: asked to advise whether such-and-such a production is libellous, they are contemptibly cautious if acting for a would-be publisher, irresponsible and inflammatory if acting for a would-be litigant. A well known writer of my acquaintance, angered by a hostile review of a volume of his collected essays, once sought out a reputable libel lawyer and was advised that he could sue to the tune of 1,000 guineas. And yet the review he complained of was nothing out of the way; it was merely a reasoned catalogue, in good round English, of my friend's literary weaknesses. I am glad to say that he soon came to his senses and dropped the matter; but the fact remains that *the advice had been given*—by a solicitor who, one may presume, knew very well that whichever way the case went he would collect a substantial fee. Although I am not qualified to assess the legal aspects of this particular case, the moral position, here as elsewhere, is surely plain. If one publishes written work, one is inviting attention and therefore comment. If that comment turns out to be disagreeable, one has no one but oneself to blame; one has deliberately stuck out one's neck and must not be offended if someone else hits it with a chopper.

This is self-evident. Yet so terrified are people these days of 'giving offence' that most reviewing now consists merely of reshuffling harmless clichés. A straightforward attack, particularly if it is conducted in salty language, arouses a great wail of protest from publishers and

authors alike: 'prejudiced', 'uncouth', 'insensitive'—
these are the labels applied to plain speaking. I was once
rebuked by Mr. Frederick Warburg for saying that
Moravia's *Two Women*, a translation of which he had just
published in this country, was a dull book. I thought so
then, and I think so now, and I'll say it again: *Two Women*,
with all respect to Mr. Warburg and his firm, is slow,
prolix and dull. Surely this is just the sort of thing
reviewers should tell the public? And just the sort of
thing they did tell the public before English letters
turned into a conspiracy of mealy-mouthed mutual
approbation. If Mr. Warburg is shocked by what I wrote
of Moravia, let him turn to reviews and essays of a
hundred years go. No quarter was asked or given; even
personal abuse was allowed; they gave blow for blow in
those days, put lead in their cudgels and took the buttons
off their sabres, and if they got hurt, they picked
themselves up as best they might and made ready to fight
another day. Only one thing was barred: no one—no one
who valued his honour—could go whining off to the
Courts.

This was as it should be and, I hope, will be again. I
myself both write reviews and, as a novelist, suffer them.
I do not complain when I am attacked, nor do I expect
others to complain if I attack them in like case.

The question of a writer who is attacked by another
writer in print is not merely a specialized one. The same
rule must apply in all regions of public life. Private
people, to be sure, must be left in privacy; but people
who set themselves up in public, whether as rulers,
entertainers, law-givers or leaders of fashion, must accept the public or printed criticism which their
performances invite. They are after great rewards; they
are often accorded great deference: they must therefore

endure, with a good grace, the occasional rotten egg. Even if the missile is unmerited, they must remember that they themselves have sought and relished the prominence which has made them targets. They stuck themselves up in the first place; so let them wipe up the mess and get on with their job—or take themselves off to the decent shelter of a private life. But let us, in no case at all, hear any more of their sanctimonious wailing in the Courts.

The Male Prostitute in London

from
Boys Will be Boys

It is no concern of mine in this article to discuss the morality of sexual deviation. I do not propose, on the one hand, to consider homosexuality as 'a problem' whether moral, social, medical, or forensic, any more than I wish to exploit it, on the other, as a source of titillation or low comedy. I merely start with the familiar and dreary truth that in London as in other large cities there is a substantial demand for the services of the male prostitute; and I hope to be able to explain, in the simplest and most concrete terms, how and in what circumstances this demand is satisfied—to explain, that is, how the boys and men concerned are procured, where they come from, in what manner and in what places they carry on their business, whether and for how long they prosper, and what fate will finally overtake them. If I have to state the point of view from which I write, I should say that my interest was *functional*. As a novelist of sorts, I simply like to know how, on a purely practical level, human affairs are conducted—in one word, how they *work*. Here is a branch, by no means inconsiderable and currently much canvassed, of human activity: how, one asks oneself, does it wag along? What happens, and where?

To start with, then, I suggest that there are some five kinds of male prostitute at present working in London. To a certain extent the categories melt into one another, but the distinctions, in the main, are clear. (Since these examples are based upon people whom I know and who have been generous with their time and information, both courtesy and necessity dictate that I should use, in all cases, a considerable element of personal disguise. I can only assert my belief that this handicap has not rendered my presentation either false or misleading in any essential respect.)

In my *first* category come young men of the armed services who are either stationed or on leave in London. Prominent among these are, of course, the members of whatever units of Household Troops are currently serving in the capital, centuries of city life having endowed these regiments with a traditional knowledge of and a notorious capacity for all sexual activities of a venal nature. If a young guardsman wishes to augment his modest pay, and if he has no objection to hiring out his person to this end, then he need only 'ask about', as a guardsman whom I shall call Tom once put it to me, and some older man (occasionally an N.C.O.) will tell him which pubs or bars to frequent, or which street corners to wait on, and will sometimes offer to accompany him in order to see fair play.

'I knew all about it happening,' said Tom, 'but I didn't mean to go myself, see? Then one week-end I was going home to see my girl, and most of my pay was owed, and on the Friday I reckoned I was at least two quid light on what I needed. So I went to a bloke I knew used to go with queers...' He was told to try several pubs in Kensington and the West End, and if still unsuccessful at closing time to take up a stance in the region of Grosvenor Gardens. Tom was not to accept less than thirty shillings in any case, he was told, and he must ask for at least three pounds if his client requested and he himself allowed the 'taking of a real liberty', by which euphemism one connotes the practice of buggery as opposed to the very much more usual manual or oral caresses. The upshot was Tom returned from his first outing without 'a real liberty' having been taken (he was not at all anxious, he informed me, for this to happen) and the better off by some two pounds ten in cash and several sophisticated items of information. His subsequent week-end with his girl was a success, having got off to a round start when he presented her with an unlooked-for pair of stockings which the odd ten shillings of his wages of sin had enabled him to buy.

Thereafter, having discovered so easy a way out of his financial afflictions, Tom found himself 'on the streets' with increasing frequency. But, I enquired, did not these expeditions do violence to his proper sexual nature? Apparently not. Tom's explanation was that he regarded 'what happened' as a form of masturbation: he would close his eyes and think about 'girls and things' while his partner provided the necessary mechanical stimulus—a service which Tom performed unthinkingly, with an almost automatic movement of the hand, in return. Thus Tom was able to persuade himself that he was not at all 'queer' by nature, and that what occurred was of no sexual significance. However, it is evident that a person who is not at least slightly homosexual in taste could never begin to tolerate such a situation; and I strongly

223

suspect that Tom, along with most soldiers who behave like him, has a definite if narrow homosexual streak. He is, in fact, bisexual—a judgement which, in its general implications, is confirmed by some remarks once made to me by a young Lance-Sergeant (also of the Brigade).

'Some of us get quite fond of the blokes we see regularly,' he said. 'You go to their flats and have some drinks and talk a bit—they're nice fellows, some of them, and interesting to listen to. And as for the sex bit, well, some of the younger ones aren't bad looking and I've had some real thrills off them in my time…'

But it would be unjust to burden Her Majesty's Guard with an unrelieved onus of obloquy. Provincial regiments which from time to time replace Household Troops in the performance of 'public duties' in London are quick enough, after a few weeks of sniffing the air, to rival the iniquity of their predecessors. Not all country boys, one must suppose, have the integrity which is popularly premised of them: show them the chance to make a little easy money, and their response is regrettably easy to predict.…I should also remark, as a final comment on H. M. Forces in this connection, that soldiers and sailors, particularly the latter for some reason, who are to be in London on leave often discover from friends the address of a 'Club' or 'Bar' where they are likely to be picked up by well-to-do homosexuals, and are sometimes told by friends to ring up 'So-and-So, who said to send my mates to him. He's very rich with a smashing flat, and he'll give you a fair old time if you don't mind being fiddled with now and again.' By this time, however, activities are within spitting distance of being amateur, and we had best proceed to the second category.

This consists of boys and young men who have full-time and respectable jobs of a more or less 'refined' nature (hairdressers, shop-walkers, low-grade couturiers or interior decorators) but who are not above improving their incomes by an occasional evening 'on the game'. The point is, of course, that their occupations reveal to these boys certain standards of elegance and sophistication which they may have the natural taste to admire but seldom the money to afford. Furthermore, such occupations have always had a strong appeal for men of an effeminate or homosexual type. Given, then, that a boy who goes in for, say, ladies' hairdressing is quite liable to be homosexual in any case, and given also that his association with a wealthy hairdressing establishment may lead him to covet luxuries which he cannot pay for, what is more likely than that he will be tempted to earn the rent overdue on too sumptuously furnished an apartment by the exploration of his unorthodox sexual leanings?

In the words of Rodney, a 'beauty shop' apprentice of seventeen-and-a-half, 'I don't like going to bars and getting picked up because I've got my own special friend of my own age. I like to save myself for him. But I've got my room to pay for, and the instalments on the gramophone to keep up, and I like nice things. So that if I can get three or four pounds extra for my trouble, it comes in very handy.'

Whereas Tom the guardsman merely wanted two pounds to go home to his girl-friend, Master Rodney wants twice that to spend on agreeable luxuries. But in fact they have a great deal in common: each of them is after a 'fuller and better life' as he conceives it—a life to which each assumes without question he is entitled. Neither considers his casual contacts of much significance (Tom considers sexual reality as being his experiences with his girl, Rodney as his connection with his 'special friend'.) And in neither of them could I discern the faintest trace of uneasy conscience—Rodney's complaint about wishing to save himself for his friend having sprung from a desire to be sexually fresh for enjoyment, not from a distaste for infidelity. Tom and Rodney, the young soldier and the young hairdresser, have simply realized, with commendable clarity, that to obtain pleasurable 'extras' it is sometimes necessary to use one's available talents in a mildly irksome or invidious fashion.

In my third category we find a type of boy who is far less prepossessing and yet would probably be found, by the moralist, to be far more easily excusable.

This is the boy of poor intelligence and low town background who has neither the ability to get a good job nor the application to stay with it if he should, but drifts round doing a series of dull, heavy, and ill-paid casual tasks (some of them verging on the illicit) when and as they can be found. Disgruntled, slow-witted, bored, such a boy is dimly aware that there are better things to be had from life and that many people are having them. It does not occur to him that his lack is in any way his own fault (that others work hard to acquire skills and establish a definite position) and still less does he have any clear idea what he is lacking. He simply knows that the world is in some manner 'doing him out of' all the things which seem to make it tolerable for others. He finally decides, making the nearest thing he can to a mental effort, that these things are obtainable only by means of something which he calls 'luck', a nebulous concept which in the end amounts to the sudden and apparently effortless possession of lots of money. If only he had 'a bit of luck', then he would (automatically) have a pot of money, and so would be as good as and probably much better than 'all of them'. But just what the money would be spent on is not specified, other than by vague and gloating references to cars, suits, and street women.

'You can say what you like,' said Len (a temporarily unemployed and half-Irish warehouse hand, whose actual dialect I make no attempt to reproduce), 'but it all comes down to luck. If that Macmillan had had my luck, then he wouldn't be where he is now. And if I'd had his I wouldn't spend my time reading to people in churches.' I do not propose here to analyse this statement into its component elements—the resentment at privilege and excellence, the half-baked notions of natural equality, the idea that everyone, no matter what his abilities, will emerge triumphant if only he gets 'a proper chance'; I merely remark that at the bottom of this underdog philosophy is nothing more nor less than a desire for easy money, and that one day such a lad will be told by a friend, in the crudest possible terms, of one method of making some.

'My friend told me,' said Len, 'that I could get some money by flogging myself to some rich geyser that liked boys. After he explained a bit, I caught on—and here I am.' ('Here' being a dim and dirty bar of a kind I shall describe in detail later and in which Len, being of recent importation, was still receiving the attention accorded to novelty in such circles.) I need hardly add that Len's resentment at 'the rich geysers', however well they treated him, was extreme (they had had all the 'luck', all the 'chances', etc., etc.), and I was not surprised to hear, a few weeks later, that he had beaten up a rich client and stolen both clothes and money from his flat. In such cases, if a 'geyser' applies to the police, he will probably be well supported. In any event, so it was here, and Len has now vanished from the scene.

All my categories so far have consisted of 'part-time' prostitutes. So it is with the fourth kind of boy, if only because he is prepared to turn his hand to anything at all other than a legitimate job (however cushy), from which he seems to recoil with instinctive aversion. This is the classical type of 'layabout', who has somehow got it into his head that the only money worth making is to be made from shady enterprises of whatever kind. These range from petty theft, dope-passing, running for low bookmakers, through hired violence and crude confidence tricks, to ordinary male prostitution which may be combined, on certain occasions with one or more of his other activities. Micky, a typical boy of this kind, differs from Len, in that while Len was stupid and essentially sluggish, Micky is quick and inventive, a man of many parts, and has the sense to know that money does not just appear by 'luck' but must be sought with effort. Micky's trouble is that as soon as he gets a little cash he spends it on clothes, drink and sexual frolics, or gambles the lot away. (When well off, Micky spends a lot on female prostitutes, though his sexual flexibility is such that he has been known to produce a very young 'fancy boy' of his own.) The result of all this is that his life varies from one of soft beds and relative splendour to one of park benches and fast-moving shifts—one of which will ultimately prove disastrous, if only because his fecklessness makes his need for money so sudden and so absolute that his shifts, though often ingenious, are not always as carefully thought out as they should be. 'I spend the lot and then look around,' he said to me once.

'But wherever I look I see steamers [homosexuals prepared to pay boys money] and suckers, so I don't have to look for long.' Perhaps not; but if he does not take to looking with rather more care, I anticipate a round misapplication of his talents.

The fifth category is that of the full-time professional male prostitute, who lives solely by his sexual trade, is anxious to improve his art and his clientele, is sometimes to be found living in very good circumstances indeed, and can often persuade a rich man, if not to set him up, at least to take him on luxurious foreign holidays. I mention this class of boy last because he is extremely rare. Among the male prostitutes, 'part-time' is the rule: the full-blown courtesan is not only an exception but is in many ways radically different, in outlook and accomplishment, from all the rest, save perhaps for the hairdresser, Rodney, who rather shoddily resembles him in manners and taste.

Conrad, one of the very few full-time male prostitutes I know, is a finished article. Polished, witty, by no means unread; highly vocal and even knowledgeable about current plays, exhibitions, and scandals; a good cook, a light but sophisticated drinker; above all, to judge from his conversation, a person of inexhaustible resource in matters of sexual technique, Conrad might well be mistaken for an amusingly epicene member of an exacting cosmopolitan set—were it not for two misfortunes: he speaks no language other than English; and this he speaks with a slight lilt, of which, try how he may, he cannot rid himself and which is quite undeniably Welsh.

So much for the boys themselves. Their family

backgrounds, I think, are important only in so far as it is true to say, in all cases, that they were in some sense unwanted in their own homes-redundant nuisances, unloved and therefore unloving. Thus Tom, the easy-going soldier, came, as might be, from a farmworker's family in the North: his father drank the money and required Tom to contribute further to his drinking, whereat the disgusted Tom went off to follow the Drum. Rodney, the soft little hairdresser, was the son of a respectable small shopkeeper in the Midlands: he disliked the grim routine of money-grubbing and chapel-going (though plainly he inherited his father's money-mindedness), was consciously out of place because of his 'refined' attitudes, and left unlamented for the big city. Len, grovelling stupidly after his share of the world, was just one of a swollen slum-family. Micky came from nowhere, whither he will doubtless return. As for Conrad, his background was Welsh and he attended a minor university: but his parents and his teachers were a preying menace and he left home for much the same reasons as Rodney—alienated from his own people by his own natural elegance. All are flotsam; rootless, or having wilfully severed coarse and ungainly roots.

More to our purpose is to enquire how these boys came to take up the practice of prostitution and how they get on when they have done so. The answer to the first part of the question is easier than many people would care to admit. Boys take up prostitution, as other boys of a better class might take up the Law or the Navy, because someone they know tells them about it, first of all painting the affair in general and congenial colours, later explaining the elementary points of application and procedure. Tom learnt from his comrades; Rodney from the whispered gossip over tea at eleven o'clock; Len from a similarly situated friend, while Micky, one may well suppose, gathered his information from the very mists and stones of the city. All 'heard'; all decided, for motives which varied from utter listlessness to deliberate career-planning, that 'it' would be both lucrative and undemanding; and so all set off, one evening and for the first time, to sell their bodies for money.

Where did they go?

They went on the street, or to one of a number of well-known pubs, 'clubs' (these latter of the 3-to-11 p.m. variety), or coffee bars. (From time to time a place gets a bad name and the police make trouble, closing it, if possible, for some technical infringement of licence; but there are always new places and people always know of them.) Once arrived, all the neophyte has to do is wait. If he is on a well-known street, he will be asked for 'a light' or 'the time'. If in a pub or bar, he will be asked to have a drink, the convention being that if he accepts he is open to negotiation. The pub could be any pub—but it isn't because it is a 'known' pub, a place where it is safe to ask people 'to have a drink'. As for the bar or 'club', it is on the first floor in a tumble-down back-street: there is a juke-box, an air of camaraderie, quite wholesome drinks at just over the average prices, an obliging proprietor, a cigarette machine, and several informally but well-dressed men, some of whom have an unmistakeably officer-like manner. One of these men has invited the new boy (after a whispered conference with the proprietor, who says that the boy is 'all right' because 'Dennis told him to come') to have first one drink and then another; and now suggests, since it is nearly eleven o'clock, that they should both go back 'to my place for another drink'. Brashly or shyly, the boy agrees. Tom might add that he is 'a little short', his older friend in the sports coat nods reassuringly. Rodney remarks that he will be needing 'four pounds for the chair-covers'; Len that it will have to be 'worth his time'. Micky (who can never, surely, have been a new boy) is there that night, but is flush and with a woman; while Conrad, who even at the start of his career avoids such places if he can, is waiting in his flat, which is just off the Edgware Road, for an expected telephone call.

So off they go, Tom, Rodney, and Len, three years on the game or three minutes (and it makes no difference now), to the nicely furnished bachelor apartment or the small house in the pretty mews. There they find drinks, a gramophone, carpets, comfort, and ease. For it is all made very easy. 'Perhaps you would like a bath?' Rodney has already had one that evening; but Tom wouldn't mind if he did, and Len ungraciously accepts, on the off-chance of being able to palm a razor or a comb. 'That's better.... You're really looking very nice.... And now....'

An hour later or so it is time to go. ('All night' is rare, save possibly at week-ends, and unpopular; clients have charwomen who arrive early, while soldiers have parades for which they must prepare, and hairdressers must be at Madame's by eight-thirty....) Tom's friend, gruff and middle-aged, crams thirty shillings into Tom's hand, asks him to come to his address at midnight the following Saturday, and says good-night briefly but with courtesy. Rodney's companion puts on his spectacles, points meaningly to the mantel (where there is a five-pound note under an ash-tray), and reluctantly hands Rodney the novel he had promised to lend him while they were drinking Crème de Menthe earlier on. Len's partner is youngish, and wishes to impress himself and his friends by being able to say, 'My dears, he adored it and didn't ask for a penny.' To lend some colour of truth to this notion, he hands Len five shillings with a kindly look, and remarks that this should see him home; but then he catches a glimpse of Len's scowling face, hastily adds a pound note and then yet another, and manages to hurry the slow-witted Len out of the door before worse befalls. Len, who will have his revenge on mankind soon but not quite yet, lopes away down the street with the money clasped in his hand (still dirty despite the bath), a purloined nail-brush in his trouser pocket, and some thirty loose cigarettes, scooped out of the open and opulent box, already crumbling to pieces in the rotting lining of his jacket.

Meanwhile, Micky has taken his improbably blonde girl to a hotel behind Victoria, reflecting, without rancour or anxiety, that by to-morrow lunch-time he will be skint; and Conrad's expected guest has arrived at the flat off the Edgware Road, bringing with him a bald head, no money but a sound cheque book, and a nicely bound volume of very curious pictures.

And what happens the next night?

The same happens the next night, and for many nights. (Unless, of course, the police step in; but this is something like a motor accident: it can happen to anyone at any time and is therefore left entirely out of the reckoning.) But just as the pubs and the bars change, so do Tom, Rodney, and Len change—change and disappear. Micky and Conrad last rather longer, because they are tough and clever; indeed Conrad, if he chooses his clientele and his lotions with care, may last until he is forty, when he will have saved enough to buy a little shop in a country town. But in this world, change is the rule: clients would soon get bored even if the boys kept their looks, and they are far from doing that. Boys will be boys indeed; but not for long.

Tom comes out all right. While serving, in Germany, he hears that his girl is pregnant, and being a decent fellow at heart he gets a compassionate leave to come home and marry her. Thereafter he settles down to soldier steadily on until finally and with a little luck he becomes a Colour-Sergeant, liked and respected by all, and even after many years occasionally to be heard giving good-natured advice, over the counter of the Company Stores, as to where 'to get the richest of them if you want something to pay for them shirts you lost'.

Rodney's fate is sadder. The attraction of his dark and sissified looks is of brief duration, and though he begins to earn more money at Madame's, he is hard put to it to pay for the little extravagances he covets. To make things worse his 'special friend' will leave him fairly soon. He begins to be resentful at what he knows he is missing and will always miss (the elegant, cultured, *rich* life of which he has received such tantalizing hints); he haunts the shadier bars more often now, and knows he is beaten on the night when he himself pays (which he can ill afford to do) to take home a boy who in a year-and-a-half will be as passé as himself. Still there are several like him; they make the best of one another and in some sort survive. Rodney scrapes along on his earnings, gives chattery little tea parties for his cronies on Sunday afternoons, and often wanders by himself along the Serpentine casting furtive, longing, and somehow reproachful looks at the younger bathers.

Len has already gone to prison for robbery with violence. The 'luck' was always against him. After all, it was these blokes corrupted him, wasn't it? But it's him in prison, mate. Why? Because the rich blokes get all the 'chances', that's why.

Micky may go to prison too, sent there by his own carelessness. Or he may get too interested in some of the drugs he is sometimes paid to carry about. Or he may just disappear—into a ditch or off to Tipperary, and no one will give a jot. Not even the police, because Micky is a very small man and even along the dope line never met anyone of the slightest importance. I shall miss him—but not much. The best one can hope is that a queer bookmaker will take a fancy to him and make him stick steadily to the business of laying small bets in the Silver Ring. The Silver Ring is about Micky's mark in life: you need quick wits, there is some entertaining bustle and enough shady practice to keep Micky happy, and he will be following his favourite game—taking the money of fools.

Conrad will be content selling fancy brassware in Barchester. He will be able to afford a week or two at Cannes every year, remember past glories in present independence, and perhaps learn a little French at last. Having earned and deserved all he has, he is careful, in the Welsh way of his Welsh fathers, to keep it.

And the clients of these young men? From the point of view of this article, which seeks to describe the mechanics of a trade, the clients wear one face only, a face which can never change. For it is the face of a currency note, always as beautiful, however faded and wrinkled, as when dew-fresh from the Mint. All that can happen to clients is that they get richer or poorer. At this time and in this country they are getting along very nicely. Wolfenden may suggest this, the Church may propose that, Mr. John Gordon deplore the other thing: but the law of supply and demand is engraven in brass, and is not to be erased by the abstract and irrelevant indignation of catch-penny public moralists.

Athens

from
Is There Anybody There? Said the Traveller

*For all the Athenians and strangers which were there spent their
time in nothing else, but either to tell, or to hear some new thing.*
Acts of the Apostles: Chap 17: v 21

These days, Athens is the nastiest and most polluted
city in Europe – in the world. It wasn't quite so foul
in 1984, when I spent a week there with a chum who had
a flat which looked out on to the woods of Lycabettos.
Although the trees were suffering from a kind of arboreal
scurvy, they weren't absolutely dead, as I expect they are
by now.

Anyhow, despite the noisy, scummy road immediately
under my chum's windows and the decaying woods on
the other side of it, it was fun staying with him for a
number of reasons: his knowledge of Athenian
antiquities, cinemas and eateries (one can hardly call
them restaurants); his deadly deadpan malice at the
expense of our common acquaintance, and his
enthusiasm for two-handed games of chance, such as
backgammon and gin rummy. But what I chiefly recall
from this visit is a process of remembering: how any site

or sight I saw provoked a melancholy comparison between what I was seeing now, in March of 1984, and what I had seen when I first came to Athens with Burgo Partridge a quarter of a century before…when the forest on Lycabettos was still healthy and Athens was still an agreeable if unremarkable city, provincial in size and air, of modest and seemly dwellings, orange-tiled and ochre-walled, instead of a huge, honking, ordurous Gehenna of smouldering streets, proletarian breeding-boxes, and brutal granite blocks.

Burgo and I arrived a few days before Christmas in 1959. The King of the Hellenes was on his throne; officer cadets of all three armed services walked the handsome avenues which led in and out of Constitution Square, gilt-sheathed daggers slung at their sides; clusters of balloons were released into the pale-blue sky and rose until they attained oneness with the empyrean.

'We shall sit down here,' said Burgo, having spotted a tin-roofed café in the Zappeion Gardens, which marched with the gardens of the palace, 'and have a drink in honour of Christmas, though neither of us, thank God, sets any store by Christ.'

Burgo ordered noxious ouzo. I ordered Fix, the national beer, thin as canary's piss but at that time the only brand available.

'Celebrating Christmas at home in Hungerford,' said Burgo, 'will be Frances my mother, Ralph my father, and their guest Isobel Strachey, whose legs are as thin as the stem of a hock glass and were said, in her youth, to open as easily and as often as a pair of nail scissors. But her youth has long since given way to what Horace calls "*canities morosa*", sour grey senescence, to conceal which she has a special hairdo which she can ill-afford even though it is only annual, before proceeding to my parents at Hungerford every Christmas. She has a fantasy, you see, about being in the train of one of the Three Kings and honourably strives, at this season, to be looking at her best. She forgets that these only had men in their entourage, noblemen and knights and esquires—witness all the pretty pictures by Sandro Botticelli *et al.* The only lady present was the Virgin; no other females, but of course lots of ogling pages. Isobel's daughter, Charlotte, looks like an ogling page. She was once married to Hamilton Glott.'

The ouzo and its predecessors were making Burgo inconsequent. To set him back on course I said, 'I know that very well, Burgo; Hamilton, as you may recall, is my publicity agent, and it was he that introduced me to Charlotte, while she was still his wife. As I told you at the time, I very much fancied her, but when she had done with Hamilton she appeared to prefer Peter Jenkins to myself.'

'Jenkins. The pink parrot of the *Manchester Guardian.* Charlotte says that he was the first man that ever made her come. I was brought up with Charlotte, you know. *We* did not come. We played together innocently in infancy and pre-pubescence. Not in pubescence, when presumably we might have come, for by that time I had been sent away to school.' He took a gulp of ouzo. 'But school is another story. Where was I before I digressed?'

'You were at your home at Ham Spray, with Ralph and Frances and Isobel, who are there celebrating Christmas.'

'Ah. My apologies. You hardly know them really. Let me explain them all.'

He gazed up at a yellow balloon which had stopped ascending and was hovering, at a height of a hundred yards, over our café.

'O yellow star of Bethlehem,' said Burgo, and tinkled his glass with a teaspoon which the previous incumbents had left lying about. 'Perhaps I am the Christ-child, waiting for the three Kings, who will not conceivably allow Isobel, even with her special hairdo, to follow in their wake, but might very well accept Charlotte as an honorary and delectable pageboy; though Charlotte will have none of them, Kings or no, as she is exclusively obsessed, just now, with Jenkers' stubby little stalk.' He tinkled so impatiently that the glass broke. This mishap restored Burgo's concentration. 'But do not permit me to stray any more,' he said, as I shook my head to warn away the approaching waiter. 'I shall now my tale unfold, as I have promised, of Frances and Ralph and Isobel and Charlotte, though not much of it concerns Isobel, except in so far as she was Charlotte's mother.

'My father, Ralph Partridge was an oarsman and a warrior, who gloried in the rank of major and won a Military Cross in the war of 1914. With this golden if philistine youth, Lytton Strachey (no less) fell in love; but meanwhile my father pined for cruel Carrington, the painter, who, in her turn, was sick with desire for bearded Strachey. Death gathered Carrington; time and chance turned Lytton Strachey to other infatuations; and my father was left free for my mother, Frances, who taught him socialism, pacifism, Luddism, and literature. He lived at Ham Spray, writing one article a week for the *New Statesman*, in the intervals of gambling cleverly for quick and marginal returns on the Stock Exchange. From these activities he took leisure to make long tours through Europe with my mother and Gerald Brenan, tours during which they deplored the condition of the peasantry as seen through the windows of their motor car and discussed what other people ought to be doing about it over dinner in the best hotel. Then I was born, a potential nuisance, but luckily there were, in those days, plenty of Spock-trained nannies with whom I could be safely deposited for liberal and non-repressive potty-training and later, of course, a tempting choice of crank schools to which I could be sent whenever I became annoying or superfluous.

'Although the 1939 war rather cramped my parents' style, they lived pretty comfortably at Ham Spray, making amusing jokes at the expense of those who were risking life or ghastly trauma to defend them, and contriving ever more ingenious schemes to "evacuate" myself to a safe distance from Hungerford. Meanwhile, their friends John and Isobel Strachey, not to be confused with lanky Lytton, had produced little Charlotte, with whom I played unhappily through the long, hot summers. My trouble was that I was convinced that nobody loved me, and this for the best of reasons: I was uniquely unlovable. At the age of nine I dug a large hole and sent Charlotte, in whose house I was staying, to fetch her parents to admire it. "What a lovely hole, Burgo," drawled Isobel; "whatever is it *for*?" "To put Ralph and Frances in," I replied. For they always made me call them "Ralph" and "Frances", though I longed to call them "Mummy" and "Daddy" like an ordinary child: one more reason why I was so horrible. On this particular occasion, John Strachey, who was busy thinking of himself, ignored my remark while Isobel laughed at it. Since they were meant to be outraged, their respective indifference and merriment infuriated me so much that I hit Charlotte with the blade of my shovel and laid her forehead open...after which, of course, I had to be sent home where, in consequence, I was loved less than ever.

'When I grew up,' said Burgo, 'I had large warts all over my body, greasy black hair, the complexion of an ill-nourished half-caste, and exceedingly smelly feet. Only one woman ever found me attractive, and she had an erectile clitoris, which I adored but dared not caress, in case she thought I was a latent homosexual. I developed a furtive manner; I slobbered when I smoked, which my nerves compelled me to do incessantly; I walked like Baron Frankenstein's monster at his first attempt; Charlotte called me "Caliban". Anyone who saw me became immediately hostile and suspicious: Englishmen thought I was a Jew; Jews thought I was an Arab; Arabs thought I was an Indian, Hindu of course; Hindus thought I was an Untouchable; Untouchables thought I was an Unseeable; Unseeables thought I was a tax-gatherer or a money-lender; money-lenders thought—indeed very well knew—that I was a natural and gutless gull, and charged me excessive interest.'

'Surely your parents didn't keep you so short that you had to go to the money-lenders?'

'No. They put me in charge of my own money affairs at the age of sixteen, making very liberal arrangements—to alleviate their guilt. But every now and then I overspent my income, and no bank manager would give me an overdraft of more than twopence, although I had ample security, because they thought I looked like a terrorist.' (As indeed the British Patrols thought when we later visited Cyprus.) 'So I had to go to the money-lenders,' Burgo continued, 'who charged me sixty per cent, instead of the usual fifty.'

'But sixty per cent is illegal.'

'I was a Lesser Breed without the law, as Kipling has it, and so forfeited its protection. Nobody gave me credit even when I did something worthwhile. I wrote a lovingly researched book about orgies*, but everyone said its success was due to Charlotte because she persuaded Hamilton Glott (to whom, by this time, she was married) to publicise it, and to my parents because they persuaded their friends Cyril Connolly and Raymond Mortimer to review it; and to Gerald Brenan because he persuaded Heywood Hill to stack a special table with it and display blown-up copies of Cyril's review all over his shop. He even conned Evelyn Waugh into buying a copy, which Waugh accidentally left in White's, where it was found by Bob Boothby ... who was excited by one of the pictures and told Maurice Bowra who told John Sparrow who told Noël Annan, thus winning the book a high reputation, which my father said was a fluke. I was, my father said, a wretchedly bad writer, ignorant, superficial, clumsy and jejune. I wish the Germans had shot him in the Great War.'

'Then you wouldn't be here now.'

'I shouldn't care.'

'I should,' I said, meaning it.

I loved Burgo; not physically, for no one, except the lady with the erectile clitoris, ever did that; but with my heart. All the same, I laughed as loudly as everyone else at the manner of his early death. He was talking to Charlotte on the telephone. Charlotte was inviting herself and Jenkins, for whom she had now left Glott, to a drink at Burgo's house in Cadogan Square. 'You're sure it's not a bore, Burgo,' Charlotte wheedled. 'Oh no,' said Burgo, and dropped dead of a ruptured aorta. Hence the story, widely current for some years, that Charlotte had bored Burgo to death over the telephone. The story was dropped after Charlotte became ill of some devilish

*A History of Orgies by Burgo Partridge. Published 1959 by Anthony Blond. Republished 2002 by Prion Books, London.

disease of the blood. She had to have her beautiful blonde hair cut off; so that she had a stubbly pate and (with the drug they gave her) bulbous cheeks. A few weeks before she died she said to some of us at dinner, 'If there's anything you want to do, do it now, while you're still here. That's what I'm still here to tell you.' Glott, with whom she had long been reconciled, took her to Kew just before she died. 'I never came with you,' she said. 'I know,' said Glott. 'I came with Peter; but after a while I didn't. I was going to try with Simon; but then my illness happened.' I wish I had had the chance to be Charlotte's lover. I always longed to kiss the little silver cunt at the fork of the fourth-former's thighs. (I once saw this ensemble, when we were bathing naked at Ham Spray.) I dream about and sometimes masturbate about it, even now.

But I must go back to Burgo, half-drunk in the Zappeion Gardens. Together we enjoyed Athens very much that Christmas of 1959 particularly, and perversely, the Roman remains rather than the Greek. We walked up Lycabettos one afternoon and talked of the disgusting food in Athens and of my early sexual experiences at my prep. school. Burgo would not believe that it is possible to come (the feeling without the emission) before one reaches puberty. At last I convinced him, describing the way in which my little prick had 'juddered'. He was intrigued, though not in the least interested in little boys, and then became jealous: 'Why didn't I come before puberty?' he said crossly. 'Think what I've missed, and missed forever*.'

---

*Had Burgo lived to have an operation for the prostate, he could have experienced precisely that type of orgasm—far more exciting (*crede experto*) than the usual adult performance. In this connection, see Ludovic Kennedy's account in *On My Way to the Club*.

After this typical instance of Burgo's resentment, we had Turkish coffee at a stall about halfway up Lycabettos—in those days you were forbidden to go further because of a military installation of some kind—and then walked down again. As we walked, we looked down on the Arch of Hadrian, beyond the Zappeion Gardens, and the Tower of the Winds away to the West, while Burgo made some more spiteful but oddly loving jokes about his father and mother. The sun shone in the pale-blue sky, and when we came to the Plateia Syntagmatos we watched some morose cadets, whose leave was to end on the morrow, stroll slowly to and fro with their hands resting on the hilts of their daggers. I gazed up, as I have always loved to ever since, at the balloons which dwindled and then, with a final flicker, vanished and became one with God who is the Good and the Beautiful, so Plato and his disciples tell us.

All that is what I was looking for in Athens in 1984, and no longer found.

The Morea

from
Is There Anybody There? Said the Traveller

I have remarked already that I was, at the period of the Glenconner luncheon, 'mildly' infatuated with Hamish. I have never quite known why. Physically he was no great catch, for while he had a handsome enough face and a well-found torso, his thighs were mean and his calves spindly – as Hamilton often used to observe when he wished to annoy him, adding that a good stint of National Service, for which he had been five years too young, might have remedied these faults and those of his character as well. The latter included conceit of his carnal attractions and intellectual attainments (mediocre); greed for flattery; covert resentment and unremitting adulation of the rich; spiteful rejection of failed or fallen friends, unless kudos was to be had, in carefully selected cases, by appearing to succour them; murderous jealousy of sexual, social, or artistic success; profligacy with Hamilton's money when Hamilton had it and extortion when he hadn't; treachery and falsehood; and the conviction that his judgements in all spheres were infallible. On the other hand, there were a few things to be said for his credit—a nice turn of phrase; his affable company during journeys or parties of pleasure, provided always that he was having absolutely his own way; his subtle talents as a chef—but not nearly enough to account for my infatuation once the debit column has been summed. How, then—*come, Muse, and tell* – did this infatuation first get a grip on me? A kindly touch early on, a pretty, passing caress of Cupid (as in the beginning I told myself it was), but cruel and enduring as the months passed, and then the seasons, and then the years.

It all started – *come, Muse, and sing a song of love in idleness* – in the Morea, more usually called the Peloponnese, a year or so before the gathering at Opsiopoulos which I have just described. In the autumn of 1971 Hamilton had been summoned back from his holiday in Corcyra a fortnight before his time; and Hamish, who was sick of housekeeping, proposed to me and his friend Alexis (one of Hamish's many heterosexual admirers) that we should leave Opsiopoulos and the Island of the Phaeacians and 'go on a tripette'.

So on a tripette we went. *Come, baneful Muse, and tell your tale of folly.* First we drove to Athens, and after paying swift duty to the Acropolis and the National Museum, we set off for Delphi, which Hamish was too restless to pause and inspect, being by now, like the nobleman in Lucretius' poem, obsessed with movement for movement's sake, thinking thus to outrun boredom and even Death. We crossed the Gulf of Corinth on a car ferry, turned east for Nauplion, were allowed by Hamish to spend half an hour en route at Tiryns but not to make the brief diversions necessary to visit Mycenae or Epidauros and, after a night at Nauplion, headed over the mountains for Black Sparta. Here Hamish became easier, for whatever reason, and let us pause to consider our journey and its stages with some care.

It was eventually decided that we should spend the coming night in Sparta, a dull rectangular conurbation, marvellously sited, however, almost at the foot of the range of Taygetus or Taïygetos and having a passable, Class A, Xenia. The next morning there would be a visit to the museum and the faintly rude Roman mosaics, then to the modest and even furtive remains of Lakedaimon, ancient Sparta.

From Lakedaimon we would proceed west to Mistra (*Come, Muse, to wake the first sweet memories of desire*), where we would patronise the spectacular assembly of Byzantine churches and despots' palaces, which climb the long, steep slope towards the Frankish castle of William de Villehardouin, the crown of the city but not of the mountain; for this surges far and high, ever farther and higher, to the summit of Taïygetos, range of Artemis the Huntress of the Peak—its lower regions having been much favoured, once upon a time, for the disposal of unwanted Spartan infants, the maimed and the female. The road across this range we would follow, over the ridge, down through the Vale of Messene and on to Kalamata by the shore of the Messenian Gulf, then famous for its fish, which these days would probably poison you on sight. Then we would motor west, across the westernmost prong at the bottom of the Morea, to Navarino, otherwise Homer's Sandy Pylos—more or less; we would see old Nestor's Palace just across the bay, and spend the night at the xenia—regrettably only Class Gamma or C—that had been named for him. The next day it would be heigh boys for the North; for Elis of the Pines; for the temple of Bassai; and Olympia of the runners, the wrestlers and the long-maned horses; then into Arcadia, which was once frequented, so the poet said, not only by nymphs and their shepherds, but also by Death. For it was He who had announced, '*Atque ego in Arcadia sum*'—'I, too, am in Arcadia.'

Our progress went much in the manner proposed until we were walking up the hill at Mistra. I was grinding on about Gemistos Plethon, the Platonist, who had lived there for much of the first half of the fifteenth century.

'So famous were his lectures,' I pontificated, 'that in 1423 they were attended by the learned Grecian, Bessarion, who was particularly impressed by —'

'—What is a Grecian, please?' said peaches-and-cream, but utterly masculine, Alexis.

'A Scholar of Greek,' I said grandly.

'Talking of Scholars of Greek,' said Hamish, 'do I not remember that your chum Paddy Leigh Fermor lives not far from here?'

'He is an acquaintance, alas, rather than a chum,' I said. 'About ten years ago I was invited with a party to a castle he was living in near Rome. A few months later Burgo Partridge and I had lunch with him in London before we went to Crete in 1959. He seemed to think we should enjoy tramping round the island with knapsacks and gave us a letter of introduction, in fluent and stylish modern Greek, to all the experts on sleeping in caves, and the concomitant horrors, whom he'd known during the war.'

'If you went to his castle *and* had lunch with him in London, you must know him well enough to call on him now. In fact it would be very impolite of you *not* to call on him now.'

'I haven't seen him for more than a decade. He lives a long distance down the Mani. Right out of our way.'

'If you telephone him,' persisted Hamish, 'he might invite us for the night. We could simply turn left for the Mani in Kalamata, instead of right for Pylos, and get there well before dark.'

I began to spell it all out. Paddy Leigh Fermor, I said, lived at Kardomili which, though admittedly less than half-way down the coast of the Mani, was only to be reached by a winding and treacherous road. If, therefore, Paddy did not ask us to stay the night, we should have a weary and perilous drive in the pitch dark, back up the Mani and then west to Navarino/Pylos – where we would almost certainly arrive too late for dinner. Since Paddy's house at Kardomili was still building, I went on, it would be difficult for him to lodge us, even if he wanted to, and why should he? The chances of our having to make a nasty, noctivagant course of some fifty miles from Kardomili to Navarino were therefore heavily odds on. These objections were compounded, I perorated, by my not knowing Paddy's telephone number, if indeed he was so ill-advised as to have a telephone, and by our being unable, therefore, to do him the courtesy of asking his permission before obtruding ourselves upon his peace.

But Hamish was implacable. *Come, Muse, and chant a lay of Ate, the dark goddess, who makes crooked the will of man.* As an habitual and hardened tuft-hunter, he had scented the propinquity of a rare and delectable tuft. For a start, he said, however disagreeable the driving, he himself would be doing it. He had heard, 'from somebody who knew the area', that the roads were now much improved (with an eye to vamping the amenities for vulgar tourism) as far down the Mani as Areopolis, and Kardomili was indisputably this side of that. Grecians and Philhellenes were renowned, he pursued, for their ample hospitality, however suddenly it might be required of them and however limited the space at their disposal, and the last thing they desired or expected was to be warned by telephone.

'So there, Simon, is an answer to all your objections.'

'Except in this respect – that such an incursion would be a hideous breach of good manners.'

'Of conventional good manners, perhaps. But men like Leigh Fermor have little time for hypocritical conventions. If you have been as intimate with him as you claim – '

'— I never claimed intimacy with him.'

'If you have been in his company as often as you have told us, it is your duty, now that you are passing so close to him in a strange country, to seek him out.'

'The country is not strange to him,' I said. 'He requires no news of England, no attention from marauding Englishmen. He came here specifically to avoid such ghastly disruptions.'

But Hamish was adamant. When we had driven over Taïygetos and come, at about tea-time, to Kalamata, he simply set his wilful face and took the turning to the Mani and Kardomili. Sweet, drowsy Alexis, who was so vague that he never knew where he was and so laid back that he didn't in the least care where he was going, appeared hardly to notice. As for myself, I knew that Hamish, when in a fit of snobbery, was impossible to deter. He had made up his mind that he was going to add Leigh Fermor to his frame of reference and tittle-tattle, and there was an end of it. We drove in silence under the Castle of Zarnaba, round and round the coastal hills as the evening crept over them, slowly making ground to the South.

At the southern tip of the Mani lies Cape Tainaros or Taenarum (Matapan); one entrance, so they say, to the world of the shadows of the dead. Devoutly I wished that that was our destination, that we could just go bumping through Kardomili without a pause, pass Areopolis and brave the road, no doubt even viler than this one, to the gates of Black Death—anything rather than disturb poor Paddy on the strength of my two or three brief meetings with him and a tenuous correspondence. But there was no escape. Hamish, like the hound of heaven, would hunt down Leigh Fermor, dragging the heedless Alexis – one more face to be fed, one more body to accommodate – and my own dismally embarrassed self behind him.

By now, as Homer has it, all the ways were dark. 'This is Kardomili,' murmured Hamish as we rattled into a benighted village that was unlit, unsigned, unnamed, indistinguishable from a dozen such through which we had passed. Hamish was, of course, right. He then discovered the only human being who was abroad in the whole peninsula, uttered a few words in formal but very clear Greek, and received back a low, demotic volley. He had a talent for languages and could have made a fortune in tips as doorkeeper to Babel.

'Paddy's house' – 'Paddy' already? – 'is half a mile further on,' he now told us, 'and one third of a mile out of the village. The house itself is almost on the sea, a furlong from the road. There is no drive, but there is a narrow path, which leads from the first bend beyond the village, over a kind of heath, to some half-finished steps which mount to a terrace.' And so it was. Hamish parked tidily and safely beyond the bend and well off the track. He examined the stone wall to the right of the track; showed us where to climb over it; found the narrow path – about six inches narrow – led us along it with the accuracy and brio of Sir John Moore leading the Light Division; anticipated the stone steps; halted the party under his command; called me forward from the rear; propelled me up the brief flight, ahead of himself and Alexis, on to the terrace.

'Now do your stuff with Paddy,' he said. 'Paddy' again.

All this time I had been judging Paddy, as I tended to judge everybody in those days, by myself: He would receive us with bare civility, I thought; offer us a drink in a tone which, like the Latin particle *num*, expected or certainly hoped for the answer 'No'; demonstrate with a gesture that he was still 'only camping' in the place himself, and helpfully opine that the hours of dinner in the distant Greek hostelries available to us were generous (as well they might be, since all food in Greek restaurants has been suppurating in lukewarm cauldrons for days or even weeks), but not sempiternal. Some such sequence of muted greeting, specious denial of resources, and smooth but swift dismissal – the swifter the better, thought I, for then there would be less time during which I must endure the shame that was already flooding my thighs and lower buttocks with crural sweat – some such formula of reluctant hail and brisk farewell I was now expecting.

The event was very different. As we walked uncertainly along the terrace, which was lit only by a storm lantern hissing on a low table, Paddy came nervously out of the house by a door at the far end, looked at us with puzzlement rather than resentment, and said: 'Simon. How nice to see you after all this time. These are your friends?'

He shook hands with me, then with Hamish and Alexis – who had, of course, no idea whatever of who or what he was; he settled us all on crude but comfortable chairs, which were ranged against the wall, did not ask us what we would like to drink but fetched retsina in a two-handed clutch of half-litre taverna pannikins, saying 'No proper jugs yet', poured for all, and raised his tumbler.

'Χαιρετε,' he said: 'be welcome to my house.'

He then told us of the Mani; its history of feuds and famines; of the pirates who had infested its coast through the centuries; of the indifference of Byzantine emperors towards the place and its people, and the love of the harsh hills borne by the Greek King Otho, who built a modest villa by the harbour of Limenaion, just north of Areopolis. He told us a legend of Cape Tainaros, one of which I had never heard, which asserts that the dead emerge from the cave there on the last night of every thousand years and fly across the sea to Cytherea, the island of Aphrodite, where they are granted real bodies with which to make love to whomsoever they choose for the single hour between eleven pm and midnight, after which they immediately revert to being shadows and return to their accustomed domicile as the last stroke of twelve ushers in the New Year, the New Century, the New Millennium.

'Of course,' Paddy expounded, 'the first time this rare anniversary occurred in the Christian Era was the year 1000 AD. The Christians of Cytherea, who knew of the legend from pagan record, were in a terrible taking lest they be seduced or raped by these spirits made flesh – presumably by the enchantment of Aphrodite and not by the authority of the church – and locked and triple-barred themselves into their houses, stopping up all apertures with boards secured by clay. The next day, the Bishop of Cytherea, who had heroically remained outside armed with Cross and crozier in order to exorcise any ghosts that might appear before they changed from larval to carnal and were capable of lustful outrage - the

Bishop, I say, reported that no revenants at all had turned up; and it was therefore assumed that Aphrodite had lost her powers since the accession of Christ the King and that there would be no further infernal and amorous invaders—who were not, in any case, due to come again for another thousand years. Next New Year's Eve, therefore, they all carried on in their usual fashion with religious and vinous excess – only to be caught unawares and molested in multitudes by swarms of horny cadavers, who had relations, as the journalists say, with just about every human being on the island between eleven of the clock and the Cinderella hour. What had gone wrong was that the Cytherans had made the stupid and vulgar error of thinking that the new millennium started and the old ended at the beginning of 1000; whereas, of course, they only start and end with the arrival of 1001, when the year 1000, the last of the old millennium, is finally seen out. So the Cytherans had shut themselves up like nuns a year too early and were wandering about in the open, totally vulnerable, when the crunch came. One sometimes wonders whether the archon (Mayor) or whoever had not purposely misled them.

'In any event, followed the most horrible trouble of every kind. What was to be done about women who had been impregnated by the visitants? Or about the babies they would bear nine months later? The dead, it appears, do not bother with condoms or *coitus interruptus* on the millennial spree. To make things worse, there was a lot of mischief from old men and women. These, having not had any sexual entertainment for many years, had been accosted by the undead, who had too little time to discriminate, and reawakened by their enthusiastic attentions. So the old now gave great offence by copulating openly with their coevals (being thoroughly overexcited by the discovery that they were up to it after all, and being in any case too old to care about appearances) and, even worse, by importuning their far more appetising juniors – who were hard put to it to fend the old pests off...or, in some cases, developed gerontophiliac tastes and techniques which inflamed the already sizzling scandal.

'As the Greeks are notorious for never learning from their own history,' Paddy pursued, 'for look how they persist in selling their few remaining trees, despite the desolation thus created by their feckless forefathers, it is to be feared that the inhabitants of Cytherea will fall into precisely the same error at the onset of the years 2000 and 2001, taking precautions on the former occasion and exposing themselves on the latter. Though of course they may just get the dates right this time, as the affair will probably, *pace* the Church, be hyped as a tourist attraction.'

Of this and other matters Paddy discoursed, beguiling us as we sat and drank lime-like retsina on his terrace in the moonless and starless night. After passing from the tale of the tumescent Tainarians, he gave some account of other entrances to the underworld, most notably that at the sanctuary of Persephone at Ephyra, with its brilliantly equipped Necromanteion and splendid view of the Acherousian Lake; and then remarked, 'I fear lest it grows late. I have but two slices of bread, and one and a half unattractive fishes. Even if one among us had miraculous powers, we would hardly wish the amount of such fare increased. But young men like you surely have sleeping bags or comparable equipment. If you wish, you may sleep on this terrace, "under the wide and starry sky". Correction: no stars. Perhaps they will emerge later.'

'I think,' said Alexis, who occasionally showed

unsuspected awareness, 'that we had best be on the road. Goodnight, sir, and thank you for your marvellous stories.'

'I shall see you along the path,' said Paddy: 'possibly you are prudent: there will be no breakfast either.'

As we trailed along in Indian file, Paddy laughed gleefully and said, ' "The night is hellish dark", to quote a character from *Mister Sponge's Sporting Tour*, but does not, alas, "smell of cheese" for our dinner, as it did in Surtees. Does anyone read Surtees now?'

'I do,' said Alexis, 'he makes me laugh.'

Hamish and I were so amazed by the intelligence that Alexis had read anything that we were stunned into silence.

When Alexis evinced no further information or lit. crit., Paddy said, 'I remember Maurice Bowra's saying that the young should be encouraged to read Surtees in place of George Eliot: Surtees would teach them about the callous, bilking, squalid nature of man as it really was, whereas George Eliot gave out an unhealthy air of moral aspiration.

'Poor Maurice,' I said: 'now that he's had that stroke, he'd be better dead.'

'Whatever do you mean?' said Paddy. 'Better dead? Maurice would never wish that. There never was a man more full of life.'

'What sort of life can he possibly have now?' I said. 'From the learned and witty Warden of Wadham he has declined into a state of geriatric ghastliness. Surely better dead.'

'I don't think Maurice would thank you for saying so,' Paddy said. 'He was always a "*dum spiro, spero*" man. "While there's life, there's hope." If you went to prison, the first thing you'd know was that Maurice was there passing fivers through the bars to rehabilitate you after your release.'

'But according to Alan Pryce-Jones,' I said – an odious piece of name-dropping – 'when you *were* released and rehabilitated, you'd better not be too happy or successful if you wished to stay in Maurice's good books. He was kindness itself to failure, implacably resentful of success. When an old friend of his was knighted, Maurice interrupted the bearer of the news with a great bellow of "Stop. *Stop*. I cannot bear THE PAIN."'

'What has this to do with Maurice's illness?' said Paddy coolly.

'Simply this: he was a great one for bringing comfort to others on their deathbeds, but was not too liberal with his congratulations if they recovered—and certainly not if they wrote a distinguished and best-selling book of their thoughts while in the valley of the shadow and married a beautiful heiress on the strength of it. This raises some interesting questions about his attitude to himself now that he is dying—or at least in serious decline. If the survival and triumph of others is so irritating to him, he must realise, as a man of sense and intellect, that his own recovery might cause grave displeasure among his acquaintance.'

'Yes, he might realise that,' conceded Paddy, 'and make a magnificent Bowra joke about it.'

Conscious that I was perversely indulging in malice and even in malignance—probably, to be fair, because of my empty stomach—I nevertheless went banging on.

'Alan Pryce-Jones says', I said as we reached the road and our car, 'that in Bowra's bottom drawer there are a whole lot of embarrassing sub-Housmanesque verses about boys and what he calls striplings. Pity the literary executor, Alan says, having to sort that lot out.'

'I'd give anything to be Maurice's literary executor,' Paddy said. 'I know those critical books are pretty damn boring, but think of all those gorgeous parodies. Lots of them have been shown to nobody at all, you know, and if those are up to the standard of the ones we have read— what a Lucullan banquet! There's that heavenly one of Hardy's verses about the sudden death of his first wife, in *Poems 1912-13*.

> 'O how you went so fast,
> Without any palaver:
> I found when I spent at last
> It was all over your cadaver.'

'Marvellous stuff,' concluded Paddy. 'One hopes there are many more like that still to be sifted.'

'What a splendid fellow,' said Alexis, as we drove north through Kardomili for Kalamata and Pylos.

'You were pretty sour just at the end,' said Hamish to me.

'I'm sorry my behaviour didn't meet with your approval. I thought that you were getting rather restless—no doubt because you weren't the centre of attention.'

'Girls, girls, girls,' said the peacemaker Alexis.

Although it seemed like the middle of the night when we arrived in Pylos/Navarino, it was not much past nine. But the Nestor was full. We drove down to the southern end of the bay, to the Castello. By this time a gibbous moon had sidled through the clouds; one could see an amusing 'Hammer Productions' castle on the slope above the hotel, and there was a notice outside announcing that dinner was served until ten o'clock and that Diners' Club cards were accepted. Spirits rose. Spirits rose still further when we inspected our rooms, all of which had 'magic casements, opening on the foam' of the Bay of Navarino. Spirits fell again when the foam immediately began to stink of human and industrial excreta, and when it became abundantly apparent that the beds were damp.

'Leigh Fermor wouldn't mind a little thing like that,' I said despondently; 'he'd have his sleeping bag anyway.'

'He'd despise the lot of us,' said Alexis, 'as silly little cissies whining about a spot of wet on the bed.'

'Mine is like a swamp,' said Hamish; 'and there are *animiculae* in it.'

'Serves you right,' I sniffed. 'If you hadn't made us go all the way down to Kardomili, we'd have arrived here in time to get into the Nestor.'

'How do you know the beds aren't damp in the Nestor?'

'Because the Nestor's a government xenia, and everything is properly done in such places.'

'The last time I stayed in a xenia,' said Alexis, 'that very grand one in the citadel of Arta, I found a used Tampax on the top of the wardrobe.'

'What were you doing, looking at the top of the wardrobe?'

'I was depositing a used French letter, as there was no wastepaper basket. Come along, chums: dinner.'

There was none at the Castello. We pointed at the notice. The manager, who had two days' growth of diseased fungus on his chin, shrugged and pouted in imbecile peasant fashion and pointed back up the bay towards the Nestor. Dinner was just over at the Nestor; but they could give us fruit and feta, the goat cheese which in those days made one's teeth squeal. We were directed to a restaurant in the square by the harbour. It was called the Clytemnestra, turned out to be Class Theta, and offered two pots of pasta so pale and swollen with lying in bilge water that one was put in mind of Mrs Hardy's corpse in Bowra's parody. We went back to the Nestor. It was locked. We banged on the door. The waiter stuck his head out of an upper window and said he hoped we had dined well at the Clytemnestra.

'As you know,' said Hamish as we trudged by the scummy waters to the Castello, 'a lot of what Leigh Fermor was telling us came straight out of his book on the Mani. He might have been reciting a prepared piece.'

'The story of the randy spooks of Tainaros wasn't in his book on the Mani,' I said.

'That was a special treat,' said Hamish, 'to make up for the lack of food. I wonder if he was lying about that?'

'I shouldn't blame him if he was. I told you we shouldn't just barge in on him like that.'

'He couldn't have thought much of you,' said Hamish, 'to turn you and your friends away hungry. You know, I think he must have got your number all those years ago when you and Burgo Partridge were having lunch with him and he was telling you what a wonderful time you could have sleeping out in Crete. I bet you put on that snooty, fruity look of yours, as if to say, "Catch me sleeping out with a load of smelly Cretans." I bet you did, and he noticed, and he thought, "Raven is a snobby soppy CUNT if ever I saw one", and that's why he couldn't be bothered to feed us.'

And so to Acherusian bed.

The Castello did not accept my Diners' card in settlement of the bill. When we pointed to the DINERS' sign, the manager prised some filth out of his fungus, rolled it into a ball, and made an obscene gesture with it.

Nestor's palace at ancient Pylos was the most boring thing out: just a plan made with stones in the turf.

'This must have been where Telemachos slept,' I said, trying to make the show go with a bit of a swing, 'on the porch. Listening to the waves from the many-sounding sea.'

'I expect he just had a wank,' said Hamish, 'all over those purple coverlets which Homer is always going on about.'

'Like what happened to Mrs Hardy,' said Alexis.

Her fate seemed to have caught everyone's imagination.

'I've never known worse value for ten drachmae,' said Hamish as we drove on towards the town of Khora, where there was a museum devoted to finds on the site of the palace: 'I vote we give the museum a miss.'

'No,' said Alexis firmly: 'we said we'd go there, and we must stick to our plan.'

Oh, Alexis. His insistence made one happy day and thirteen dismal years.

In the museum at Khora were swords and cups, palatial pottery and fragments of fresco which made one understand what an exciting and seductive place Nestor's palace would have been to live in; with its long view of the sea and the curving beach, on to which, before the time of the classical harbour, brilliant and distinguished guests would disembark, pulling their ship up over the whistling sand, to be feasted and filled with wine, there and then on the beach itself as like as not. After which they would sing, on request, for their supper, telling their tall tales of Troy and Crete, and Aulis and old Nile. The jewels and wine-jars in the little museum conjured such a scene for us, there among the grimy glass cases and the hawking curators; and suddenly Hamish said what Nestor had once said as he handed the cup to a newly come guest.

' "Ευχεονυν, ω ςεινε. . . Pray now, stranger, to the

Lord Poseidon, for his is the feast whereon you have chanced in coming hither ... δοσ και του τω επειτχ ... then give thy friend also the cup, the cup of honey-sweet wine.'" He mimed the passing of a wine-cup from himself to me.

Whereupon ∝τη (até), Infatuation, bane of mortal man, sent for his affliction by the gods that are forever, entered my soul and set me to loving Hamish. I owe Alexis no thanks, after all, for bringing us into the museum that morning. *Say, Muse, what manner of man was my beloved*: a more lethal object of love, or even affection, than Hamish would be impossible to conceive.

However this was not, for the time being, apparent. The next few hours passed in a light, bright air of enchantment, as we drove up what was little better than a goat-path from the coast through Phigaleia – an appropriate place, as the ancient inhabitants and, for all I know, the modern, have a reputation for witchcraft – and on to the temple of Bassai, which Pausanias tells us was built in gratitude to Apollo for lifting a local plague.

He did not lift my plague.

A lunch of no character, food in any case now a matter of indifference, at Andritseina in an unremarkable xenia; then on to Karyteina, where is the thirteenth-century castle, with its faery turrets, of the Lord Geoffery de Bruyère, 'the best knight in all Romany', as Alfred Duggan tells us; the very pattern of Morean chivalry, a glutton for intrigue and adultery. We missed the way to Olympia as evening fell; but what cared I for that, so long as I was being driven by my own knight of the Morea, ever potent in my besotted eyes against dragons and the dark? In any event, we very soon found the road again and by six of the clock were entering the marble halls of the Old Railway Hotel (SPAP), where wispy, Jamesian ladies and gentlemen sat on wicker chairs and quizzed the trio of Hamish the demigod, Alexis the smiling faun, and their attendant and gawping pantaloon.

'Not a woman was allowed in the place,' I said to Alexis and Hamish the next morning as we walked round the gymnasia and temples of Olympia. 'No women, tradesmen, aliens or slaves were allowed inside the sacred precinct. The brothels and the eating-places and all the fun of the great fair were to be found over there, west of the river.'

'The Games were only for men?' said Alexis.

'Only for gentlemen. For a start, only gentlemen could afford to come here. It was a long and expensive journey from most parts of Greece. True, some cities subsidised competitors. But since no one except gentlemen would have been trained, no one except gentlemen received subsidies.'

'Some one once told me,' said Hamish, 'that they had mule cart races here. Not a very gentlemanly sport.'

'They didn't last long. They were considered to have neither antiquity nor dignity in their favour.'

'I see,' said Hamish. 'Pindar would not have approved. It was Pindar who wrote odes in honour of the winners?'

'Yes,' I said, much fancying my pithy style of calling up the past in front of two such, as I then supposed, sympathetic listeners. 'Odes which he was paid very handsomely to compose by posh families, when little Dio or little Telly had just won the junior wrestling, or by municipal sponsors who had, say, entered a chariot. The odes were commissioned on the understanding that they would contain much praise of the families or townships that were paying for them. In theory such praise was confined to legendary ancestors and aboriginal founders, but Pindar was not above accepting an extra twenty per cent to pop in a complimentary couplet about little Dio's daddy or some of the contemporary town councillors.'

'So Pindar,' said Alexis, 'was a sucker-up?'

'An arse-licker,' Hamish said.

'Also a remarkable poet,' I urged.

In silence we surveyed the massive platform on which stood – or rather sprawled – the Temple of Zeus, then walked along the remains of a colonnade to the western end of the stadium. It was a dank, ungracious day. The Pines of Elis on the hill above the precinct clothed the summit like a cowl; the pines in the precinct itself, black, sullen and absolutely still, dripped steadily. Not a day for love; a day for nagging or disillusion. I was only twenty-four hours gone in my folly, so of course nothing could disillusion me, yet; but even so, early ugly doubts could start squirming into the mind, if not the heart.

'Any competitor who cheated or took bribes could be publicly flogged,' I said, as we gazed at the dreary length of the stadium.

'What a pity,' said Alexis, 'that this regulation has been discarded from the modern Olympics.'

'Amateurs and gentlemen could be whipped in public?' said Hamish.

'Only if they disgraced their gentility.'

'Shall we go?'

'Why? There's no hurry,' said Alexis.

'I'm sick of all this rotting rubbish,' Hamish said. 'Greek Antiquity. "An old bitch gone in the teeth," Ezra Pound called it: "a few hundred battered statues". I'm sick of the reverence we are expected to lavish on it, just because it is old. Why can't we pay more attention to modern Greece, to modern problems in this country, modern pastimes? Living people, warm blood, quivering flesh? Here's Simon, spends half an hour a day, as he claims, reading Homer or Plato in the original —'

'—With the help of a crib,' I interposed, trying to draw off this bile, to soothe this facile protest that had come without warning or provocation.

'But you can't speak a word of the demotic, you never try. You make no effort at all to understand modern Greeks or what they say, or even what they write.'

'It's a matter of personal preference,' I said. 'I enjoy archaic and classical Greek literature—and *some* modern Greek literature: Cavafis, Kazantzakis —'

' —Only because Cavafis and Kazantzakis write about the same things, gods and goddesses and pretty little boys romping about,'—he gestured at the stadium—'the same things as all that classical crew. You don't give a damn for modern Greek political ideals or economics or social ethics —'

' — I like the classics,' I said, 'both Greek and Latin, because they are about the excitement, the charm and the transience of physical pleasure, and about the operations of time, chance and death. These are the great human themes. Why should I bother with the greed and trickery of modern Greek politicians and the squalid whores whom they take as their mistresses? If I want to read about that kind of thing, the classical authors have done it with ten times the style and wit of your demotic tabloids.'

'But the classical authors write – wrote – about the dead.'

'And where's the odds in that? The trashy lot now in power in Athens will be dead soon enough.'

'They are alive now. Their ideas and aspirations affect those that live here and now.'

'They don't affect me,' said Alexis. 'I never listen to any politicians, least of all the shower of shit here in the

Balkans. They desire power, and must therefore be contemptible as men. I value only independence.'

'And what happens,' I said, 'when the politicians' hankering for power interferes with your taste for independence?'

'Luckily we're English,' said Alexis. 'In England politicians aren't allowed to interfere with people's independence. Or not so's you'd notice.'

'Just you wait a while,' said Hamish. 'Until you get rich.'

'I shall never be rich,' said Alexis. 'I only want enough money to spend from day to day in minding my own business and amusements.'

'They'll get round to you in time,' said Hamish. 'You are - or soon will be if present trends continue— what Orwell's socialists in *Nineteen Eighty-Four* called a "thought criminal". Somebody who despises current political fads, even though he may keep quiet about it for the sake of peace. They're going to hate you worse than they hate anybody.'

'Because they can't touch him,' I said. 'Or not in England.'

'Not yet,' said Hamish. 'I dare say they're working on it.'

I was so much in agreement with his last two or three remarks that I forgot, for that day and many days, that this discussion had started with Hamish's petty and contrived complaints about the classical Greek past and those that love and study it.

Isherwood Gored

from
Bird of Ill Omen

' **I**f you like,' said the studio representative, 'we can send a girl over to the Beverly Hills Hotel to help you with the typing.'

'I think I can manage it myself.'

'You're sure now?'

'Oh yes.'

'Well, that's up to you. We thought you might like company. With a little persuasion and a drink or two, she'd probably go down on you.'

'It's very kind of you,' I said, 'but I think I'd better stick to the job myself.'

The studio representative laughed stridently down the telephone.

'Suit yourself, Si,' he said.

For the first time in my life I was in Hollywood, or thereabouts, trying to write a film script, or at any rate a treatment for one. The book that was to be filmed was Gore Vidal's *Burr*. I now rang up old chum, Howard.

'Gore there?' I asked.

'Yes. He's having his portrait done. Or rather, a

preliminary drawing. By Chris Isherwood's friend, Don. And Mistress Tynan is here too.'

'What does she want?'

'What does anyone want?' said Howard. 'Fame and fortune.'

'So since Gore's clearly a bit preoccupied, perhaps you can answer a question for me. The studio representative has offered to send me a girl to help with my typing. He says that "she might go down on me". What does that mean?'

'*Soixante-neuf* without the *neuf*. When is she coming?'

'She isn't. I declined.'

'Very prudent, I'd say,' said Howard, who enjoyed an Anglicism from time to time. 'Those girls are not for you.'

'Unhygienic?'

'Not physically. Mentally. Once they start they won't stop. They want to prove something.'

'What?'

'Difficult. Let's put it this way. I have a friend who comes around from time to time. He is taking a course in muscle building. He has an excellent degree from Yale, no less, in mathematics and physics, but all he can think about is muscle building. He wants to be a professional wrestler or a weight lifter. Yale has offered him an important teaching post with plenty of time for research. All he thinks about is staying here in California and lifting weights. When I ask him why, he says, "Because I'm sick". Asked to elucidate, he says that he wants to prove that he can do it. He knows he can do math and physics, you see, so there is no point in going on with them. He doesn't know yet whether he can become a pro wrestler and he wants to find out.'

'Why wrestling?' I said. 'Or weight lifting, come to that?'

'Because he was a skinny, weedy boy and everyone at Groton laughed at his drumstick arms and legs. So he has this obsession, to prove that he too can be like Joe Louis. Same with those girls from the studio pool. They were brought up real nice, most of them. So now they have to convince themselves that they can go down on a guy all day long. It means they're liberated – they think. Like those queens that go running and skipping into the naughty part of the park six times a day. *They* have to convince themselves not only that they're liberated but that they're still capable of doing it. Reassurance, that's what all these people want. And of course the more they get reassured the less convincing the reassurance. Mistress T. with her writing, or those studio girls with their gobbling, or my friend with his muscles, or those queens with their antics – they're all watching pots that take longer and longer to boil each time and finally will go dry before they do boil. It's called the law of diminishing returns. The only thing that doesn't diminish is the degree of mental sickness. What are *you* queer for? What's your obsession?'

'Peace and quiet,' I said.

'A people hater, eh? People hater, reader of books, onanist, gambler, lone drinker. Right?'

'Not far out,' I said.

'Solitary cathedral and museum crawler?'

'Yes. I thought I'd go to the Getty Memorial Museum. Since no one's coming here to go down on me, I shall have plenty of time to do my work and take the afternoon off.'

'The Getty Memorial Museum?' said Howard. 'All on your own? Boy oh boy oh boy, are you sick?'

In the gas-guzzling monster I had hired from Hertz, it

271

was impossible to turn the wireless off without turning off the whole engine. You could change stations but you couldn't have silence. If you turned the knob to where there wasn't a station – which was a labour of Hercules – you got a mournful bleeping noise that was even worse. So all the way along Sunset Boulevard to the Pacific Ocean I had compulsory music and chitchat, which were, however, interrupted every seven minutes or so by a far superior entertainment in the form of the local news. From this it appeared that an aphrodisiac artist was infesting the campuses of California, doping and having his wicked will with the more succulent students of either sex, leaving them bound and gagged, naked and, when male, priapic (from the residue of the julep), in witty places like the Principal's comfort station. What lifted him to a very high level of comedy, indeed of wizardry, was the incredible ubiquity of the fellow. In the first item I heard about him he had apparently just finished doing his number in a campus cafeteria near Los Angeles; seven minutes later it was announced that fresh and typical victims had just been discovered way up the West Coast. During my (admittedly lethargic) run between Beverly Hills Hotel and the sea, he had scored some nine or ten times, an average, say, of 1.29 victims every seven minutes, in venues which varied from Berkeley to San Clementis.

Pondering on this versatile exhibition, I turned into the entrance of the Getty Memorial Museum and was stopped at a barrier by a courteous but very firm black man. Had I, he enquired, fixed my reservation? No, I hadn't. Well, he explained, what I should have done was to request the bell captain of my hotel to ring up the museum and arrange a parking reservation. Normally, my gas guzzler and I would not be admitted without one.

However, since I was a guest in the country and since today there were plenty of spaces free, he himself would now allot me one. No, there was no charge.

I parked my vehicle on the numbered rectangle I had been appointed to (feeling like a captain who has finally docked an aircraft carrier) and wandered through an open court with many pools and fountains. I couldn't see whether it was intended to be late Roman or early Renaissance (the former, I fancy); either way I found it very agreeable. Acquaintances had told me it was vulgar, but when, I ask you, did a little vulgarity do any harm? At the bottom of the court and at the entrance of the museum proper, I was asked for my reservation number and waved on my way, still free of charge.

It had now been made clear to me, by the black man and a number of notices, that only those who arrived in cars or taxis were admitted to the museum at all. In certain cases, a certificate of travel by public transport (what there was of it) would be allowed as *bona fides* for admission; in no case whatever would a pedestrian be let in. It soon became clear to me why not. Whatever one might have thought of the exhibits (and, candidly, in 1979 they were mostly rather draggy sticks of furniture, as Howard might have said), there was no question about the sumptuous amenity. Restaurants, rest rooms, halls of repose…all invited the jaded sightseer to relaxation and indulgence with the dreamy magic of Spenser's Garden of Adonis or Bower of Bliss. The wonder was that anyone did any sightseeing at all. Now; clearly the place would have been a paradise for travel-worn hippies or whomever, a danger fully realised and guarded against by the administration on behalf of Mr Getty. No pedestrians here; I should just think not.

Reflecting on the uses of democracy, I relieved myself

among imperial pillars, ate an elaborate snack under titanic murals and then sat down to recuperate from these adventures in a *trompe-l'oeil* grove of tamarisk, where I might admire primly tripping nymphs and satyrs, and listen to a somewhat repetitious recorded nightingale.

Back in my aircraft carrier and reluctantly leaving the many-sounding seashore for the depths of LA, I was once more diverted by the antics of the Campus Comus, who had had several further triumphs while I was lolling in the Getty Museum. The trouble was, he was now losing his good taste and sense of humour. He was choosing elderly, ugly and sickly victims, and abandoning them in nasty situations, such as the municipal rubbish dump. Since incidents were now spread over hundreds of square miles, it had at last been deduced that there was either a copy-cat sequence in progress or else that there was a syndicate of widely separated members. That a rogue rapist was now committing vicious acts of cruelty was giving concern and spoiling the joke; and of course before I even got back to Beverly Hills, someone had overdone it and actually throttled a lady in her nineties, then chopped her up and been apprehended feeding her minced fesses to the tigers in his local zoo. A sad end, I thought, to a very passable jape: why are Americans always so excessive?

Soon after I was back in my room, Howard rang up. Apparently Gore had excited Don (Isherwood's portrait-making friend) with the news that I had known E. M. Forster at King's College, Cambridge. Don had departed bubbling with the intention of imparting this news to Christopher, who had 'adored' Morgan Forster.

'But Isherwood knew this perfectly well already,' I told

Howard. 'One of the very few times I ever met him was with Morgan Forster…who was giving us a dinner of spectacular sparseness in his rooms in King's.'

'I thought your college did that sort of thing rather well,' said Howard, who knew the proper form.

'It does. Morgan Forster didn't. He was the meanest man that ever drew breath.'

'Ah. That is Gore's view. He has decided to ask you and Christopher and Don to a little dinner to discuss the matter – and indeed assess Forster from several other aspects.'

'Aren't you coming?'

'No. I'm spending the evening with my muscle man. How are you getting on with *Burr*?'

'All right. The structure of the novel is rather complex.'

'The studio will like that. They think complexity of structure is a sign of important literature.'

'But do they want it in a script?'

'They will tell you they do. In fact what they want is something very simple and easy to follow but which keeps changing direction.'

'*Burr* is a story within a story. What shall I do about that?'

'Cut from one to the other,' said Howard, with the assurance of Gore himself.

'That means flashbacks,' I said wearily. 'Everyone hates flashbacks these days.'

'You sound a bit low. I told you that going to the Getty Museum would do you no good.'

'I had an interesting time in the car,' I said defensively, 'listening to radio reports about that man who's cruising around with the aphrodisiac.'

'There are dozens of them. There must be,' said

Howard.

'They've caught one of them.'

'That won't stop the rest. It's become a craze. Before you can say "Morgan Forster" everyone will be joining in. Californians are very imitative. The trouble is that it will create such a bad impression, coming at the time of Princess Margaret Rose's visit.'

'We don't call her that any more. Just Princess Margaret.'

'What a pity. The rose is the emblem of England.'

'Perhaps she doesn't want to be the emblem of England any more,' I said, 'now that it's so disgusting.'

'My word, you are low. Let's hope this dinner party will cheer you up.'

'Why should talking about E. M. Forster cheer anybody up?'

'You can talk about Princess Margaret Rose as well. Gore knows her, you know. He may be going to give a party for her. Do you know her?'

'No. But I was once quite near to her in King's chapel. She was with her parents in the Provost's box, and I was just below in a scholar's stall. I'll never forget it. I got so nervous that I had to go out to pee in the middle of the "Nunc Dimittis".'

'Was there comment on the platform?'

'No. Since I was a scholar I was a steward for the royal occasion. I just walked out with a purposeful look as if I was on steward's business, like ejecting someone that was being sick. If you act strictly in your official character no one ever notices you.'

'So Princess Margaret Rose didn't notice you?'

'Nor did the King; nor did the Queen; nor did the Provost, or I should have been told off afterwards.'

'But how do you know the Royals' – well done,

Howard – 'didn't see you? They would have been much too polite to tell you off afterwards. Did Morgan Forster come to the service?'

'No.'

'How rude.'

'He didn't approve of the Chapel and he didn't approve of Royalty.'

'Did he approve of you?'

'No. I tried to borrow money from him.'

'If he was as mean as you say, you must have known it wouldn't be any good.'

'I was desperate. I went round the college calling on everyone I knew. He was on staircase A, so he was the first. A very discouraging start: he said that he wasn't interested in me or my money.'

'Well, well, well,' said Howard. 'You'll have a lot to tell Christopher. Would you like to come to Gore's party for Princess Margaret Rose? You could ask whether she noticed when you walked out during the "Nunc Dimittis".'

'That was in 1951. She might not remember.'

'Well, think about it. The party, I mean. Meanwhile, this dinner for discussion of Forster is the day after tomorrow. Gore is taking you all to a Mexican restaurant where they have Tequila.'

'What's that?'

'A Mexican spirit. Malcolm Lowry, the *Underneath the Volcano* man, used to get sozzled on it. This restaurant you're going to uses it in long drinks. They taste delicious but they're lethal.'

'Thank you for the tip.'

'One more thing,' Howard said. 'Gore will pick you tip in a taxi at eight o'clock and will brief you about Christopher on the way. The thing is, you see, that

THE WORLD OF SIMON RAVEN

Christopher is very sensitive about being English. He can't forgive or forget all those nasty things which English people like Evelyn Waugh said about him and Auden at the beginning of the war.'

'What else did he expect?'

'You must try not to make any mention of it in front of Christopher. I'll leave Gore to explain the details.'

'The point is,' Gore told me as we drove to the Mexican restaurant in our taxi, 'that to Christopher and all that lot their decision to break with England and settle over here was the crisis of their lives. Never mind that it was forty years ago, that everyone else in the US and the UK has long forgotten the whole business, *they* think that the world is still discussing it as assiduously and as ferociously as in 1939. Therefore they are perpetually on edge, ever ready to take umbrage and make aggressive scenes. Somebody was talking about Aldous Huxley the other day, saying that it was possible to take two views of his mescalin caper: the first, that it was a valuable and courageous exploration of the frontier territories of the mind; and the second, that it was all a farrago of nonsense and set a very bad example to the young, who now swim in all kinds of dope on the specious excuse of spiritual experiment. Christopher, who was present, flew into a temper and said that this second opinion was simply a rehash of the British prejudice against Huxley: they'd never forgiven him for getting out of England just before the war, Christopher said, and they'd always belittled and ridiculed his splendid research with mescalin out of sheer spite. Then the chap who had made the original comment on Huxley said that he wasn't thinking about any of that, he was simply making a common-sense assessment of a kind which, sixteen years after Huxley's death, was very much called for. Whereupon Christopher muttered and gibbered and eventually went off in a sulk. In one word, he is still paranoid.'

'Tonight,' I said, 'we are to discuss E. M, Forster. I don't think any of that war-time bit need come into it at all.'

'But, dear boy, that's the whole point about Christopher. Everything, from Greek tragedy to the Quantum theory, is sooner or later reduced by him into terms of his own epic struggle – as he sees it – to break free from England, the land of the copybook headings, and escape to America, land of the equal and the free. Now, you've only met him once or twice, I gather, and not for very long: so you'll find he will not rest, or let you rest, until he can extract an opinion from you about that seminal period of his life and his migration to the US.'

'I take the Evelyn Waugh line,' I said, 'and have done ever since I read *Put Out More Flags* at the age of seventeen, when the war was just ending. Auden and Isherwood equal Parsnip and Pimpernel.'

'I.e., Auden and Isherwood were just a couple of fags who chickened out?'

'Right.'

'You'll oblige me by keeping this sentiment to yourself during this dinner. He is, after all, my guest.'

'That I appreciate and of course I shall suppress discourteous utterance in the matter. But what act do you want me to put on instead?'

'Just pretend you were too young to know about it.'

'If he thinks all this is as important as you say he does, he'll be pretty offended by that.'

'You can imply,' said Gore, 'that the whole thing is simply accepted by your contemporaries as a *fait accompli.*'

'If I've got you right, he wants to be applauded, not just accepted.'

'What view did Forster take?'

'Difficult to say. Any talk of the war made him feel inferior. He loathed any reminder that a lot of us had been officers during or just after it. He took the Chinese view, I think, that all soldiers were quite ridiculous. There's a lot to be said for it, as you'll know for yourself having been one. But when there is a war, soldiers are necessary – a simple fact that Forster couldn't really bear to admit. I'd say that his view was that now the war was over we must just pretend it never happened. You see, not only did mention of the war make him feel inferior, it made him jealous, just as Cyril Connolly was jealous of an old friend's armoured car. It was something that took people's minds off *him.*'

'So as far as all that goes, he would probably have approved of Christopher's desertion?'

'Yes. But I can't think that any of this will be very fruitful ground. What needs to be discussed is Morgan Forster's capacity for being a silly, interfering old woman ... and his admiration of "Goldie" Lowes–Dickinson, who was an absolute embarrassment to anyone who was any kind of a man at all—homosexual or other. There was a large section of the world they just didn't know about or acknowledge—the world of action. Not only soldiers upset them, but barristers, huntsmen, explorers, scientists, politicians, sportsmen – anyone that actually *did* anything. All Forster and Co were ever good for was to sit about having lovely thoughts, and to complain about those that moved about a bit on the ground that they made a noise, and then Forster and Lowes–Dickinson couldn't hear each other twittering.'

'Well, just play it by ear, dear boy. But remember that Christopher adored Morgan Forster and he's an old man who mustn't be unduly upset.'

'Goodnight, Mr Vidal,' said the taxi driver as we got out at Montezuma's Human Abattoir.

Gore liked to be recognised: a good start, I thought, to the evening.

In the end, the discussion about Morgan Forster took a line that no one could have predicted or even deemed possible. It was, as it happened, my fault.

Asked by Isherwood how well I had known Morgan at King's, and seeking about for a pleasant and not wholly boring answer, I remarked that we had once been to the cinema together, on my suggestion, and that Morgan had seemed to enjoy the film.

'And what film was that?' said Christopher.

'Walt Disney's *Peter Pan*,' I said.

In fact this was untrue. The film we had been to was Alfred Hitchcock's *Strangers on a Train*, a marvellous thriller which Morgan, despite his dislike of violence, had indeed appeared to enjoy, possibly because of its artistry. *Peter Pan* I had seen with Morgan's old chum, J. R. (Joe) Ackerley. Since I closely associated the two men in my memory, I had mixed up which film I went to with which and now saw no particular reason to correct my error – indeed, as it turned out, had no time to.

'Morgan,' said Isherwood, 'would never have gone to any rubbish of Barrie's.'

'I suggested it,' I replied. 'He had never seen a full-length animated cartoon before and I thought it might amuse him.'

'How could it have done? Just before the war I once proposed that we should go to *Snow White and the Seven*

Dwarves, which was the first full-length cartoon ever to be made. He replied that he didn't like those Germanic sort of fairy tales in which the heroine is turned into a corpse – even if the prince does revive her later.'

'But that was an objection to those grisly stories by Anderson or Grimm,' said Gore, 'not to the idea of a full-length cartoon. After all, he might have liked the idea of *Peter Pan* done in such an unfamiliar medium.'

'I just told you: he hated J. M. Barrie.'

'So much the more fool him,' said Gore. 'For though I agree that a lot of Barrie is muck, the character of Captain Hook, the old Etonian pirate, is a splendid invention, as is his enemy, the ticking crocodile.'

'Morgan did not like fantasy.'

'But he did. Look at his own. Thomas Browne as the coachman in *The Celestial Omnibus*. All those little boys in Italy that kept on turning into Pan in the middle of picnics and making their aunties hysterical. What is all that if it isn't fantasy?'

'Admirers of E. M. Forster,' said Don carefully, 'are quietly and reluctantly agreed that his stories of that nature are – well – untypical. It is thought that he himself was later embarrassed by them.'

'There are enough of them,' said Gore. 'He made no attempt to have them suppressed. I remember, very clearly, one such story in which the boy who turned into a faun or a satyr or whatever it was put down his Bovril sandwich, stripped naked, and went rushing off to join all the other fauns and satyrs. Somewhere near Florence, that happened.'

'Could you get Bovril in Florence?' enquired Don.

'I was speaking figuratively,' said Gore. 'For "Bovril sandwich" understand appropriate food for a little English boy. Now anyone who can get up a tale like that about an English prep. school boy in Florence for the hols, must surely be able to tolerate *Peter Pan*.'

'You haven't understood me,' said Christopher. 'It is a question of quality. Morgan's fantasy at least had a basis of truth – the existence of the wild creature that lurks in every one of us. *Peter Pan* was just commercial slop.'

'What he seemed to enjoy,' I improvised, 'was that dog, Nana, that took care of the children.'

Montezuma's Human Abattoir was very hot. Gore had just ordered a third round of long Tequila fruit drinks.

'But Morgan hated dogs,' said Christopher, and took a slurp of Tequila plus Tamarind. 'I remember Joe Ackerley saying that he never would have Joe's dog, Queenie, to stay with him. It made for a lot of bad feeling.'

'The thing about that,' I said, 'was that dogs weren't allowed in King's College guest rooms.'

'The other thing was,' said Gore, 'or so I was told by you yourself, that Queenie was almost permanently on heat, and couldn't travel. Joe had to stay in London with her and couldn't go to Cambridge or anywhere else.'

'But that's just it,' said Christopher. 'Morgan bitterly resented the fact that Joe couldn't come to stay because Queenie was on heat. It made him hate Queenie and by extension all other dogs even more than he'd hated them before. He simply cannot have enjoyed the character of Nana.'

'What he enjoyed,' I said, 'was the idea of Nana's taking care of the children. He said it reminded him of Romulus and Remus being suckled by a she-wolf, and also of Chiron the Centaur's bringing up Jason and Achilles.'

'I can't relate all this to the Morgan Forster whom I

knew,' said Christopher. What with confusion and Tequila, his neck had gone scarlet under his exaggerated crew cut, which was like a pudding-basin job on an aging band-boy.

'I think that what we have to recognise,' said Gore, 'is that Forster was in many ways a very silly man.'

'Inconsistent,' I said, and decided to tell the truth for a while. 'During my last year at Cambridge, there was rather a good comedy on at the Arts Theatre, with Roland Culver, about a member of Parliament who had trouble keeping his wife away from his mistresses, because they all liked each other much better than they liked him, and were forever meeting for giggly lunches and even entire weekends. A pretty flimsy affair but quite witty. When Morgan was asked what he thought of it, he said that he didn't care for the thing because it was full of "immorality flats". He didn't object that the play was frivolous or light-minded or eminently forgettable: simply that it was full of immorality flats, the idea of which he detested. Now, as his friend, Patrick Wilkinson, the Horatian scholar, pointed out very succinctly, Morgan Forster had spent his life in immorality flats. As soon as he got free from his mother, he had immorality flats all over Europe and most noticeably in Alexandria during the First War. He was full of praise for Cavafy and his friends, all of whom lived in immorality flats, and someone in one of his novels—someone he rather likes—keeps a mistress in one. So what on earth was he talking about when he said he detested the idea of them?'

'Precisely,' said Gore. 'He was a man of double standards—one for himself and one for the rest of us. And so intolerant. The only man in his oeuvre that ever played a game—the only man in all his books who was a proper man—was killed off almost immediately, "broken up" in a game of rugby football. He had to be punished, you see, for actually doing something, instead of sitting on his arse and bitching about the moral insensitivity of everyone else in a "world of telegrams and anger".'

'You are deliberately distorting it all,' said Christopher as his fourth Tequila (refused by Don and myself) was placed in front of him.'

'I have asked you here purely in order; said Gore, 'that we may have a quiet and rational talk about Forster.'

'So Don said, and that's why I've come. But all this talk of *Peter Pan* has misled us – it has taken us off down a totally wrong path.'

'Not at all,' said Gore. 'It has compelled us to discuss a side of Morgan Forster that his admirers studiously ignore. A captious and foolish side, puerile, vacuous and winsome; a side that explains the total fiasco of the Malabar Caves, for example, and that quintuply blush-making father and son relationship in *A Room with a View*.'

Christopher took a violent pull at his Tequila, opened his mouth to retort, started wagging his cropped head from side to side like a mechanical clown and toppled into the arms of the expectant Don...who took him out, rather officiously assisted by Gore. I wondered what would have happened if I'd got the thing right at the start and told them all that it was really *Strangers on a Train* which Morgan and I had seen together. As far as I remember, he had much enjoyed the villain's simpering and incestuous mother, so where that would have got us, God knew. Together with the Tequila, I thought, it would probably have got Christopher on the floor, just as *Peter Pan* had.

Gore came back.

'Don's taking him home,' he said. 'A very neat

evasion, I thought, of all the problems we discussed on the way here. Did you *really* go to the cinema with Forster?'

'Oh yes.'

And I swear I did. The old Royal in Cambridge.

'Well now. Our next enjoyment. As I think Howard has told you, I shall be giving a party for Princess Margaret. Today week. I'd like you to come.'

'I wrote the script of a serial,' I told him, 'about Edward VIII and Mrs Simpson. The Royal Family didn't enjoy it much, I'm told. Of course, they probably don't know the name of the scriptwriter – nobody ever does – but they just might and then it would be embarrassing for me to meet Princess Margaret.'

'I shall tell her you wrote that script,' Gore said. 'That's why I want you to come – to see what she says to you.'

'I'd much sooner not. I hate parties.'

'You were quite a star at the party we've just had.'

'A small dinner party with people I know is one thing,' I said. 'A crush of celebrities and princesses is quite another. My brother and I used to hide in the lavatory when we went to smart children's parties until it was time to go home. We couldn't even endure the conjuring show – in case the conjuror called one of us out for some trick.'

'You must have grown out of that by now. Someone said you were a great partygoer at Cambridge.'

'For a brief period in my frothy youth. It is long since gone.'

'You can't refuse the Royal Command.'

'It's only your command.'

'Most people in Hollywood would give their eyes to come. Don't you like your Royal Family?'

'I start crying whenever they appear on television. Particularly the Queen Mother.'

'Well then?' said Gore.

'Loyalty is one thing. Introduction is another. Princess Margaret would not want me crying all over her.'

'You won't when it comes to the point.'

'Gore…why are you being so persistent about this?'

'Simon…why are you being so stubborn about this?'

'I told you. I prefer to adore from a distance. Anyway, she hasn't come here to meet Englishmen, but to mix with your lot.'

'The trouble with you is that you're an inverted snob.' Suddenly I had an inspiration. I took out my wallet and showed Gore my air ticket home.

'It's for the day before your party,' I said.

'Change it.'

Christ.

'I'll ring up the airport,' I said feebly.

'No. You'll take your ticket to your bell captain. He'll do it all for you. I'll come in with you when we get to your hotel and give him full instructions.'

The story ends with a whimper. The planes that week were all full. I had to leave on the flight on which my seat had been booked. Why Gore was so keen that I should meet HRH, I shall never know.

He reported to me later on the transatlantic telephone that she had formed a poor impression of *Edward and Mrs Simpson*, complaining that her family did not talk remotely as I had scripted them.

'Ah,' I was able to tell him, 'the director and the actors changed a lot of it. That makes it their fault.'

' "Actors are cattle," as Hitchcock used to say. What a pity they won't believe it.'

'Talking of Hitchcock,' I said, 'I can now confess. The

film I saw with Morgan Forster was not *Peter Pan* but *Strangers on a Train*.'

'Never mind. Christopher had so much Tequila that he's forgotten the entire story. Don has persuaded him that he argued us into the ground and then fainted because of the heat. There's no truth anywhere these days.'

'None,' I agreed.

'But here's some for free. The chap who was interested in Burr has left the studio, having been poached for more cash by another. So they'll never make *Burr* now. The new man won't want his predecessor's leavings. No true Yankee will walk in a dead man's shoes, however well cut.'

'No hope, Gore?'

'No hope, Simon. You won't get half the money you might have done. Neither shall I.'

So if there is little truth in the world there is some justice, I thought, seeing Christopher's crew-cut head as it wagged in despair while he toppled, deceived and helpless, into the arms of his friend.

Birthday Treat

from
The Erotic Review,
edited by Rowan Pelling

' What an attractive woman,' said my old
Cambridge friend, K—, who had popped in to
sponge my Calvados and was now prying through one of
my scrapbooks.

'Which woman?'

'The one with very short shorts, sitting on the steps of
a beach hut, drying a small boy. She's just beginning to
get his bum-bags down.'

'That was me and my mother,' I said, 'in 1938.'

'What a pity we can't quite see your dear little doodah.
I bet you were as stiff as anything, being mussed about
between a pair of thighs like those.'

'I was only ten.'

'Byron got hard-ons at the age of nine,' said K., 'he
says the Nursery Maid saw to that.'

'As it happens,' I said boastfully, 'I got a hard-on at the
age of eight. But with chums at prepper, not with my
Mama.'

'Didn't you fancy your Mama—as young and pretty
as that?'

'It is not permitted,' I said priggishly, 'to fancy one's Mama.'

'You'd be surprised how many boys do. Remember that French film some years back – *Le Souffle au Coeur* it was called – all about a very pretty little *garçon* who was in short, white socks when the film began, but was just getting pubescent. He couldn't find anyone to do it with because he was so delicate that his *maman* wouldn't let him play with the other boys and girls; so he began to nag at her to have it off with him, and eventually she was part bored and part flattered into the thing. They both enjoyed themselves like all get out; they got a lot of amusing ideas for the future, and the boy's health improved *instanter*. One of the critics said that any proper boy would fancy his mother if she was as sexy as that boy's was.'

'That was only a film, and a French film at that. I never,' I said resolutely, 'fancied my Mama.' Time for getting a bit of my own back, I thought. 'Did you?' I asked.

'No' said K. 'She fancied me.'

'What an unchivalrous thing to say. Were you upset …disgusted…frightened?'

'Frightened of my own mother? No. I was interested.'

'But you said you didn't fancy her.'

'Once things were getting started,' said K., 'it would have been ungrateful and ill-mannered not to join in.'

'But your mother,' I said, 'wasn't a bit sexy, not at all like that lady in the film.'

'This was all a goodish time ago. My mother was handsome then. Well-made. Lots of wholesome flesh to – let's say – handle. When I think of her now I think of that poem of Browning's, the one where the dying bishop promises his sons that if they build him a splendiferous tomb, he'll pray to the Virgin Mary to send them mistresses 'with great, smooth, marbly limbs. That was what my mother had,' said K., with relish: 'great, smooth, marbly limbs. Very appetising.'

'I never looked at your mother's limbs. I didn't think they were relevant.'

'Neither did I,' said K, 'until the night before my fourteenth birthday. I'd been taken to the cinema (Michael Redgrave and John Mills in *The Way to the Stars*) and I was in my room, having a glass of milk and putting on my pyjamas. I'd just put on my pyjama jacket and taken off my underpants, when midnight struck and there was my mother, stark naked, posing in my bedroom doorway like the Venus de Milo. "Happy birthday, darling," she said. Then she beckoned and vanished. By this time I was thoroughly, alerted. So I set off down the corridor in my pyjama top – I'd grown a lot lately and it only came down to my navel. Suitable kit for what seemed to be in train, I thought.

'The bathroom door was open and the light was on. 'In here darling,' said my mother's voice, and there she was, sitting on the loo with her legs splayed, pissing like a carthorse.'

'How very off-putting,' I said.

'Nonsense. There is nothing more exciting,' said K, helping himself to a quintuple Calvados, 'than a woman with her legs splayed, pissing. Rowlandson has a special picture about it, called "The Family Outing". The mother is peeing from the "at ease" position, holding up her skirts so as not to wet them. The two daughters (seventeen and twelve, by the look of it) are squatting. The family dog is careering round with a dotty look on its face; and the son of the family is standing on the box of their barouche, clutching a colossal erection in one hand and his driving whip with the other.'

'The trouble with Rowlandson,' I said, 'is that he can't do penises properly. They all look like pencils with angry red ends.'

'Still, he got the micturating women right. In my mother's case there was a bonus. She had a very prominent, Brigade-scarlet, semi-erect clitoris. 'Hullo, darling,' she said: 'if you want to go pee-pee, there's just room through here.' And she pointed to a triangle made by her two thighs (which she now splayed a little further) and the front of the seat. She took my cock and depressed it to aim through the gap. 'Thank you, mummy,' I said, 'but I don't actually want to pee.' 'How silly of me,' she said, 'of course you don't, with a boner like that.' She let it return to its former angle and fondled it very lightly with both her capable hands.'

'Boner?' I enquired.

'American for erection. My mother,' said K., 'was American'.

'Perhaps that explains it all.'

'She was also Jewish; but she didn't take that very seriously,' said K., 'she never had me circumcised. So now she was able to slide my foreskin backwards and forwards…'My little boy,' she intoned, 'with his pretty prick standing up stiff for his Mummy.' Then she suspended her operations on my foreskin. 'You mustn't worry about a thing,' she said. 'I'm not worrying. Darling Mummy, just go on … doing what you were doing.' 'I promise I shan't keep pestering you,' she said, in a bright chatty voice: 'I'm only doing it this once, in honour of your birthday and because you're growing up and I think I ought to show you things. But I find I'm enjoying it much more than I ought to be, considering that it's all supposed to be educational. I've never been so wet between my legs in my whole life. Perhaps I really ought not to carry…' 'Never mind all that,' I almost shouted, 'please, Mummy, don't stop.' 'Well, all right,' she said, 'so long as we're both quite clear that it's just for your instruction.'

'Then she stood up,' K. continued, 'and slipped her left knee between my legs. She cupped my bottom with her left hand and arranged me in such a way that when she put gentle pressure on my bum, my willy skidded up and down the inside of her thigh. 'I'm still not sure it's quite right,' she muttered, 'so much pleasure in teaching.' 'And in learning,' I said.

'I wonder…' she began again, and stopped her rhythmic propulsion of my bottie. But by then I was fully able to keep going on my own. 'Too late now, Mummy,' I said, 'much too late… CHRIST, MUMMY, CHRIST, MUMMY, JESUS, JESUS.' Four fierce squirts and a long, juddery dribble. When I started, my mother got some of my stuff on the fingers of her free hand. She applied it liberally to her clitoris and then guided my hand down to massage it under her direction. By the time I'd almost finished coming but not quite…'

'While the long juddery dribble was going on?' I suggested pruriently.

'I felt Mummy's thigh start to quiver and the muscles just under her bush jerk like a jack-in-the-box. Then she started to laugh, not a normal laugh, but a high, thin, tweeting giggle … followed by a kind of sepulchral moan, while the whole of her stomach seemed to heave.

'She sat down again on the loo so suddenly that I found myself riding cock-horse on her thigh. 'My little boy has made his Mummy come,' she sort of crooned, 'what a dear, good little boy.' 'My lovely Mummy has made me come,' I babbled, 'lots and lots and lots, what a dear, kind, beautiful Mummy. And, oh Mummy, I'm still coming.' And indeed my weenie was still twitching feebly in the mess around Mummy's upper thigh.

'Then, visibly trying to take control of herself, my mother said, 'His mother always knows a boy best; she should always be the one to show him. Now back to beddy-byes.' She prised my buttocks off her thigh with a kind of squelching noise, turned me round, patted my head, and, 'Off you go, darling,' she breathed, 'Happy Birthday.'

K. helped himself to more, much more, Calvados.

'And was that the end of it all?' I said sadly,

'Not quite. A few days later I went to her and whispered in her ear that I hoped another round of 'educational activities' would be in order as I'd missed some of the finer points the first time. She put her fingers on her lips and shook her head, not guiltily or crossly, but very firmly. So I rather lost heart. After all, she had stipulated 'just this once'. However, when my fifteenth birthday came, and my sixteenth and my seventeenth, there she was naked at my door at midnight, and off we went to the bathroom, to do what we had both been longing for the whole year. Every time there were a few appropriate variations in the dialogue…'my big rorty boy' when I got to be sixteen, 'Mummy's brave soldier laddie' when I'd started my National Service. And there was always something new on the agenda, in the cause of education, of course. The year I was commissioned into the Dragoons ('Mummy's knight with his long curving sabre') she went down on all fours above me and rubbed me off between her dangling breasts. And on my first birthday after I was demobbed, she tickled my fesses and my balls and my pego with a peacock's feather and a powder puff, till I ejaculated so violently I almost fainted.

'Very instructive, that,' she said: 'it'll teach you not to overdo it.' And so on, till the end.'

'When was that?'

'Not long after I first went up to the old college. We'd been celebrating my twenty-first by *soixante-neuf* in the bath. Wonderful. Being in a hot bath solves all the hygienic problems. Anyway, I was just leaving in my short pyjama top—I kept that going as a tradition—when my mother called out, '*Hélas, cheri, ils sont fini, tes amours avec maman.*' She'd been teaching me the French words, you see, for everything like pubic hair and masturbate and spermatozoon, so she found it easier to carry on now it was time for the bad news. 'Why?' I called back. 'I was hoping to fuck you next year, Mummy.'

' "That's just the trouble. I knew you'd want to fuck me, sooner or later, and if you really wanted to I shouldn't be able to resist. So I shall make a point of being as far away as possible on your next birthday. However educational it might prove, fucking would really be going too far.' 'Why Mummy?' I whined at her. 'It's really desperately simple, darling. One must not commit incest,' my mother said.'

The Amateur

from
Turf Accounts,
edited by Mike Seabrook

'What about a trip to the September meeting at Perth?' I said.

'No,' said Rollo Rutupium very firmly, 'not Perth.'

'Why not? It's one of the most attractive courses in the kingdom.'

'So I used to think,' said Rollo. 'I changed my mind.'

'Why?'

Rollo thought heavily for half a minute.

'Once upon a time,' he said at last, 'I had an affair with a very appetizing undergraduate in Trinity Hall.'

'What's she got to do with it?'

'He. This was over forty years ago…before all those women shoved themselves in where they weren't wanted.'

'Oh, come on, Rollo,' I said. 'It must be rather jolly there now, with plenty of girls around.'

'There were plenty forty years ago, if you knew where to look. The thing was that they all had their own colleges and had to go back to them for most of the time. A man could get away from them if he wanted to. They weren't in one's room giggling and whining and demanding and wearing out the furniture all day and all night – which is what it's like now, my nephews tell me.'

'Well, that's their worry. This catamite of yours in Trinity Hall – what's he got to do with Perth Racecourse?'

'He wasn't my catamite, for a start. A catamite is a boy whom you bugger. Although I have always been in favour of widely varying sexual practice with all the genders, I absolutely drew a line at buggery. Messy, painful, and (as it now turns out) potentially lethal.'

'All right,' I said, 'this fancy boy of yours. What's he got to do with Per—'

'He wasn't a fancy boy either. Definitely not mincing or dainty. He was butch and wholesome and just a little bit bandy. Played cricket and rugger for Trinity Hall. Blue eyes and Viking blond hair and a slightly snub nose. Medium height. When he played tennis in white shorts, his bonny bow legs (smooth as silk) used to flash and twinkle all over the court like magic.'

'Steady on,' I said, 'that's enough.'

'No, it isn't,' said Rollo. 'If you want to appreciate this story, you must first know all about Micky. Micky Ruck, he was called. I sat next to him by accident in one of Professor Adcock's lectures on the late Roman Republic. Adders was buzzing away about that crook Clodius, and suddenly there we were, Micky and I, playing footsie and kneesie and thighsie like a pair of demented fourth formers…Mind you, I was quite a dish myself in those days. Tall and languid and sinuous…hardly a hair anywhere on my body, except a small blob of pert pubes.'

'Love at first sight?'

'No love about it. Sheer randiness. Yearning for flesh and skin. But there *was* affection. I enjoyed his sort of accommodating naivety, while he admired my upper

298

class demeanour and cynicism. So in no time at all we were lusty bedfellows – he used to laugh a lot, I remember, just before he came – and excellent occasional companions, playing squash and watching cricket at Fenner's. However, there was just one cloud in the sky.'

'Scandal?'

'No. We usually met in my own college, King's, and in King's in those days nobody worried about that kind of carry-on. However, the trouble was that Micky was afraid that because he liked doing it with other boys he might turn into a full-time homosexual. The Classics master at his school, unlike the Classics master at mine, hadn't pointed out to him that the norm both in Greece and Rome, at any rate among the best people, was an easy-going bisexuality. So I now made this plain to him, quoting chapter and verse, and just to set his mind at rest I arranged for my cousin, Heather Sopworth of Girton, to give him a go. As I told you just now, you could always find a girl if you needed one, even then – long before they infested the entire University.'

'And how did he get on with Heather Sopworth?'

'Spiffing. Heather was a grand girl, as I knew well enough; we'd been intimate playmates since we were twelve. She told Micky that he was the best she'd ever had except me, and explained that a taste for boys made boys far more attractive to girls (jealousy and curiosity) and also made girls far more attractive (by sheer contrast) to boys. He could have the best of all possible worlds, she told him, but he should remember that he had only a limited time in which to enjoy them: boys will be boys, but not for long. When he became a man, she said, he'd probably still be pretty attractive, but by then women might expect him to be faithful to them, or even to marry them, and that would be a bore. So gather ye rosebuds while ye may, Heather urged, on both sides of the garden path.'

'I still don't see,' I said, 'what any of this has to do with Perth.'

'Patience,' Rollo said. 'So Micky was gathering rosebuds in all directions, Heather's and mine and God knows who else's, when it occurred to me one May morning that I should be going down for good in June, after which I should have National Service for two years, much of it very likely abroad, and that there would be an end of Micky Ruck. I therefore decided to extend my stay in Paradise by arranging a last spree with Micky the following August and September, before he must go back to Cambridge and I myself must list for a temporary lancer. Micky and I would have a Grand Sporting Tour, taking in Festival Cricket Weeks – there were plenty of those then, before the game was put in the charge of a money-grubbing inquisition from the Corporals' Mess – and lots of tennis tournaments, both real tennis and lawners, and plenty of golf and racing. We could start at Lord's, make our way up through England and then Scotland to Gleneagles, and then on to the goal and crown of the whole expedition, the September Meeting (here we are at last) at Perth.'

'Bravo,' I said.

'One possible obstacle, however, was Micky's adoring mum, who liked her little boy to be with her during the hols. Luckily she was a howling snob. I hadn't inherited then but she knew who I was, so to speak – Micky never really understood all that, bless his heart – and she was very pleased with our friendship. As for the idea that "something" might be going on, it didn't bother her. She wasn't fussy. I did have to pay a toll of a night in bed with her – but it was no trouble. Like her son, she roared with laughter when she was coming; and she kept on calling me "Micky darling" by mistake, which had interesting and rather exciting implications. Anyway, I soon had her imprimatur for our journey.

'And so off we went, Micky and I, in that Lagonda I used to have, playing in the odd match for the Butterflies and IZ – Micky belonged to neither but a few smiles at the right people soon settled that problem – watching the late county games, going to early National Hunt meetings at Hereford and Stratford and Sedgefield (proper country meetings, none of those pimply pimps and lacquered whores that you get at the meetings near London), popping in at Doncaster for a bit of Flat, di-da, di-da, some tennis (Royal) at Chester and some Shakespeare in Edinburgh, until at last we came to Perth, where we put up at a very decent pub in the forest some miles north of the course.

'We had a day spare before the racing started, and so, since Micky was getting into one of his periodical states about being too queer – he'd been laughing like a satyr all the way from London and was afraid he was enjoying himself too much – I took him to see Penny Pertuis, a busy widow whose husband had been in the same regiment as my father. Penny was a versatile lady, who now taught anthropology at the University of St Andrew's; she showed us round the golf course as far as the ninth, where we retired into the bushes for a picnic followed by a tremendous three ball. I let Micky do most of the actual fornicating, to restore his confidence, and what with him laughing and Penny bawling obscenities, which was her way of showing gratitude, I thought we'd have the entire Committee of the Royal and Ancient charging down on us like a squadron of the Greys. But no, we were only spotted by a redheaded Scots laddie looking for lost balls to sell, who happily made up a foursome – nothing so rorty as a wee ginger Scot.

'Blissfully tired after a long day in the fresh air, we set out back towards Perth, taking Penny, who had decided to come to the races with us the next day. We telephoned the pub to book her in and order our dinner, and on the way back we paid a visit to the Palace at Scone. Although the place had just closed when we reached it, Penny knew a private way in. In any case the purpose of our call was not to see the Palace itself but to inspect a remarkable graveyard they have there, in the woods near the Chapel, because Penny the Anthropologist had some theory about eighteenth-century burials in that part of the world and she had heard that there might be something helpful there at Scone.

'Now, Penny's theory had to do with the sepulchral use of the obelisk. There was, so they said, a particularly fine obelisk at one end of this very grave ground, an obelisk which had been put up over the remains of one Purvis Pride, the eldest son of Purvis Pride the Pride of Birnam – the Prides, then as now, being great men in the county and devils for hunting. The Pride under the obelisk had been killed steeple-chasing in 1789, at the age of nineteen…this during a cross-country race, which had started in the hills up at Belbeggie and ended (so Penny told us) at a tavern which then stood by a copse in the middle of the meadow that formed the centre of the modern circuit. Young Purvis, when well in the lead, had broken his neck at the last obstacle of all – the stream in which the good woman of the tavern did her washing. She'd hung a huge night-shirt out on a hedge to dry, and the wind had got up and blown it straight on to horse and rider, blinding them both just as they were about to jump the steeply banked stream. The horse, a stallion called

Jupiter Tonans, had perished with Purvis and was buried with him.

'Penny's theory,' Rollo went on, 'was that obelisks were reserved for the remains of gallant men – soldiers and sailors, explorers and adventurers. What she wanted was to read the inscription on the Pride obelisk, which was said to include a phrase which would explain why Purvis Pride, a mere local huntsman and stripling amateur jockey, had been allowed the full funereal apparatus of a proven man of action.

'Having climbed a bolted postern in the wall, which ran parallel to the Perth-Balmoral road, we approached the burial ground through graceful conifers and along a sunken path. This opened out in a delta at the east end of the cemetery, where the trees gave way to the ranked monuments. Although evening had not yet fallen, the grave ground in front of us (about one hundred yards by fifty) was diffusing its own shade of subfusc illumination from the lolling mounds and crumbling pedestals, the black slabs and sweaty cylinders, which made up the assembly of seventeenth- and eighteenth-century sepulture. We filed through the stones, Penny leading, Micky and I, seeing as little as possible of the spikes and balls and skulking crosses, until we came to the far end, the end nearest the Chapel (which was just visible through high bush and ladybirch) and the Palace itself, about a furlong beyond, on the far side of a broad, trim lawn. But our attention was soon distracted both from Chapel and Palace by the grave, which we had come to see. A marble obelisk, of a tall man's height and topped by what looked like a mortarboard without its tassel, stood on a small grass island, which was surrounded by a moat of dark water about seven foot wide.

' "Apparently it's quite deep," said Penny, "not for

wading. And anyone that jumped it would break his napper on the obelisk. Luckily I can read the inscription from here with my race glasses."

'She took these from their case...the ones her husband had used all through Italy.

' "Take it down," she told me, and glinted through the glasses at the inscription on the side of the obelisk, which was facing us.

' " 'Brave rider, Purvis Pride'," she read, " 'brave stallion had to ride; *Jupiter Tonans* him did call, who slew both by cursed fall.' Not a high standard of verse," observed Penny. "But there's a bit more – in Latin. '*Nonne quidem stuprorum poenitet animum equitis hic sepulti in saecula saeculorum cum nobilitate equi sui?*' Interesting use of the abstract: 'the nobleness of his horse' instead of 'his noble horse'."

' "In sum," translated Micky, looking over my shoulder at the transcript, " 'surely the soul of the horseman repents of his *stuprorum* – debaucheries – buried here as he is for ever with his noble horse?' Informing us that the horse, *Jupiter Tonans*, is in there too."

' "That we knew," said Penny, "though it is useful to have it confirmed. The glowing tribute to *Jupiter Tonans* obviously explains why Purvis Pride's tomb was dignified with an obelisk. Clearly the obelisk is for 'the noble horse' rather than his rider. But there remains a slight mystery: it seems that Purvis was guilty of certain *stupra* of which, it is hoped, he will repent at leisure, perhaps influenced in this by his 'noble' companion. Evidently these *stupra* were considered no great matter; otherwise this memorial would not have been allowed an obelisk in the first place however great the fame and nobility of *Jupiter Tonans*. The nice question is, exactly what were they, these *stupra*? Micky has translated them as 'debaucheries', but what specific debaucheries?"

' "The word is commonly used both in Latin prose and verse," said Micky the classicist, "of any sexual misdemeanour and in particular of orgies or adulteries. Perhaps Purvis Pride junior went round tumbling the local wives? Not much of a crime for a well-connected young man in the eighteenth century."

' "A considerable crime in Scotland," said Penny. "The Kirk would not have stood for it...and would certainly not have permitted him this kind of interment in this kind of place."

' "No doubt," I myself put in, "Father Pride the Pride of Birnam had a liberal palm for greasing other palms. Come to that, the Kirk or the episcopalians – whichever administrated this place – might not have been too keen on a bloody great stallion being permitted Christian burial."

' "Good point," said Penny. "A nice fat bribe covers the difficulties all round. No doubt Father Purvis squared it for both of them – for *Jupiter Tonans* and for little Purvis."

' "It would still be amusing," said Micky, "to know precisely what he squared in the way of *stuprorum*." He stooped down and looked into the black moat. "Purvis Pride, Purvis Pride," he intoned, "what naughtiness did you get up to?"

'Answer came there none, except for Penny's comment: "Pretty boys should not go close to still waters. Remember little Greek Hylas, who was hauled in by the water nymphs."

' "They don't have water nymphs in Scotland," Micky said, "the Kirk would never allow it." '

***

'The next day,' continued Rollo, 'we all went to Perth races. The course, as you know, is not far from Scone; indeed, if you stand by the second jump out from Tattersall's you can see a bit of a rampart or whatever through the trees which separate the circuit from the Palace gardens. So here we came and stood for the big race, a very long steeplechase during which the horses and their riders would take this fence three times.

' "You will observe," said Penny as we walked across the meadow from the Enclosure, "that the Purvis family is well represented. Purvis Pride – surely a descendant – is to ride his gelding, Long John Silver. Black and White halved with Black Cap."

' "Same colours as the Hall," Micky said. "Trinity Hall," he explained to Penny, "my college. We call it the Hall for short."

' "So I surmised," said Penny.

' "Of course I've backed him," bubbled Micky. "The layers gave me a hundred quid to a tenner."

' "Extravagant boy."

' "It's well worth a tenner," Micky said, "just to be standing here in this lovely place."

'One quite saw what he meant,' Rollo pursued. 'In front of us, the other side of the course, were the trees up the gentle slope to the peeping Palace; behind us was the meadow and two hundred yards away the copse near which had stood the vanished tavern, by a stream that had also vanished, where the eighteenth-century Purvis Pride had broken his neck. Beyond the far end of the course the countryside idled away, pine and bracken, to a semi-circle of low hills.

' " 'What are those blue remembered hills,' " I quoted, " 'what spires, what farms, are those?' "

' " 'That is the land of lost content,' " murmured

Micky, continuing Housman's poem, while a single tear ran down the left side of Penny Pertuis's nose.

' "Pay attention to the racing, boys," she said huskily.

' "They're off!"

'It cannot be said that young Purvis Pride's Long John Silver distinguished himself. Nor did his rider. A series of blunders, the first of them at the fence by which we were standing, soon put him a good twenty lengths behind the rest of the small field (seven in all). The second time round he was trailing even further; but he managed to stay upright for a further circuit, and as he went past us for the third and last time he appeared to be rallying slightly and drawing nearer to the pack of six horses in front. When the field emerged from behind the copse, with half a mile to run, Long John Silver had come level with the last horse and seemed to be making good ground. Over the last ditch, with two plain fences still to jump, he was lying fourth…but thereafter reverted to his previous form, sagged back to the rear of what was now a forlorn queue. Ye Banks and Braes, the only mare in the race, was going to win by a corridor: Long John Silver passed the post last by thirty lengths.

' "So much for my tenner," said Micky; "boring race."

' "I don't know," said Penny. "For a time he quickened rather bravely. Then something took the heart out of him."

' "I don't think there was ever much heart there."

' "He seems to be showing a bit more now," Penny said.

'And indeed, having barely flopped past the post, Long John Silver with Purvis on his back in his black and white colours had started to gallop again and was coming very fast round the bend and towards the fence at which we were still standing.

' "He's riding very long," said Micky. "I didn't notice that before."

' "Perhaps he's lost his stirrups," I said.

' "No," said Penny. "He's riding long." She concentrated through her glasses as horse and jockey drew closer. "And he isn't riding Long John Silver," Penny squawked, "he's riding a stallion, dear Jesus—"

'The stallion veered to its right, jumped the rails between the course and the meadow, set straight at us, came swiftly closer. The rider, a wedge-faced youth with a shapeless black cap and no helmet, lent down and across, seized Micky by the scruff of his jacket, tensed and hauled him up like a circus act. He wheeled his horse (Micky now being bunched in front of him like a parcel), jumped back on to the racecourse, then over the hedge on the far side, and galloped away through the scattered clumps towards Scone.

' "Now we know," said Penny, shivering and jerking, "what form Purvis Pride's *stupra* took. The dead Purvis Pride. I told Micky he shouldn't have looked into that moat. You see what's happened?"

' "I think so," I retched. "It must have cost the Pride of Birnam a pretty penny in bribes to arrange for that monument if his son's tastes were known when he was living."

' "They must have been known. *Stupra*. Abomination. Perhaps they thought he would be…safer…in consecrated ground. Perhaps they forced his father…to add an obelisk to keep him down…a moat to keep him in …just in case, they thought. Just in case."

' "What now?" I said. "Shall we go to the graveyard?"

' "No point," Penny said. "We can't compete…"

'Nevertheless we did go there. And saw nothing we had not seen the day before. The waters of the moat were dark and still as ever. We went back to the pub – what else could we do? – and ordered dinner.'

'Halfway through dinner,' said Rollo, 'Micky came back. He was shrivelled and yellow and taut. He ate ferociously, and didn't talk till he had finished. Even then he spoke mostly in monosyllables, at once clear, courteous and impersonal, as if he did not know to whom he was speaking, as if he were the voice of an answering machine. He named neither of us and made no reference to what had occurred, beyond saying, "I am there. We must go to me there. You must take me to me."

' "Now?" asked Penny.

' "Tomorrow," stated what was left of Micky Ruck.

'And so the next morning we took him there to him. We called his name. Poor, shrunken Micky leant over the moat, while Penny and I stood discreetly just behind him. "Micky, Micky Ruck," Micky called. His reflection appeared in the dark water, the reflection of a rosy, laughing boy with blond hair and a snub nose, full of jollity and juice.

' "Micky, Micky Ruck," Micky called.

'But the reflection laughed the more, waved happily, and faded.

' "Please take me away," said Micky to Penny and me, as if he were addressing two complete strangers and asking for a lift.

'And now you know,' said Rollo Rutupium, 'why I shall not, if you will kindly excuse me, be accompanying you to the September meeting at Perth.'

Conclusion

from
Is There Anybody There? Said the Traveller

'Where shall we stop on the way home?' said O.
'Where we like. There is plenty of time. I had
thought of Cahors and Millau. Then somewhere like
Brantôme on the way north.'

'Wasn't there a man called "Brantôme"?'

'He was, I think, count of the place. He ended up as
abbot of the monastery there. He did a deal with the
Huguenots, to stop them sacking it.'

'Money?'

'No. Charm.'

'I never thought of him as an abbot. I thought he was a
courtier and a gambler and a seducer – lots of amusing
things like that.'

'He was. He wrote about them – about women in
particular – with appreciation and wit. Then he got
bored,' I said. 'He just didn't want any more of it.'

'In India,' said O., 'when a man of wealth and worldly
fame reaches a certain age, he renders an account of his
assets to his heir, then puts on the clothes of a beggar and
wanders over the country, seeking to become a holy man.

Was it like that with Brantôme?'

'No. What he wanted was peace and quiet. He wanted to cease from hustle.'

'That's what these Indians are after. If you give away everything, you need worry about nothing.'

'Brantôme wanted a different kind of peace. He wanted to be at leisure to sum up, without disruption or intrusion, the lessons of his worldly career, and to compare these lessons with those formulated by others. He wanted the peace of a well-stocked library. These Indians you speak of want nullity. That is *their* idea of wisdom.'

'What I said they were seeking was "holiness".'

'Rather a long order.'

The little ripples lapped on the pebbles of the beach where we were having our picnic.

'The point about Brantôme,' I went on, 'at least as I see it, was that he wanted to draw up his conclusions about the world in an intelligent and civilised fashion. Those Indians of yours want to dispense with knowledge and intelligence; they want to merge with the eternal. They want to be absolved from the personal effort which is an essential part of being an individual, even an individual who has retired, like Brantôme, into a monastery.'

'You seem to be saying,' said O., 'that Europe and the West believe in private intellectual endeavour, whereas most Indians and Orientals just want to surrender to oblivion.'

'I'm saying just about that.'

'Like your friend, Hamish M'cSass, who's always going to India? Who never reads a book, you say, and is always blathering about meditation?'

'Rather like him,' I said. 'He hasn't exactly given away

his worldly goods but it amuses him to pretend that he has none, not least as this excuses and assists his parsimony.'

'He gets a high out of not spending money?'

'You could put it like that.'

'And of course,' said O., 'it must be very economic to spend the whole day just meditating.'

'Oh yes. No cash needed – and little enough in the way of mental exertion. You just let your mind go blank.'

'Isn't that rather difficult?'

'Not if you're ignorant and ill-read. Like most Indians. And like Hamish. The difference is, of course, that Indians can't really help being in that condition, but Hamish can. He went to Cambridge; he has a very fair intelligence. He simply decided, at a very early age, that it was easier to find someone else – Hamilton – to carry him through life and pay for his treats, than to be his own man and make his own efforts. The rest, from his youthful "marriage" to his middle-aged meditation, follows easily enough.'

'Aren't you being rather spiteful about Hamish?'

'Yes.'

'Why?' said O.

'Because he threw me over. I began to bore him and he threw me over. It is the duty of a true friend to put up with being bored. God knows, I had been bored enough by him over the years; but because I loved him in my way, I put up with it. . . as I did with his avarice, with the horrible companions whom he produced from time to time, and with his enormous conceit of his mediocre intellect and his fading beauty. Now that he has finally spurned what I have to offer, he has released me from any further obligation. Like Brantôme, I can retire to a well stocked library and compare the lessons which I have learned with those recorded by other and wiser men.'

313

A SELECTION OF PRION HUMOUR CLASSICS:

AUGUSTUS CARP ESQ
Henry Howarth Bashford
introduced by Robert Robinson
"much funnier and darker than *Diary of a Nobody*, with which it is
often compared" *Independent on Sunday*
1-85375-411-0

SEVEN MEN AND TWO OTHERS
Max Beerbohm
introduced by Nigel Williams
"the funniest book about literature ever written" Nigel Williams
1-85375-415-3

THE FREAKS OF MAYFAIR
E F Benson
introduced by Brian Masters
"acid-tongued… peerless" *Kirkus Review*
1-85375-429-3

THE MARSH MARLOWE LETTERS
Craig Brown
introducted by Craig Brown
"I doubt there is a better parodist alive" Matthew Paris, *The Spectator*
1-85375-461-7

DIARY OF A PROVINCIAL LADY *
E M Delafield
introduced by Jilly Cooper
"an incredibly funny social satire… the natural predecessor to
Bridget Jones" *The Times*
1-85375-368-8

A MELON FOR ECSTASY
John Fortune and John Wells
introduced by John Fortune
1-85375-470-6

THE PAPERS OF A J WENTWORTH, BA
H F Ellis
introduced by Miles Kington
"a gloriously funny account of the day-to-day life
of an earnest, humourless and largely ineffective
school master" *The Daily Mail*
1-85375-398-X

SQUIRE HAGGARD'S JOURNAL
Michael Green
introduced by the author
"marvellously funny spoof of the 18th-century
diarists" *The Times*
1-85375-399-8

THE DIARY OF A NOBODY
George and Weedon Grossmith
introduced by William Trevor
"a kind of Victorian Victor Meldrew" *The Guardian*
1-85375-364-5

THREE MEN IN A BOAT
Jerome K Jerome
introduced by Nigel Williams
"the only book I've fallen off a chair laughing at"
Vic Reeves
1-85375-371-8

THE UNSPEAKABLE SKIPTON
Pamela Hansford Johnson
introduced by Ruth Rendell
"A superb comic creation."
The New Statesman
1-85375-471-4

SUNSHINE SKETCHES OF A LITTLE TOWN
Stephen Leacock
introduced by Mordecai Richler
"there is no-one quite like Leacock, and no-one quite so good"
Tatler
1-85375-367-X

HERE'S LUCK
Lennie Lower
"Australia's funniest book" Cyril Pearl
1-85375-428-5

THE AUTOBIOGRAPHY OF A CAD
A G Macdonell
introduced by Simon Hoggart
"wonderfully sharp, clever, funny and cutting"
Simon Hoggart
1-85375-414-5

THE SERIAL *
Cyra McFadden
introduced by the author
"an American comic masterpiece" *The Spectator*
1-85375-383-1

THE UNREST-CURE AND OTHER BEASTLY TALES
Saki
introduced by Will Self
"they dazzle and delight" Graham Greene
1-85375-370-X

THE ENGLISH GENTLEMAN
Douglas Sutherland
"extremely funny" Jilly Cooper
1-85375-418-8

My Life and Hard Times *
James Thurber
introduced by Clifton Fadiman
"just about the best thing I ever read" Ogden Nash
1-85375-397-1

A Touch of Daniel
Peter Tinniswood
introduced by David Nobbs
"the funniest writer of his generation"
The Times
1-85375-463-3

Cannibalism in the Cars – the Best of Twain's Humorous
Sketches
Mark Twain
introduced by Roy Blount Jr
"as funny now as when it was written in 1868"
The Independent
1-85375-369-6

* for copyright reasons these titles are not available in the USA or
Canada in the Prion edition.